THE ELUSIVE EDEN

THE ELUSIVE EDEN

Frank McMullan's Confederate Colony in Brazil

by William Clark Griggs

University of Texas Press   Austin

Copyright © 1987 by the University of Texas Press
All rights reserved
Printed in the United States of America

First edition, 1987

Requests for permission to reproduce material from
this work should be sent to:
  Permissions
  University of Texas Press
  Box 7819
  Austin, Texas 78713-7819

LIBRARY OF CONGRESS CATALOGING-IN-PUBLICATION DATA
Griggs, William Clark, 1932–
  The elusive Eden.

  Bibliography: p.
  Includes index.
    1. Americans—Brazil—History—19th century.
  2. American Confederate voluntary exiles—Brazil—
  History. 3. United States—History—Civil War, 1861–
  1865—Refugees. 4. São Paulo (Brazil : State)—
  History. 5. McMullan, Frank. I. Title.
  F2659.A5G75 1987   304.8'764'081   87-6024
  ISBN 0-292-72057-2
  ISBN 0-292-72059-9 pbk.

Contents

Preface   vii

1. Design and Destiny   1

2. The Search for Lands   15

3. Steamers from the South   28

4. Gathering at Galveston   43

5. The Isles of the Lotus Eaters   56

6. A Hankering for Brazil   64

7. The Promised Land   79

8. Under the Southern Cross   91

9. Life in El Dorado   108

10. Straitened Fortunes and Baptized Souls   116

11. The End of El Dorado   127

12. The Last Exile   136

APPENDIX A.
Census of the McMullan-Bowen Colony, As Taken by William
Bowen, November 9, 1867   149

APPENDIX B.
Sarah Bellona Ferguson List, May 29, 1935   153

APPENDIX C.
List of the Names and Families of the American Emigrants on the
River Juquiá, by George Scarborough Barnsley, March 4, 1915   155

Notes   157

Bibliography   191

Index   205

Photographs and maps begin after page 78.

Preface

To most southerners, the news of the surrender of the Confederate States of America was devastating. Although they knew that the end of the war was near, neither the rebellious army nor the citizenry found it easy to adapt their thinking to the social adjustments they would face as a conquered nation. The guidelines for regaining United States citizenship remained blurred, and most former Confederates felt anxious about the uncertain future. "We are surrounded by gloom," wrote one Georgia woman, "not even hope to sustain us. My heart is filled with an intensity of hatred toward the authors of our misery, that I cannot mollify. There is no happiness within or without. I cannot reconcile myself to this wretched servitude."[1]

In another extreme example of depression, Edmund Ruffin, the man who reputedly fired the first shot at Fort Sumter, loaded his pistol, wrapped himself in the Confederate flag, then committed suicide. Adding to the southern feelings of uncertainty and fear, some northerners, particularly radicals like Congressman Thaddeus Stevens of Pennsylvania, clamored that a harsh, demanding reconstruction policy should be adopted toward the South. In reaction to such pressures, many southerners decided to leave the United States for another nation where they would be free from fears of Yankee domination, the humiliation of anticipated rule by former slaves, and the imminent possibility of criminal action for treason.[2]

One Georgian who later emigrated to Brazil expressed the fear of some southerners: "It is true that our horison [sic] is dark, but political prosecutions have not commenced. The crash and thunder of contending factions at the north are almost heard." Commenting on the possible loss of freedom in the South, the *Galveston Daily News* editorialized that "the radical programme of depriving the people of the South of the last vestige of liberty is about to be carried out, and . . . our unhappy country is about to be made the theatre of the most despotic rule the world has witnessed in modern times." Although the fears of former Confederates were, in most cases, not realized, potential emigrants discussed the relative merits of dozens of countries. Canada, Mexico, Cuba, Honduras, and England received consideration by many, but most talked of Brazil, where land was cheap, where slavery was still legal, and, above all, where southern emigrants were actively courted.[3]

Although officially neutral during the Civil War, the government of Brazil refused to comply with continued Union demands that Confederate ships be treated as "pirates." Although such actions were not official imperial policy, Brazilian port authorities allowed southern ships to secure provisions, take on coal, and, in some cases, to "dispose of their captures." When the United States warship *Wachusett* went so far as to fire upon and capture the Confederate ship *Florida* in the port of Bahia, a "frenzied mob" of irate Brazilians defiantly ripped the American flag from the consulate. "Citizen police" in Rio de Janeiro were detailed to guard the residences of the American consul and minister "against possible violations from the infuriated populace." According to historian Lawrence Hill, matters "might have taken a serious turn" except for other diplomatic problems that demanded the immediate attention of Brazilian officials.[4]

The wartime differences between Brazil and the United States must have resulted in some affinity for the southern cause, and on the close of the conflict, agitation began in Brazil to encourage Confederate emigration. Many in Rio de Janeiro discussed the possibility of luring badly needed agriculturalists and technical experts from the South. The newspaper *Diário de São Paulo* pressed for a liberal emigration policy, arguing that southerners "cannot submit to the new order of things and live on a footing of equality with their slaves. . . . If our government loses this favorable opportunity to draw them to our country, it will not find another." In January, 1866, prominent Brazilians held a meeting in São Paulo for the express purpose of forming an association to promote emigration.[5]

All over the South serious plans were drawn for settlement in Brazil. In Chester County, South Carolina, Joseph Abney was elected president of the newly formed Southern Emigration Society. Lansford Warren Hastings, a pioneer in both Oregon and California, made plans for a colony on the Amazon River. Alabama's George Grandioson Gunter determined to lead a flock to a home on the Doce River in Espiritu Santo Province. Dr. James McFadden Gaston, a South Carolina physician, made an extended survey of southern Brazil, then wrote a lengthy treatise called *Hunting a Home in Brazil*. Probably sponsored and subsidized by the Brazilian government, Gaston's volume became a textbook for many who planned to go to South America. One of the best-known colonizers, Reverend Ballard S. Dunn, an Episcopal preacher of New Orleans, acquired a tract of land near Iguape, São Paulo Province, on the Juquiá River. Dunn named the settlement Lizzieland in honor of his late wife, Elizabeth, and declared the spot to be a refuge for the South's oppressed. He edited a book, *Brazil, The Home for Southerners,* which promoted emigration and incorporated the reports of several other empresarios. In what ultimately became the most important colonizing effort, Frank Mc-Mullan of Hill and McLennan counties, Texas, led a group of friends, relatives, and like-minded southerners to the São Lourenço River in São Paulo Province.[6]

In an attempt to fill a major gap in the history of Confederate emigration to Brazil, this book traces the colonizing attempt of Frank McMullan, who, with his partner William Bowen, guided the only organized colony from Texas to South America. Although several important manuscript sources have been available to historians for over forty years, no scholarly study was written specifically about the McMullan colony until a master's thesis and subsequently a doctoral dissertation were completed by the author of this book. After detailed research, a large number of primary materials were located in a number of private and public collections. Blanche Henry Clark Weaver, whose work on Confederate emigration began in the 1930s, generously allowed the use of her papers, including all personal correspondence on the subject. In addition, the Weaver papers contain several items that were vital to this work, including a 1935 manuscript by Sarah Bellona Smith Ferguson, a young girl in 1867 when she sailed with the McMullan emigrants. Eight large collections of Barnsley family correspondence were found, five in the United States and three in Brazil. All include valuable letters by George Barnsley and his brother Lucian, both McMullan colonists, from Brazil to family members in the United States. Duke University, the University of North Carolina, the University of Georgia, the Tennessee State Library and Archives, and Emory University were extremely helpful in providing microfilms of items in their collections.[7]

Brazilian sources were also invaluable in the study of the McMullan emigrants. Several very important documents were located in the Archives of the State of São Paulo, including surveys, reports, letters, and an 1867 census of the colony. The National Archives of Brazil and the Brazilian Institute of History and Geography in Rio de Janeiro provided valuable data on Brazilian emigration contracts in addition to other in-depth correspondence. The National Archives also yielded many other McMullan-related materials, including the official 247-

page survey of colony lands and numerous letters concerning several North American emigration attempts. One of the most important sources of information about the McMullan Colony was reviewed in the archival collection of the Palacio de Itamaratý in Rio de Janeiro. A large number of manuscripts from this institution, principally information relating to the efforts in behalf of North American emigration by the Brazilian consul in New York, were published in 1943 in the *Revista de Imigração e Colonização*. Included is a storehouse of correspondence from and to Frank McMullan, the consul, and authorities in Rio de Janeiro.[8]

Personal interviews with descendants of George and Lucian Barnsley, especially Harold Barnsley Holland of Jacareí, S.P., Julia Barnsley Macdonell of São Paulo, and Olga Barnsley Schuenstuhl of Rio de Janeiro, were especially important in obtaining primary information. In addition, all three provided invaluable manuscript material; Holland alone loaned or copied nearly 800 pages of letterbooks and other correspondence relating to the life of former Confederates in Brazil. Betty Antunes de Oliveira of Rio de Janeiro, also a descendant of Confederate emigrants, was extremely helpful in providing previously unknown manuscripts, maps, and photographs. In addition, she provided many helpful suggestions after reading a draft of this book. Appreciation must also be expressed to members of the McMullan family. Rachel "Kelly" McMullan White provided invaluable information in two different interviews. Frank McMullan of São Paulo (Ney McMullan's youngest son) provided information not available from any other source. The late Wiley Dyer McMullan, who also lived in São Paulo, provided valuable data.

It may properly be said that although a single author is usually listed on a book's title page, no historical study is the work of one individual. The historian must draw on the compositions of those who have gone before and the assistance of those who provide help in scholarly endeavors. This work is certainly no exception to that rule, and appreciation is therefore expressed to the following persons in addition to those already noted: Adelaide Alba of the Instituto Historico e Geografico Brasileiro in Rio de Janeiro; Margaret Ross of the J. N. Heiskell Library of the *Arkansas Gazette* Foundation, Little Rock; Sharon E. Knapp and Robert L. Byrd of the William R. Perkins Library at Duke University; Ann Graham of the Benson Latin American Collection, the University of Texas at Austin; Kent Keech and Ellen Brown of the Texas Collection, Baylor University; Raul Lima, Former Director-General of the Archivo Nacional do Brasil in Rio de Janeiro; John Thweatt, the Tennessee State Library and Archives; and Carolyn Wallace, the Southern Historical Collection at the University of North

Carolina; as well as the Archives of the State of São Paulo; the Bridwell Library of Southern Methodist University; and Virginia J. H.
Cain, the Robert W. Woodruff Library for Advanced Studies at Emory
University. Special thanks are due to Blanche Henry Clark Weaver,
formerly of Vanderbilt University, who generously made available her
extensive collection.

The author also wishes to acknowledge Professor Alwyn Barr of
Texas Tech University, who provided invaluable criticism and suggestions. Appreciation is also due professors Robert Hayes, Joseph King,
Jacquelin Collins, and Dan Flores of Texas Tech. Professor James V.
Reese, now of Stephen F. Austin University, and the late Ernest Wallace of Texas Tech gave much-needed critical evaluation in the early
stages of this book. Seymour Connor, formerly of Texas Tech, should
receive credit for initial suggestions for research methodology on the
McMullan colony.

Much of the research that was completed in Brazil could not have
been done without the opportunity of the author to teach for one semester at the Casa de Rui Barbosa in Rio de Janeiro under the Ful-
bright program. Although the purpose of the professorship was to
teach museum studies and not conduct research on the McMullan
colony, the opportunity was nevertheless provided, and the weekends
and evenings that were spent in archives or in interviewing descendants allowed a huge amount of work to be done. Sincere appreciation is therefore due the Institute for the International Exchange of
Scholars and the United States Information Agency.

Finally, my thanks and appreciation go to my wife, Joan, and to my
children, Nancy and John, for their understanding during what must
have seemed to them an interminable project. All endured long hours
of work at odd hours and innumerable miles of travel spent in the
search for information about Frank McMullan and his Brazilian Eden.

CHAPTER 1

Design and Destiny

T HE END OF THE Old South brought to many southerners an emptiness in defeat that today few understand, a loss akin to the death of a dear friend who never again would experience the zest for life. The conclusion of the conflict meant massive change: a reevaluation of the meaning and purpose of life; a transition from war to peace, from master to servant, from ruler to ruled. Some tolerated the reversal and approached the hectic pace of Reconstruction in the same rational manner in which other adversities were borne. Others, feeling the loss more emotionally, chose to cast aside the defeat as well as the past and search for a new life and home far from their familiar surroundings. Many followed trails to America's West, where they worked the gloryholes of Colorado, tracked the wandering buffalo on the plains of Texas, or pursued the still strong lure of gold to California. A few, believing their break from the reunited Union to be complete and final, searched for new starts in Mexico, Central America, or Europe. Other southerners, in measured actions that rejected impulse and required extensive planning, made the more difficult decision to sail for Brazil, far from family, friends, or even the comfort of an easy or inexpensive voyage home should they make the decision to return to the United States. For these erstwhile Confederates, the break with former days signaled a search for a fresh loyalty—a new Valhalla to which their dreams might be tied. Some followed erratic stars that led them farther and farther into obscurity. But one young man, keenly feeling the results of surrender, retrieved the romantic wand of adventure from the conquistadors of old and began anew the search for El Dorado, a quest begun over 400 years before by the likes of Raleigh and Pizarro for a legendary lake of gold which, like the Golden Fleece, seemed to appear, then vanish, then reappear at another time in another place. Unlike his predecessors, however, Texan Frank McMullan and 154 of his friends and family hoped to settle the new land, reap its harvest, and accept its treasure if or when it was found.[1]

The genesis of McMullan's saga predated the War Between the States, and it was closely tied to southern expansionism, one of the principal roots of the conflict. In 1857, with other men of similar persuasion, McMullan sailed from Mobile for Nicaragua on the schooner *Fashion* as a lieutenant under filibuster William Walker. Primed for a fight, confident of victory, and certain of the need of the South to expand into the "Golden Circle" of Central America, the adventurers rallied to the cause of the "Grey-Eyed Man of Destiny" to promote the cause of their beloved Southland.[2]

As is always the case when time hangs heavy and men are lonely and far from home, the soldiers gathered in knots on the ship's deck listening to narratives of exotic lands, lost treasure, and beautiful women. As story after story was told and enthusiasm was whetted by Cuban rum, an old sailor determined to recite once again the incredible legend of João Aranzel and the golden sands that rimmed the banks of a lost lake high in the coastal mountains of Brazil. "João Aranzel was guilty," the ancient seaman commented as he began his story:

> He committed the murder because of a question concerning the honor of his wife. No matter that the accusation was true; one does what one has to do under such circumstances. But the court offered no sympathy, and the honorable man was sentenced to die. With help from friends, João made his escape and fled into the *sertão*—the backwoods of coastal Brazil—making his way south through the mountains to the village of Conceição, then to an Indian settlement named Peruibe where he found Father Ancheita, a Jesuit missionary. The priest advised Aranzel to flee again into the back country and to stay there until sufficient time passed that it might be safe once more to return to civilization.[3]

The sailor detailed every aspect of the story and commanded the rapt attention of the young southerners. He told the legend of how the escapee wandered deeper and deeper into the mountains, following the course of a tropical river that wound toward a high peak that shined like polished metal in the midday sun. One morning, the seaman continued, Aranzel awoke to find himself on the shore of a crystal-clear lake, surrounded by trees, with a beach of fine sand that glittered like gold. As the fugitive examined the shiny material he discovered that it was indeed gold and in huge quantities. Although Aranzel was sorely tempted to return to the settlements, he realized that the advice given to him by Ancheita was sound and that he must stay in the wilderness until the seriousness of his crime was dulled by passing time. He remained in the *sertão* for nearly two years, relishing the mild climate and existing on the abundance of nuts in the forest.[4]

Aranzel became increasingly anxious about his family, according to the narrative of the sailor, and decided to attempt to return to civilization, whatever the price. He gathered as much gold as he could carry and started down the river, then up the coast to his home in the village of São Paulo. Because of his long absence, he found that feelings against him had softened, and with his newly found wealth he purchased a pardon. He was reunited with his family and provided a large dowry for each of his two daughters. Aranzel was repeatedly questioned about the source of his fortune, but he refused to divulge the secret, even to members of his family, until he realized that he was about to die.[5]

As if to lend an aura of confidentiality to his story, the old seaman leaned forward and, with a crook of his finger, urged the young soldiers to move closer. Then, in a soft voice that was almost a whisper, he continued his intriguing tale. "Aye, there's a lost lake of gold still hiding from those who search for it. And I, my lads, have the instructions one needs to find it, written on his deathbed by old João Aranzel himself. A hidden El Dorado, high in the mountains of São Paulo, just waiting to be found. We located it years ago, Dr. Rath and I, but the *jacarés* [alligators] that guard it would not let us near." The old man then reached into a bag tied to his waist and pulled from it a small package carefully cased in oilcloth and tied with a raveled string. "You don't believe me?" he queried in an indignant tone; "then look at this." An ancient document written on parchment in flowing script drew the attention of the interested but skeptical young men who surrounded him. As the time-weary sailor carefully unfolded the manuscript, all instinctively pressed closer for a better view.

The seafarer critically eyed each of the seven soldiers, then slowly, almost reverently, handed the yellowed instructions to the young officer at his side. "Read it to them, Lieutenant McMullan; they don't believe me, but perhaps they'll listen to a gentleman." Carefully holding the document at an old tear, Frank McMullan slowly recited the contents of the message said to have been the last words of João Aranzel:

> The way to the Lake of Gold: From the village of Iguape, take canoes to the rio Una, go up the river to the foot of the serra behind the peak of the São Lourenço, there leave the canoes, go on foot to the top of the serra, keeping along the banks of the stream which is above the rapids, again navigable; and on the 2d day a great Figueira will be found, covered with saucupemos, due north, about a league and a half is the Lake of Gold.[6]

As McMullan paused, the group was quiet, and for an instant the filibusters almost forgot that they were on their way to Nicaragua to attempt to capture the small nation. Every one among them vicariously lived the excitement of canoeing up a South American river and locating the body of water upon whose shores could be found huge amounts of gold. Yet only one of those who heard the story of the supposed treasure would make an attempt to find it.

Frank McMullan's search, combined with a legitimate colonization effort, would result in changes of incalculable value to Brazil and enormous impact upon those with whom he chose to share his dreams. Desperation, fatigue, and illness, buoyed by hope, enthusiasm, and persistence, shaped the next few years of McMullan's life. The search for an elusive Eden in a Confederate colony its Texan members called El Dorado would be the basis for one of the most dramatic adventures to result from the forlorn hope and dashed expectations of the Civil War.

Frank McMullan was born in 1835 in Walker County, Georgia. He came from a venerable and respected family, for tradition related that his grandfather, John McMullan, was an Irish baron who emigrated to the United States during the American Revolution to serve as a military advisor to the Americans. He left family and fortune in Ireland, it is said, when it became apparent that his wife had no desire to come to the New World. John McMullan's son, Hugh Milton, followed him to the United States and married Nancy Dyer, the daughter of Wylie Dyer of Virginia, in 1834. The couple settled in northern Georgia and were among the first to live in the village of Chestnut Flat, a farming community north of La Fayette. Although Hugh McMullan was a farmer and a stockraiser, he also served as a lawyer for those who lived in that remote section. McMullan became the "local advocate of the Whig cause" and frequently engaged in heated debates with neighbors who championed the Democrats.[7]

As a boy in Georgia, Frank McMullan exhibited qualities that were to serve him well in later years. He was a natural leader, an outstanding student, and a close companion to the sisters and brothers who were also born in Walker County. His real name was Francis, but he always preferred to be called Frank. Sister Martha Ann, two years younger than Frank, was affectionately called "Matt." Milton, born in 1840, became "Bud," and Eugene, born in 1843 and the youngest at that time, was dubbed "Nuck." Frank had as a companion and friend a young Negro slave named Jasper. Like the rest of the children, he had a nickname, "Jap," which he kept the rest of his life.[8]

The growing number of settlers that had converged on Walker County by 1844 convinced Hugh McMullan that the time had come to move farther west. Like other frontiersmen, he could not resist the temptation to sell property at a high price in older, established areas and to buy cheap uncleared land in new settlements. In Mississippi Hugh and Nancy found a home that suited them as well as the one in Georgia. The country was still relatively unsettled, land was inexpensive, and the neighboring pioneer families were to their liking. The birth of three more children added to the joy of the new surroundings. In 1845 another daughter, Victoria, arrived, and two years later she was joined by sister Virginia. After the birth of Louise in 1849, the tradition of nicknames soon changed the correct names of the three to "Vic," "Jennie," and "Lou."[9]

As early as 1837 Nancy McMullan's father, Wylie Dyer, became convinced of the opportunities in Texas and went there permanently. In preparation for the move, he sold some of his Georgia property as well as land acquired years before in Lawrence County, Kentucky. Dyer went to Smith County, Texas, where in about 1842 he purchased 640 acres of land for fifty cents an acre. He brought five slaves to the Texas farm to help construct a house, then prepared to buy land for each of his sons so that they might follow him to Texas. In 1847 Dyer started back to Georgia to get his family. Near Daingerfield, Cass County, Texas, his horse stumbled and threw Dyer to the ground. His rifle discharged when it hit the rocks, killing Dyer instantly. He was buried by the side of the road.[10]

Despite the tragedy of Dyer's death, the glowing letters written by him before the accident convinced Hugh and Nancy McMullan that the time had come for them to move west once again. The details of the outstanding grazing lands and rich farming areas watered by large rivers were tantalizing, and consequently by mid-1853 the family had located in Hill County, in the north central part of Texas, where Nancy's brothers Simpson and James Dyer already made their homes. The McMullans settled on a 320-acre plot of fertile farmland located near Pecan Creek, formerly owned by widow Martha Wyman and situated on the "old government road running from Fort Smith, Arkansas, through Texas." Although the structure had only two rooms with a "dog trot," it served the McMullan family well until additions could be constructed. Hugh McMullan also purchased a 640-acre tract from John A. Carothers shortly after the family's arrival. This property was located on a site later chosen for the town of Hillsboro.[11]

Nancy's brother, James Harrison Dyer, was a strong influence on the McMullan children, particularly Frank. With his wife, Amanda, Dyer arrived in Texas in 1847 from Georgia, and by 1851 he and his brother Simpson had built the first dam and mill on the Brazos River. In January 1853, Dyer was elected as the first chief justice (county judge) of newly formed Hill County. Years later a friend described

Judge Dyer's character in this way: "Judge Dyer was of [the] type of President Lincoln. He was not very cultivated, nor very learned in book lore, but from what I knew of him [he] had a naturally well-balanced mind, quick insight into error, and he was honest. He was one of those men on the frontier of Texas who would let an innocent man off and be sure that a culprit got his deserts by hanging or shooting."[12] Frank McMullan and his uncle developed, aside from family ties, a friendship that was to continue all of their lives.

Shortly after the arrival of the McMullan family in Texas in 1853, another son, Edwin Ney, was born. Like his oldest brother Frank, Ney inherited a spirit of adventure and romance that was inspired and nurtured by legend and challenge. Little Charley, born two years later, lived only until 1858 and thus did not share the interesting future of others in the McMullan family.[13]

Hugh McMullan's unexpected death two days after Christmas, 1855, put twenty-one-year-old Frank in a responsible and restrained position as the executor of his father's estate. Routine sales of property, surveying, and paperwork were uninspiring to Frank, and he yearned to get away, perhaps to New Orleans and the excitement that only a port city could offer. After his mother agreed to become administrator in October, 1857, Frank left Texas for adventure and wealth. He was to have much of the first but none of the second.[14]

By the summer of 1857 it was no secret that William Walker, an American filibuster who was ousted from Nicaragua on May 1, planned to return with another army in an attempt to regain control. He established a recruiting organization called the Central American League with offices in many parts of the United States. Colonel William K. Rogers, a longtime officer and confidant of Walker, led the effort in New Orleans. After arriving in the Crescent City in November, 1857, Frank McMullan learned of the league and determined to meet Rogers, whose headquarters were in the St. Charles Hotel. The would-be recruit impressed the recruiter with his surprising knowledge of international affairs, his broad understanding of southern goals, and his acquaintance with Walker's past campaigns. The captain was convinced that the adventurous Texan had the qualities of leadership and would serve well as a junior officer. McMullan was sworn in as a lieutenant, apprised of the army's plans, and told to be ready to sail for Nicaragua by November 11.[15]

William Walker was extremely careful not to expose his army as anything other than a legal emigration party. A telegraph dispatch from New York, however, revealed to the press the nature of the organization and disclosed that the filibusters were to leave within a week. When the news was published in New Orleans newspapers, federal authorities moved quickly to prevent any violation of U.S. neutrality laws. Just before midnight on November 10, they arrested Walker and escorted him to a federal judge. Walker was freed only after posting a $2,000 bond.[16]

The release of Walker concerned authorities who knew that the steamer *Fashion* was in port and that it had been advertised as a regular packet of the Mobile and Nicaragua Steamship Company. The customs officials searched the *Fashion* as well as its cargo but found nothing incriminating. Consequently, they had no grounds for detaining the vessel in New Orleans, and it lifted anchor for Mobile, Alabama, a few hours after Walker's arrest. That afternoon Walker, ignoring the bond that he had posted, boarded a mail boat for Mobile with several of his followers, including Frank McMullan.[17]

New Orleans authorities telegraphed officials in Mobile as soon as it was known that Walker had escaped. Orders were given to rent a steamer, board it with a marshal and a posse, and catch the *Fashion*. For an unknown reason, the message was never delivered. Mobile port inspectors did make a cursory inspection of Walker's ship, but found the cargo to be "above suspicion" and the men aboard to be "legal emigrants." The *Fashion* left the United States with Walker and 195 men on November 14.[18]

As soon as the ship was at sea, Walker organized the men into four companies, and veterans began training the new recruits. In order to ease the tedium of shipboard life, the men on board were encouraged to compete with each other in various sporting events, especially wrestling. To the surprise of many, it was not one of the toughened fighters of foreign wars who won the prize as champion wrestler of Walker's army but Frank McMullan of Texas.[19]

To the chagrin of the American filibusters, however, the second Nicaraguan campaign of William Walker was to be as futile as the first. As the *Fashion* entered the harbor at San Juan del Sur, the U.S. sloop-of-war *Saratoga,* commanded by Frederick Chatard, lay in wait. Although unwilling to initiate open combat on the small army before it disembarked, Chatard's sailors harassed the adventurers in their camp with threats, near misses with howitzers in "target practice," and demands for surrender. When the English ships *Brunswick* and *Leopard* and the American steamer *Fulton* arrived to reinforce his enemies, Walker realized that his efforts were useless. At 1:30 P.M. on December 8, Walker ordered his Nicaraguan banner lowered and surrendered to the vastly superior forces. Within a short time Walker and most of his men were on board the *Fulton*. Twenty of the officers boarded the *Saratoga*. Among those included in the official listing was one "Lt. McMullen." On January 5, 1858, the *Saratoga* arrived at the

Norfolk Navy Yard. The second try to capture Nicaragua ended in failure. Discouraged but still enthusiastic about the future of the South, Frank McMullan returned to Texas.[20]

Frank's family treated him to a joyous homecoming. Fires burned in the two fireplaces of the McMullan cabin on Pecan Creek, warming the interior from the gusts of cold February air that regularly swept down from the Texas plains. The table was piled high with food, and the children crowded close to their globe-trotting brother, eager for a word about life on the high seas or descriptions of the tropics. As days passed, however, the unusual became commonplace once again, and Frank quickly returned to the family responsibilities he had shouldered before going out into the world. But he knew that for him life would never be the same. He was confident that he would soon leave again to get an education, a relatively rare commodity for a young man on the Texas frontier.[21]

On Monday, October 1, 1858, Frank McMullan arrived at McKenzie Institute, a college in Red River County, Texas, operated by John Witherspoon Pettigrew McKenzie and sponsored by the East Texas Conference of the Methodist Church. McMullan chose the Lingual and Mathematical Department and paid $130 for board and tuition. He registered for courses in geometry, algebra, philosophy, and Spanish, as well as two courses in Latin. The restrictive new life in a church school must have seemed strange to someone like McMullan, who already had ventured into a violent world. Like all students, he was required to be in his room every morning and was forbidden from "playing at cards, billiards, and other unlawful games, or raffling." College rules also prevented a student from being absent or tardy at prayers or recitation and condemned smoking and the possession of firearms.[22]

Frank McMullan, later described by a fellow student as "a remarkable young man of cool courage [and] undaunted resolution," enrolled for a second year at McKenzie Institute in the fall of 1859. His studies proceeded on schedule, and he generally enjoyed the mental challenges that could be found in a college environment. Too, he developed a real liking for the "Old Master," a name affectionately given to the headmaster of the school. Course work, however, had become more difficult. In addition to the studies of Tacitus and Homer, McMullan studied surveying and navigation, Greek testament, the *Bucolics* and *Georgics* of Virgil, and Xenathon's *Cyropoedia*, Anton's. Plane and spherical trigonometry were added as a bonus.[23]

Columbus "Gus" Wasson of Grimes County, "a conspicuous fellow" who was "into all sorts of mischief but nothing vicious," became Frank's

closest friend at McKenzie Institute. The two men saw eye to eye on
the political situation of the time, especially slavery and southern
rights, and soon established a genuine rapport. During semester
breaks, the two often traveled together to Hill County, where Wasson
met the McMullan and Dyer families. During the visits Wasson became attracted to young Harriet Dyer, James and Amanda's pretty
daughter. As a result, Wasson became a regular visitor to the McMullan home.[24]

Like the McMullan farm, Hill County and the frontier were quiet in
the last part of the 1850s, but in other parts of the nation, particularly
Kansas and Virginia, developments were occurring that set the stage
for war. Although the Kansas-Nebraska Act of 1854 provided for
popular sovereignty in those two territories as they entered the Union,
both northerners and southerners reacted violently when elections
were called in Kansas. A free-state constitution for the territory was
finally approved in October, 1859, but southerners generally disap-
proved of the outcome, adamantly insisting on their right to take
slaves into any territory in the nation. They believed that this privilege
had been legalized in December, 1856, by the Supreme Court of the
United States in the case of Dred Scott, a Negro who sued for freedom
because his owner had taken him into territory where slavery was out-
lawed by statute. In its decision the court ruled that Scott was not free
and that slave owners could not be deprived of liberty or property
without due process of law. John Brown, fresh from violence in Kansas in his efforts to secure abolition, attacked Harper's Ferry, Virginia,
in October, 1859. With only eighteen men Brown captured the U.S.
arsenal as well as a nearby rifle factory, hoping that slaves would revolt
and join his crusade. When none came forward, Brown was captured
by federal troops after a two-day siege. Charges of murder, conspir-
acy, and treason were filed. Virginia courts found Brown guilty and
he was hanged, much to the horror of northerners. Many southerners
believed that Brown was an instrument of the abolitionists and felt no
remorse at the quick execution of the religious fanatic. Brown's capture and death heightened fears of slave revolts and forced sectional
tensions to new heights.[25]

As a result of the political situation and violence, Frank McMullan
became energetically involved in Texas political affairs. Although still
enrolled in McKenzie Institute, he obtained leave to return to Hill
County in February, 1860, when local Democrats scheduled a convention to prepare for the forthcoming state meeting. On Saturday, February 11, the chairman brought the proceedings to a quick start by
appointing ten men, including Frank McMullan, to a committee that

would "draft resolutions expressive of the object of the convention." The group retired and formulated a statement that reflected the general feelings of most southerners.

The thirteen-paragraph resolution also echoed Democratic policy on a state and national level. It reconfirmed the right to take slaves into the territories and declared that the states were in themselves sovereign and "co-equal members of the American Confederacy." The statement defended the right of ownership of slaves and called for no compromise. Furthermore, the resolution continued, the hostility of the North required "that the Southern States meet in convention, to consult upon the means necessary to secure their peace, security, and safety." Finally, the Texans reaffirmed their devotion to the United States but declared that loyalty was dependent on the retention of the rights of the South: "Whilst we claim to be second to none in patriotic love and devotion to the Constitution and Union of the States, nevertheless, it is our solemn and deliberate opinion that, without *all* the rights to *all* the states, which that instrument guarantees, the Union is not worth preserving."[26] As a final action of the Democratic meeting in Hillsboro, the chairman named the delegates to the state convention in Galveston, a list that included Frank McMullan and his uncle, Judge James H. Dyer.[27]

After the Galveston convention Frank returned to McKenzie Institute. Soon after his arrival at the college, however, McMullan realized that his physical condition was quickly deteriorating. Not understanding the symptoms of tuberculosis as they developed, he attributed his cough, his shortness of breath, and his weight loss to a long-lasting cold. As he became worse, he found that he was no longer able to maintain the hectic pace of his studies, and he asked J. W. P. McKenzie for advice. A friend as well as McMullan's professor, McKenzie recognized that the young man had consumption and advised him to go immediately to the high, dry climate of Mexico. There, McKenzie reasoned, the illness would no doubt improve and McMullan would be able to continue his studies in Spanish, a language for which he showed considerable aptitude. Not yet willing to admit the seriousness of his situation, McMullan returned home in August, hoping that some change in his health might occur that would make the long trip unnecessary.[28]

The effects of the disease worsened instead of improving, however, and a crisis developed when the family decided to move to White Rock Creek in McLennan County. In an effort to appear healthier than he really was, Frank gave his all to the task. The charade backfired, and he collapsed from exhaustion. Bedridden for days, McMullan might have died without constant care from his mother and sisters. The scare convinced Frank of the wisdom of McKenzie's advice, and in mid-1860 he left for Mexico.

Later that year the festering political developments between North and South came to a head. On December 20, South Carolina's secession from the Union triggered a chain of events that eventually resulted in the formation of a new southern confederacy. The next month, five more states broke away. In Texas a mass meeting in Brazoria called upon each county to elect delegates to a January 8 convention to determine the position of the state and, in all likelihood, to secede. Governor Sam Houston did his best to slow the emotional pace but was unsuccessful. On January 28, the convention, by a vote of 152 to 6, called for Texas to leave the Union. In addition, the convention repealed the U.S. annexation agreement, adopted a list of reasons for leaving the Union, then drafted a secession ordinance. It then set February 23 as the date for a statewide referendum on the issue. The election was decisive; 76 percent of those going to the polls favored secession. The vote was 46,129 to 14,697. On March 23 the convention adjourned after ratifying the constitution of the Confederate States of America.[29]

Texas rallied to the Confederate banner, and Hill County was no exception. As early as December 8, 1860, Judge James H. Dyer joined John T. Eubank and Jackson Puckett in a plea to Governor Houston to call the legislature into session "for the purpose of taking into . . . deliberate consideration the best mode of action for the safety of our property, lives, and honor." After Texas left the Union, Joseph Wier, a delegate to the Secession Convention and the editor of the *Hillsboro Express*, melted down his type to make bullets and organized Company A, Twelfth Texas Cavalry. John B. Williams, Frank McMullan's brother-in-law and an early Hillsboro merchant, organized Company A, Nineteenth Texas Cavalry. Other southern loyalists organized units wholly or partially composed of Hill County men.[30]

In Mexico when the war began, Frank McMullan was able to help behind the scenes, and perhaps he made an even larger contribution than he would have had he been in the South. His association with a Dr. Knapp, his physician, gave him the opportunity to serve as an intermediary in negotiations between pro-Confederate Mexican merchants and John T. Pickett, the Confederate consul. Little is known of this confidential association, however, and only scraps of correspondence that mention "Doctor K" and family tradition link him to the southern effort. It is significant, however, that after his return to Texas at the end of the war, he was generally referred to as Major McMullan even by veterans just returned from southern battlefields.[31]

McMullan's health improved drastically during his stay in Mexico.

Although his cough remained, it became less severe. Too, he gained weight and began to resemble the Frank McMullan of old. He continued to study and practice Spanish, and his proficiency advanced to the point that he spoke almost as well as a native. He even wrote a Spanish grammar textbook before his return to Texas.[32]

When Frank McMullan crossed the Rio Grande into the United States in 1865, he encountered a terrible feeling of uncertainty about what would happen to southerners. Yankee troops began to occupy the South, and, although President Andrew Johnson seemed to be following a conservative line, his amnesty proclamation of May 29 left many unanswered questions. Fourteen classes of persons, including those who held civil or diplomatic positions with the Confederacy, as well as those with taxable property valued in excess of $20,000, would have to seek individual pardons.[33]

Typical of northern opinion, the periodical *Harper's Weekly* vehemently demanded that "traitors" be brought to the bar of justice. Its editorial writer argued that if the law was not to be enforced, then it should be changed. If "public conviction" did not dictate that the law should punish treason with the death penalty, then the statute should be rewritten. "If it is to be unchanged," the journalist continued, "it is not necessary for the vindication of the law that all convicted traitors should be hung; but it is surely necessary for the purpose of the law that all shall not escape."[34]

Although there were large numbers of northerners who were not as vindictive as the editors of *Harper's*, there was considerable public pressure for the legal action called for by the news magazine. The courts, however, moved slowly on the issue of treason, preferring instead to prosecute persons who had committed criminal rather than political acts. One of Morgan's Raiders, a man named Champ Ferguson, faced arrest and trial for alleged murders while pursuing guerilla activities for the Confederacy in Tennessee and Kentucky. He was found guilty and hanged on October 20, 1865. On November 10, Captain Henry Wirz met the same punishment for mistreatment of prisoners at Andersonville Prison. Some northern periodicals, although not questioning whether such men as Ferguson and Wirz should be executed, began to wonder how widespread retribution should be. "The question," said one journal, "really becomes a serious one—are all the traitors *par excellence* to be pardoned while these cheap scoundrels are sternly executed?"[35]

Southern newspaper humorist Bill Arp expressed the thoughts of many former Confederates. Writing to his fictional friend Mr. Happy, Arp discussed the situation in easy-to-understand but somewhat exaggerated terms:

How is it now, Mr. Happy? They conquered us by the sword, but they haven't convinced us of nothing much that I know of. All is lost save honor, and that they can't steal from us nor tarnish. If they had held out the hand of friendship, we would have made friends and buried the hatchet. But the very minit they whipped us, they began to holler treason from one end of the country to the other just like they had made a bran new diskovery. It seemed to strike them all of a sudden like an X-post facto law, and they wanted to go into a general hangin business and keep it up as long as they could find rope and timber.[36]

Although Arp had a way of making a desperate situation humorous, there was little to laugh about in the South. Whole towns lay in ruins. Former slave owners worried about confiscation of land and scarcity of labor. Even more critical was the lack of seed and the money to buy it if it were found. One northerner, traveling on a survey mission in the South in 1865 for the president, said that the southern landscape "looked for many miles like a broad black streak of ruin and desolation—the fences all gone; lonesome smoke stacks, surrounded by dark heaps of ashes and cinders, marking the spots where human habitation had stood; the fields along the road wildly overgrown by weeds, with here and there a sickly patch of cotton cultivated by Negro squatters."[37]

Although Texas was spared much of the destruction suffered by other parts of the Confederacy, despair was widespread, and some Texans shared a feeling that the freedom of the slaves would create a new and somehow impossible social order in which Negroes would have not only equality but legislated superiority. The feeling was reinforced by the arrival of Negro occupation troops in some areas soon after the surrender at Appomattox. Rumors of Negro atrocities, most fictional but some true, fell on anxious ears and further increased feelings of hopelessness. One southern girl expressed a general sentiment when she wrote that "there is complete revulsion in public feeling. No more talk about help from France or England, but all about emigration to Mexico or Brazil. We are irretrievably ruined." The fears, as it turned out, were excessive in comparison with the events that actually transpired in the South. But the massive changes in society, combined with the inability of southerners to predict the events to come, made their apprehensions seem legitimate.[38]

Frank McMullan shared the concerns of other southerners regarding the impending results of Reconstruction and sought personal answers to the best way to cope with them. He yearned for freedom—a commodity that he believed would be in short supply as northern troops occupied Texas. He also wished for an opportunity to create a new South where the principles of the one just lost might be continued, where slavery was still a vital institution, where agriculture was the principal industry, and where land was cheap. Brazil offered this new frontier, and McMullan determined to go there with his family and friends. But perhaps, just perhaps, Frank McMullan's yearning for Brazil was reinforced by the occasional examination of a keepsake stowed in a little black trunk in which he kept those items he considered most precious. From time to time, he weighed in his hand the leather pouch that contained an oilcloth-covered package, tied with raveled string, given him years before as the parting gift of the old boatswain of the steamer *Fashion*. If wealth might be the handmaiden of freedom, so much the better.

CHAPTER 2

The Search for Lands

A LTHOUGH THE LOSS of the Civil War was a principal motivation for many southerners to go to Brazil, knowledge of and interest in the South American empire were evident many years before the war. As early as 1845, Reverend Daniel P. Kidder wrote a best-selling two-volume work entitled *Sketches of Residence and Travels in Brazil,* which found a place in many southern libraries. Southern intellectual Matthew F. Maury touted the outstanding qualities of Brazil in such prestigious publications as *De Bow's Review,* which prompted a U.S. study to determine the feasibility of forcibly opening the Amazon River to international trade. In 1853 Maury called for a conference for that purpose and suggested that the Amazon basin might also serve as a satisfactory place for the relocation of southern slaves.[1]

Spurred by the international interest, the Brazilian government wrote legislation in 1860 that formalized the nation's invitation to free and self-governing colonies of emigrants. As a geographically huge but sparsely settled country, Brazil welcomed the possibility of additional technological expertise and an increase in the labor force. Lawmakers realized that colonies of emigrants would open roads, harness rivers, and increase agricultural production. The law provided that established colonies could receive financial support for roads, schools, and even churches. It gave free land to prospective colonies and even allowed the government to subsidize the construction of temporary colony buildings. Although the 1860 law originated primarily as an aid to immigration from Europe, the defeat of the U.S. Confederacy caused many Brazilians to become even more zealous in their support of a policy that would bring "new blood" to their country. In 1866 the International Society of Immigration was formed in Rio de Janeiro to create new interest in and to encourage legislation for new and beneficial immigration programs.[2]

The idea of immigration from the South to Brazil was a logical one, and throughout the Civil War discussion about possible cooperation between the Confederacy and the government of Brazil persisted. As late as December, 1864, newspapers such as the *Richmond Examiner* editorially discussed the possibility of an alliance between the two countries. With the war's end, Emperor Dom Pedro II officially encouraged former Rebels to consider Brazil as their new home. For their part, southerners expressed interest in the hospitable country that had agriculture as its economic base, allowed slavery, and promised favorable terms and advantages for the emigration of former Confederates. They were particularly pleased with the low prices of land and the extended payment terms offered by Brazil. Other economic benefits, including the ability to repay ship passage over a period of several months, were also inviting to poor southerners. In addition, many from the South felt a kinship with Brazilians that they did not sense so strongly in other nationalities. One South Carolinian, after an extended trip to South America, remarked that in Brazil there was "a dignity and a hospitality . . . that correspond[s] in many respects to the lofty and generous bearing which characterized the Southern gentleman in former times. We find people in Brazil capable of appreciating the Southern character, and ready to extend a cordial greeting to all who come."[3]

The reasons for emigration to Brazil were as varied as the people who elected to go there. One relatively wealthy emigrant expressed his sentiments in this way: "I left . . . because of anarchy which I expected to prevail—of the poverty that was already at our doors and the demoralization which I thought and still believe will surely cover the land." Another colonist to Brazil had similar thoughts, stating that he fled to escape "an obscure existence, with a . . . constant struggle against poverty." Brazilian sociologist José Arthur Rios, discussing the reasons southerners chose Brazil rather than some other country, concluded that the geographic similarity and a farm-based culture were the principal magnets. "Brazil was chosen because of the cultural traits it had in common with the Old South," Rios observed. "Like the antebellum South," he continued, "Brazil was governed by a rural aristocracy which had as the main supports of its power and prestige the latifundia—the cotton, sugar, and coffee farms."[4]

Although large numbers of southerners simply booked passage from New York to Brazil and planned to take their chances on making a place for themselves after their arrival, many believed that their plans would be better served by joining one of the several colonization efforts being organized by various entrepreneurs. By September, 1865, a writer for the *New York Herald* suggested that as many as 50,000 persons might leave Dixie. He noted that already twenty agents were

in Brazil, sent by various southern organizations to look for colonization sites. One of the first to leave was General William Wallace Wood,
a multitalented Mississippian who became the emigration agent for
many southerners from Louisiana, Virginia, and Mississippi. By the
time he sailed from New York on the *Montana* on October 3, 1865,
nineteen other agents from across the South had decided to entrust
their business to him.[5]

Wood and his entourage received an enthusiastic reception from
Brazilians in Rio de Janeiro on October 3, 1865. Upon their arrival, a
brass band playing "Dixie" provided a sympathetic welcome that was
followed by three days of entertainment. When the time came for the
Americans to leave the capital city, the overgenerous Brazilian government furnished an engineer, a guide, and an interpreter as well as
letters of introduction to all provincial officials who might conceivably
be of service. Wood and his examining party left Rio on October 12 en
route to Santos by the packet steamer *Santa Maria*, then proceeded to
São Paulo Province by railroad. There they examined a huge block of
land on both sides of the Jahu and Teite rivers. Thoroughly impressed
with the agricultural lands, the climate, and the abundance of timber,
Wood canceled plans to visit other Brazilian provinces and returned
to Rio de Janeiro to discuss land acquisition. Upon completion of a
pact, Wood boarded the steamship *South America* on January 2, 1866,
and sailed for New York. Following his arrival on January 25, he returned to the South, supposedly to make his reports. For unknown
reasons, however, Wood lost all interest in Brazil after his return and
dropped out of the emigration picture, much to the dismay of the
Brazilians.[6]

At the same time Wood's prospecting expedition searched São Paulo
Province, another Confederate, Major Lansford Warren Hastings, investigated colonization prospects on the Amazon. After his chances of
gaining a presidency or at least a governorship in California vanished,
the famous trailblazer of the American West attached himself to the
southern cause. Hastings supported slavery, became a Confederate
officer, and devised a scheme to capture both Arizona and New Mexico for the South. After receiving permission direct from Jefferson
Davis to implement the plan, Hastings dropped the idea, probably because of a decision of southern military leaders to deny him complete
authority in the operation. After the end of the war, he became one of
the first to endorse emigration to Brazil.[7]

In December, 1865, while other southerners still debated the ethics,
opportunities, and fears of leaving the defeated South, Hastings was
on his way to Brazil with a colony. He chartered the schooner *Neptune*
at Mobile, Alabama, and sailed on December 27 for Rio de Janeiro

with forty-two persons. On January 4 the ship was wrecked by a storm twenty-six miles from Havana after a defect in the ship's compass took it off course. The Americans made their way to the Cuban capital, where they dispersed: some continued to Mexico while others went to Florida. A few of the passengers, wishing to return to Alabama, boarded the steamship *Guiding Star* for New Orleans and thence to Mobile. According to Hastings, most of the colonists vowed to renew the effort to go to Brazil after a visit to former homes and friends.[8]

The Brazilian government expressed concern about the wreck of the *Neptune* and the possibility of losing the persons aboard as colonists. It began an effort to locate the passengers and made an official offer to provide free transportation for any of them to continue to Brazil. When the colonists were located, the consul was to offer, "in the name of the government, passage gratis to this country, where they will have the liberty to choose such mode of life and place of location as may suit them." Although the passengers of the *Neptune* were so scattered that the effort was generally unsuccessful, no question existed about the intentions of Lansford Warren Hastings. He would sail for Brazil as soon as he could gather another contingent of colonists, and on March 26, 1866, Hastings and thirty-five southerners left Mobile on the steamer *Margaret*. Bad luck seemed destined to plague Hastings' efforts, however, for only a few days from shore, smallpox on board ship forced the captain to turn back to the United States to face a quarantine in Mobile Bay. Before it was lifted, eleven of the would-be colonists had died.[9]

By the summer of 1866 Hastings was back in Brazil, this time 1,000 miles up the Amazon. He obtained a huge provisional grant of sixty square leagues of land at the confluence of the Tapejos, Curea, and Amazon rivers. The price of the tract was only twenty-two and one-half cents per acre, payable at the end of the third year. Hastings also received other inducements to settle in Brazil and declared that he was "fully satisfied with the country and the government," and that he intended to make Brazil "his permanent future home."[10]

Hastings returned to the South in the fall of 1866 and immediately began recruiting additional colonists for the Amazon River tract. In July, 1867, he left Mobile for Pará with 109 persons on the *Red Gauntlet*, an iron steamer that had long been on the South American run. The ship had mechanical problems at the island of St. Thomas and was unable to proceed further. Consequently, the Hastings emigrants were forced to board the regular packet to Brazil, then complete the voyage on an Amazon River steamer. Hastings later assembled another shipload of emigrants for his colony, but he died on board ship as it made its way to Brazil.[11]

Another colonization venture to Brazil began in late 1865 when William Hutchinson Norris and his son Robert C. Norris of Alabama went to São Paulo Province in search of lands. They bypassed the city of São Paulo, preferring instead to go about eighty miles into the interior where they located rolling farmlands that were easily adapted to American-style agriculture. They then sent for their wives and children as well as other southerners who desired to emigrate. The Norris family sailed from New Orleans in a small ship, the *Talisman*, accompanied by twenty-six other Alabamians. After sailing off course for eighty-nine days, the *Talisman* finally docked at Rio de Janeiro on April 19, 1867.[12]

James McFadden Gaston, a southerner from an old aristocratic family in South Carolina, arrived in Brazil on September 12, 1865, to search for suitable colony sites. He arrived just before the prospecting party headed by General William Wallace Wood and at times worked in concert with the Mississippian in land exploration. Gaston eventually decided on property on the upper Ribeira River near the town of Xiririca. He kept an extensive log of his travels and, upon his return to the United States to recruit colonists, wrote a detailed book entitled *Hunting a Home in Brazil*, which later became a standard reference work for many who considered emigration.[13]

Another Alabamian, Charles Grandioson Gunter, made plans to take an extensive colony to the Doce River near Lake Juparanão, north of Rio de Janeiro. Described as a "tremendously large man with a voice like the rumblings of distant thunder," Gunter predicted that "fifty Southern families from Alabama, Florida, Louisiana, Mississippi, Texas, and Virginia would go with him to the tropics." Gunter was so vehemently anti-Union that after his arrival in Brazil he instructed his son in Alabama to "settle my affairs as if I were dead in the United States. I shall never go there again, unless I go on business for this government." After extensive negotiations with Brazilian officials, Gunter supposedly obtained five million acres of land which he planned to develop into twenty settlements.[14]

One of the most carefully planned efforts to plant a colony in South America was formulated by the Southern Emigration Society of Edgefield, South Carolina, with Joseph Abney as president. The society sent Major Robert Meriwether and Dr. Hugh A. Shaw to Brazil with instructions to explore the entire southern part of the country for a suitable location. After the completion of the survey, the two men recommended the area around the town of Botucatu in São Paulo Province. Despite the efforts of its agents, the Southern Emigration Society never actually sent additional colonists to Brazil, although both Meriwether and Shaw remained.[15]

Another early attempt at Confederate settlement in Brazil began in the summer of 1865 when Colonel M. S. Swain and Horace Lane of Louisiana selected property on the Assunguay River in Paraná Province in the southern part of the country. By October the two men had been joined by thirty-five other southerners, most of whom were from Missouri. This American colony continued to grow, principally on the basis of letters to the editor of the *Daily Missouri Republican* by Dr. John H. Blue, who constantly urged the home folks to leave the "radicals" and come to Brazil. Several families accumulated large land holdings and others became financially independent after starting a firm to manufacture barrels to hold *herva-mate*.[16]

On November 11, 1865, the Reverend Ballard Smith Dunn, Rector of St. Phillips Church, New Orleans, and during the war a chaplain and ordnance officer of the Confederate army, left Rio de Janeiro in an effort to locate lands for a colony for those who "from manly motives" were "seriously contemplating emigration." Dunn's plans called for a search of the Province of Rio de Janeiro as well as the southern part of Espirito Santo Province. After a long and unsuccessful search, Dunn and his companions finally went to São Paulo Province, where, on February 2, 1866, he found lands that he believed would be suitable, the "magnificent valley of the Juquea [Juquiá River]." Here Dunn planned to establish a colony that he would call Lizzieland in honor of his late wife Elizabeth. On April 14, Dunn returned to Rio de Janeiro in preparation for his return to the United States to recruit colonists.[17]

On December 9, 1865, the ship *Ann & Lizzie* arrived at Rio de Janeiro from New York. Among the passengers were three Texans, Major Frank McMullan, Colonel William Bowen, and Major S. S. Totten. The three had left Texas for Brazil to explore the possibilities of emigration and to search for lands that might be secured for a colony composed of relatives and friends from Hill, Navarro, Bosque, and other Central Texas counties. Colonel Bowen was a veteran of three wars—the Texas war for independence from Mexico, the Mexican war of 1847–48, and the Civil War. He shared McMullan's anti-Union sentiments and was eager to find a new home not threatened by northern occupation. A widower, Bowen also sought a suitable place to raise his seven children. Silas S. Totten was a bona fide southern hero famous for his leadership in the Battle of Dove Creek. Known as a first-class machinist, Totten was particularly interested in the potential for manufacturing in Brazil.[18]

The initial stop of the three men in Rio was the office of the First Secretary of Agriculture, Commerce, and Public Works, Antonio Francisco de Paula e Souza. The Brazilian was delighted to see the Texans and vowed to do everything possible to ensure the success of their search for lands. On January 8, Paula e Souza wrote a letter to the president of the coastal steamship line authorizing free passage for the three. He also notified authorities that the men were to be honored as guests of the Imperial Government and given free transportation on all public thoroughfares. They also received letters of introduction to the heads of all municipal governments through which they might pass with instructions to the Brazilians to furnish information and facilitate movement through the country as much as possible.[19]

On the afternoon of January 9, the three men boarded the coastal steamer *Dom Affonso* in preparation for sailing the next morning for Cananea, a seacoast city where they were to meet Major Ernesto Dinez Street, the Inspector General of Public Lands for the Province of São Paulo. Southerner Arthur M. Hanson, a "very enterprising [man] with a fine presence and a copius flow of good language," also joined the party. On the morning of January 10 they began the 400-mile trip down the coast. After passing the port of Santos, they came in sight first of the town and mission of Conceição, then the village of Peruibe, and finally legendary Iguape—remembered as the point of departure for those who would search for João Aranzel's fabled Lake of Gold. McMullan could not help but dream of the possibilities of finding the treasure as he viewed the town and its imposing church, Bom Jesus de Iguape. Although his surveying task would not allow him to stop at that time, he was eager to return to the small coastal city. But the unimposing skyline of Iguape was soon obscured by low hills, and the trip to the south continued. At 4:00 P.M. on the thirteenth, after what one passenger called "a most unpoetical voyage in a slow, comfortless steamer," they reached their destination, the little town of Cananea. There McMullan, Bowen, and Totten met Inspector General Street and began making plans for their trip into the interior.[20]

That evening McMullan had his first opportunity to study an accurate and detailed map of São Paulo Province. As expected, McMullan located the towns of Conceição, Peruibe, and Iguape as well as the rivers that were to play such an important part in his plans. The Una River flowed into the Ribeira de Iguape north of the town of Iguape, and the tributary of the Juquiá, the São Lourenço River, traveled a circuitous course through the mountains between Iguape and Conceição. Nearby, the cartographer designated a mountain known as São Lourenço Peak. Called by many the "Finger of God," the elevation is visible from any point on the coast of Brazil between Conceição and Iguape, and it is said to "shine like polished metal in the noon-day sun."[21]

During his stay in Cananea McMullan also learned of another legend concerning gold in the *serra* of coastal Brazil. The story was attributed to Father Ancheita, the venerated Jesuit apostle to the Indians who was the confessor and advisor of João Aranzel, the criminal who was said to have found the Lake of Gold. For hundreds of years, McMullan was told, the natives of the region passed from generation to generation the cryptic information that "between mother and son lies a great treasure." The "mother," McMullan learned, signified the little convent in the town of Conceição—Our Lady of Conceição—and the "son" was interpreted as the church that graces the center of the town of Iguape, the entry to the Juquiá River. São Lourenço Peak, mentioned by João Aranzel as one of the keys to finding the Lake of Gold, is almost equidistant between the two municipalities. McMullan resolved to determine as soon as possible whether the area in the region of São Lourenço Peak was available for colonization grants and, if so, to take steps as soon as possible to try to secure the properties.[22]

In his first general conference with Inspector General Street about the availability of lands in São Paulo Province, McMullan made inquiries about several possible colonization sites, including the headwaters of the Juquiá River and the area around São Lourenço Peak. Street acknowledged that that area was one of many that were available to McMullan. In addition, Street noted that the price for the property was the same as the other in the region—twenty-two and one-half cents per acre. Further, the Inspector General stated that it would be possible to inspect the area in the course of looking at other sites.[23]

After five days in Cananea, the travelers began their explorations. They followed the Jacupiranga River to the town of Botujuru, then made a search of the Bananal River valley. Upon discovering the magnificent falls of the waterway, Major Totten and Captain Hanson resolved to become partners, secure the property, and open a sawmill. McMullan and Bowen were also impressed with the region, but McMullan insisted that they continue. They had not yet seen the São Lourenço.[24]

After another fruitless foray up the tributary of the Jacupiranga, the explorers shifted their quest toward the Ribeira de Iguape, a huge waterway into which almost all of the rivers of the area eventually flow. This leg of the trip covered some of the most rugged country they had traversed. The route followed "a dim trailway, often barely perceivable for the first eight miles." The group of six men, including *cameradas* to carry baggage, had only two horses, and these, said McMullan, "without bridle or saddle—our blankets answering for the former, while thongs of bark, tied to the under jaw of the animals, made substitutes for the former." They finally reached the "lovely and inviting village" of Xiririca. There they were met by townspeople who were extremely friendly to the Americans and expressed a desire that they would locate a *municipio* in the area. To ensure future hospitality for the travelers, the *delgado* of Xiririca gave letters of recommendation to McMullan and Bowen so that they might receive warm and courteous treatment as they proceeded up the river.[25]

Using Xiririca as a base, McMullan and his party traveled extensively throughout the upper Ribeira River valley, even climbing small mountains described by McMullan as "much like the mesas of western Texas." Eager to inspect more likely properties, however, McMullan convinced Bowen, Totten, and others to return downriver to the coast and the town of Iguape. The old port city intrigued the visitors with its beautiful buildings, wide avenues, and beautiful churches, and the town provided a civilized respite after the rigorous days and nights spent in rugged river valleys and on mountain trails. After securing rooms in the local hotel, McMullan and Bowen began making plans for future exploration.[26]

As they discussed their business with town leaders at Iguape, Mc-Mullan and Bowen learned that another American was also there, and with similar objectives. After a short search they located Reverend Ballard Dunn, the minister from New Orleans. Speaking of the area in glowing terms, Dunn declared that he had already located riverfront property on the Juquiá River, where he planned to build a colony he termed Lizzieland. When Dunn invited McMullan to accompany him to the colony site, the Texan responded quickly and enthusiastically, as he knew that Dunn's properties were near the upper Juquiá and the São Lourenço, the headwaters near São Lourenço Peak, which he was eager to inspect. McMullan and Bowen agreed to meet Dunn in four days at the Ponta Grossa, another tributary of the Ribeira de Iguape, then proceeded from there to the Juquiá River. Totten and Hanson, not eager to begin another wilderness trek and pleased with the properties they had already selected, left the McMullan party for good.[27]

The trip up the Juquiá River with Reverend Dunn was an enjoyable one to McMullan and Bowen. The waterway was 150 yards wide at its mouth, McMullan noted, and was deep enough for large steamers. Compared with properties already inspected, the countryside was extremely impressive. Upon arriving at the future site of Dunn's colony, however, McMullan privately expressed concern. The lower Juquiá, although beautiful with broad, flat riverbanks, appeared to be floodprone, a concern that would be confirmed within a year.[28]

After expressing appreciation to Reverend Dunn for his friendship and hospitality, the McMullan party continued upriver, eager to see

the waters of the São Lourenço, a region that might offer fine farmland as well as mineral wealth. Indeed, it could be the best of all possible worlds. McMullan was not disappointed. "On the upper Juquiá
and São Lourenço," wrote McMullan, "we found a country that did
our hearts good, and made us feel that we had at long last found the
place we had been looking for for so long. There, in this delightful
region, we determined to locate." Not unexpectedly, the properties selected by the Texans lay almost exactly within the limits of the area
described in João Aranzel's directions to the Lake of Gold.[29]

Since the lands available for colonization were not directly on the
lower watershed of the São Lourenço and thus not easily accessible for
river transportation of crops, McMullan immediately began talks with
Inspector General Street about acquiring legal right-of-way to riverbanks. After receiving verbal assurances, he set out for Rio de Janeiro
to ask the emperor to appoint a competent person to make the grants
as well as to confirm all other agreements in writing. "We were not
suspicious," said McMullan, "of any 'intentional' fraud on the part of
the people, but were only desirous of seeing our way clear, and guard-
ing against future contingencies." McMullan worried that his caution
would be misinterpreted by the Brazilians, but the request was granted
without question. McMullan subsequently asked for written answers
to a number of questions which, like the grants, might be forgotten or
misinterpreted if not set down on paper. He forwarded the inquiries
to Bernardo Nascentes de Azambuja, the Third Secretary of Public
Lands and Colonization:

1. Please state again the price of lands, including the price of
measurement.

2. Restate, in writing, that McMullan and Bowen are to have sole
regulation of the amount of land that each emigrant will be able
to buy.

3. Provide assurance that the lands received by McMullan and
Bowen will have provisionary title, clearly written, with the limits
clearly outlined, and that this title can be exchanged for others which
will be definitive after the payment of the value of the lands purchased.

4. Say in writing that the emigrants who come will be able to im-
port, free of duty, all of their farm implements, manufactured items,
utensils, and other objects which they carry with them for their use.

5. Acknowledge in writing that the government will unilaterally
make arrangements for the reception of the emigrants upon their
arrival.

6. Concerning transport. Please say again that the government will
pay the cost of leasing one or two ships that will be leased by McMullan

and Bowen to carry emigrants. Or, as an alternative, say that the government agrees to pay the cost of passage of the emigrants after their arrival in Brazil, and that we will be allowed to repay this money over a period of three or four years. Please acknowledge that this responsibility will become effective upon the assumption of lands that are purchased in the empire.

7. Please state again that the emigrants will be able to dock at Iguape without passing through Rio de Janeiro. Any communications are to be received through the intermediary of the Brazilian Consul, or Vice Consul, of the mode and time needed to expedite the precise orders to this end, without visiting the customhouse of the port.

8. Please acknowledge that McMullan and Bowen have guarantees concerning the unexplored lands that exist on the São Lourenço River and its tributaries, as indicated on the map that is on file in the archives of the Secretary of Public Lands and Colonization.[30]

The same day, Street wrote a declaration about the measurement of the lands in which he said that the McMullan-Bowen lands encompassed sixty square leagues, or five hundred thousand square *braças*. He stated once more that provisional title had been issued and declared the property eligible for measurement in order to determine definitive legal ownership.[31]

After receiving provisional title from the Inspector General, McMullan and Bowen left Rio de Janeiro on April 6 for the Juquiá–São Lourenço area to "make a more thorough examination of the Government lands included in the survey which we had selected." The men went up the São Lourenço, "half a day's run," to the home of one Joaquim Pedroso, who invited them to spend the night. With Pedroso as guide, they took canoes and went about eight miles upstream, where they left the water and proceeded on foot to colony lands. Upon arrival, they found the site to be of "very superior quality, well situated, and above all overflow." The land, they felt, could easily support twenty families and, just as important, they could unhesitatingly offer it to their friends. The Bigua, a "beautiful creek" that ran through the lands, flowed over "a bed of clean, white sand, with a delightful valley spreading out on each side a distance of from three hundred yards to more than a mile, and this skirted by high hills covered with fine, large timber." Returning to their canoe after a strenuous and tiring walk, McMullan and Bowen stopped for the night. The next morning by 10:00 A.M. they began their descent of the river and within a short time arrived again at the home of Sr. Pedroso.[32]

After refreshments and rest, the Texans again headed their canoe up the São Lourenço to look at the remainder of the lands. Throughout the day, they passed farms and coffee *fazendas* on the river's edge and marveled at the beauty of the area. By early evening they were "snugly resting under the friendly roof of Sr. Captain Lui Leite." This gentleman, "being well acquainted with the country above, volunteered to accompany us," said McMullan, "and on the morning of the 30th of April we were up the river again."[33]

Within two hours of leaving Leite's home they found themselves at the head of steamboat navigation on the São Lourenço and at the mouth of a tributary called the Itariri. After a stop for the night they proceeded up the smaller stream, where they saw several falls and passed the mouth of the Peixe (Fish) River. By noon they were at the mouth of the Rio de Azeite (River of Oil), "decidedly the clearest, most transparent, and purest water we have ever seen in any country. As small a thing as a pin is clearly perceivable at a depth of ten feet as though it were on the surface."[34]

Going up the Azeite one and one-half miles the prospective colonizers found an extensive plain from four to ten miles wide and twelve to fifteen in length, "covered with large, straight timber, and [with] a hundred rivulets dancing over beds of yellow gold-like sand. The land," said McMullan, "will be easier to clear than any others we have seen in this country, being of loose, yellow loam, and with plenty of sand to make them pleasant to cultivate." He also noted that the lands at this point were dry and always above the river during overflow. "This day, May 1, 1866, was," according to McMullan,

> the happiest day we had spent in the Empire; we felt that our hopes were realized, that the great Giver of all good had blessed our honest endeavors to find and secure homes for a brave but unfortunate people. Here the homeless may find a home, and the outcast "a resting place, with none to molest or make him afraid." Here are lands equal to any in the world and within three or four days' run from the great Capital of the nation, a climate unsurpassed, neither hot nor cold, and where frost is never known, water as cold as the mountain spring, and so equally distributed as to allow every man to run his plantation machinery from it. Here also everything grows, and grows well, too, that is calculated to minister to the health and comfort, not to say luxury, of man.[35]

After spending several days in what would be their new home, McMullan and Bowen began their trek back down the river. On their way to Iguape, they stopped long enough for Frank to purchase, for cash, a small *fazenda* on the Juquiá River that McMullan proposed to use as a headquarters for colonists when they arrived from Texas.

Called Morro Redondo (Round Mountain), the farm boasted a large number of well-cultivated coffee trees. Leaving the Juquiá, the two men continued to Iguape, where they said good-bye. Bowen agreed to stay in Brazil to make final arrangements with the government as well as to begin the preparations for the arrival of the colonists. McMullan boarded a steamer from Iguape bound for Rio de Janeiro, where he arrived on March 14 and made his final report to the Secretary of Agriculture. Near the end of that document, McMullan expressed his faith in the Brazilian government and voiced his hope for the future: "We have the best system of government known to man; while it combines all the elements of strength requisite to insure its stability against every emergency, it guarantees PRACTICAL EQUALITY to ALL its citizens, and administers justice with a firm and willing hand. We have a monarchy (thank God!) in name, and a TRUE republic in practice; and under the wise administration of our good Emperor, our destiny must be onward and upward to a degree of prosperity unknown to other countries."[36]

The report chronicled almost every movement of McMullan and Bowen from the day of their arrival in Brazil until the return to Rio de Janeiro. Well-written, it presented an in-depth analysis of the geography, the people encountered, and the prospects for success in the new land. It consumed nearly two months in preparation, but was finally delivered on May 24, 1866. On June 2, McMullan received a reply from Bernardo Nascentes de Azambuja that satisfactorily answered and put in writing all of the concerns expressed in the April 4 letter. Thus the stage was set. The site for the colony was located and provisional title obtained. Finally, Frank McMullan could return to Texas.[37]

CHAPTER 3

Steamers from the South

WHEN A WEARY BUT pleased Frank McMullan sailed on the *North America* on June 3, 1866, from Rio de Janeiro to New York, he felt that a huge weight had been lifted from his shoulders. His six-month inspection of lands in Brazil was over and a comprehensive report to the Brazilian Secretary of Agriculture was complete. In addition, McMullan and his partner William Bowen owned over fifty-four leagues of land on the São Lourenço River, and the boundaries were officially designated. But work remained to be done by the two men. Rather than return to the United States, Bowen elected to remain in Brazil and construct a large temporary structure where the former Americans might live until they could build their own homes. Bowen also promised to begin negotiations with officials of São Paulo Province concerning the construction of a wagon road from colony lands over the Serra do Mar, a coastal mountain range, to the city of Santos. McMullan, on the other hand, planned to conclude travel arrangements with the Brazilian minister in New York and then return to Texas to make final plans with prospective colonists. He did not imagine that plans which seemed so simple would go awry.[1]

McMullan was eager and confident of success when he arrived in New York on June 28. His enthusiasm quickly turned to disappointment, however, when he learned that Minister Joaquim de Azambuja was out of town and that he would not be able to conclude his transportation and travel arrangements on schedule. McMullan became even more unhappy when the minister's aides told him of a pact that was being negotiated that might cast doubt on the arrangements for leasing a ship that Brazilian officials had approved before he left Rio de Janeiro. A tentative agreement between the empire and the United States and Brazil Steamship Company contained provisions whereby the firm would be the only authorized carrier for the transportation of American emigrants to Brazil. The accord outlined a table of rates, with prices from southern ports, and provided for a special agent who would clarify all conditions to prospective colonists as well as issue Brazilian passports, a condition for boarding ships. In addition, the proposed pact contained conditions for advances to emigrants for travel costs, repayment terms after arrival in Brazil, and the Empire's freedom from reimbursement conditions to the company. Although many of the proposal's conditions were not in themselves objectionable, the tone of the accord was such that earlier promises to McMullan could be undermined.[2]

McMullan contended that he was not affected by the new pact; as a naturalized citizen of Brazil, he was no longer an emigrant. Furthermore, his June 2 correspondence from Bernardo de Azambuja, the Third Secretary of Public Lands and Colonization in Rio de Janeiro, stated in writing that he was authorized to lease a ship, the cost of which would be reimbursed by the imperial government when the colonists arrived in Brazil. McMullan also argued that he did not desire to dock in Rio de Janeiro as provided in the new agreement. Rather, he wished to land at the port of Iguape, a city much closer to colony lands. This concession, too, was granted in writing to McMullan in Secretary Bernardo de Azambuja's letter of June 2.[3]

Without Minister Joaquim de Azambuja, the consul's staff could not reconcile the pending contract terms with those already promised by the Brazilian government to McMullan. To clarify the situation, the aides suggested that McMullan write to the minister, outlining his objections and asking for clarification. Before departing from New York on July 2, McMullan did as the aides requested, although he hesitated to leave for the South without the answers he needed. When Minister de Azambuja returned to the consulate on July 5, he promptly replied to McMullan, who by that time was en route to Texas. The correspondence did not, however, provide answers to the questions that had been raised. Minister de Azambuja wrote that he regretted that he did not have the opportunity to discuss the situation personally with McMullan because he could have "explained better the instructions I received from my government on the subject of emigration." The minister outlined the terms of the proposed contract in considerable detail; then he stated that he had no special orders authorizing him to act in McMullan's case. Nevertheless, he did promise that he would correspond with officials in Rio de Janeiro so that he could discuss the matter more intelligently. Minister de Azambuja also advised McMullan that he was aware that many southerners would find it difficult, if not impossible, to get to New York and promised that he would do everything in his power "to give all the assistance and solicitude they may want from this Legation."[4]

True to his word, the minister did write to Secretary of Agriculture Paula e Souza and requested detailed information about McMullan's situation. He complained that he was confused by what seemed to be contradictory policy. He said it appeared that McMullan, according to Bernardo de Azambuja's letter of June 2, was officially authorized by the imperial government to "lease ships for emigrants." This permission seemed to be in direct opposition to new imperial policy, as the proposed agreement would limit all emigrant travel to the ships of the United States and Brazil Steamship Company. Consequently, the minister said he would not recognize McMullan's authority to contract independently until he received further instructions from Rio de Janeiro. On the other hand, de Azambuja reasoned that McMullan's plan seemed "to promote emigration directly from Louisiana or other states of the South without the necessity of bringing persons to New York to approve grants, passports, and other favors that are today at the disposal of the Imperial Government to confer." In another letter of the same date, Minister de Azambuja concluded that allowing emigrants to board steamships at southern ports would be more reasonable than departing from New York. The tone of de Azambuja's letters, although expressing loyalty to his superior, reflected a bias toward the more logical approach suggested by McMullan.[5]

Despite Minister de Azambuja's personal opinions concerning the logic of emigrants departing from other than southern ports, he soon learned that his government had concluded the agreement with the United States and Brazil Steamship Company on June 20, 1866, which did not contain this provision. In an attempt to clarify official policy, de Azambuja wrote a letter of inquiry to Secretary of Agriculture Paula e Souza (who signed the new agreement for Brazil) in which he declared that his office did not have complete knowledge of what was happening and that the "convenience of facilitating passage directly from the ports of the South disappears with the contract celebrated by . . . [Paula e Souza's] agency." He was clearly distressed by what he considered a contradiction in emigration policy by his government.[6]

On June 30, ten days after Paula e Souza and the United States and Brazil Steamship Company completed their pact, Secretary Bernardo de Azambuja wrote an official letter from Rio de Janeiro to Ballard S. Dunn that was almost identical to the one addressed to McMullan and Bowen on June 2. Like the Texans, Dunn specifically received permission to act as his own contractor, including permission to lease a ship, for bringing emigrants from the South to Brazil. Obviously, confusion still reigned supreme in the Brazilian bureaucracy.[7]

Within thirty days after the signing of the pact between the steamship company and the Brazilian government, difficulties began to surface that neither party originally anticipated. To the chagrin of company president C. K. Garrison, the Brazilians modified their position by stating that the new contract did not invalidate an old agreement that called for a 30 percent discount for "first class" citizens. Garrison answered that he could not operate profitably under those terms and refused to answer further correspondence from Minister de Azambuja on the subject. Garrison also declined to implement other provisions of the June 24 contract. The problem festered when three men from Arkansas were refused tickets by the steamship company under the reduced fare. Minister de Azambuja attempted to discuss the matter with Garrison, but, once again, he was ignored. In a letter to Rio de Janeiro, de Azambuja suggested that the legation in New York be given the power to contract all passages of emigrants because of "the apparent prejudice of . . . [Garrison's] company against emigrants from the South."[8]

The questions of steamship service to southern ports, discounts on tickets, and extended payment terms were of immense importance to the Confederate emigration movement. No doubt these and other questions were in Frank McMullan's thoughts as he left New York for Texas to complete final arrangements with prospective emigrants for his colony in Brazil. He would no doubt have to answer questions such as these, and he knew that in some cases it would be difficult to do so.

Another reason for going home, other than to recruit colonists, was to be present at the August 9 wedding of his sister Jennie to George L. Clark, a former Mississippian who farmed and taught school at the community of Bosqueville, McLennan County, Texas. Also attending were most members of the McMullan family, including Frank's mother Nancy and his youngest brother Ney. In addition, Frank saw his sister Vic and her husband of one year, affable William T. Moore, a Bosqueville dentist. He also renewed ties with his brother-in-law, John Odell, a former Hill County neighbor, and his sister Lou. McMullan's sister Matt and her husband John B. Williams were also present for the occasion.[9]

The wedding also gave Frank the opportunity to discuss colonization plans with Judge Dyer, his uncle and strongest family ally in the plans to emigrate. Dyer, already living in New Orleans so that he could facilitate arrangements for departure for Brazil, reported to his nephew that he did not anticipate any problems in enrolling a number of people adequate to fill a small ship. Already McMullan's mother, his sisters Lou and Vic and their husbands, and his younger brother Ney were making plans to emigrate, as was McMullan's old college friend Columbus Wasson. The judge planned to bring his wife Amanda as well as his two sons Wylie and James and his daughter Harriet. Other friends and family from Hill, Navarro, Limestone, Freestone, Grimes, and Brazos counties already had determined to follow the young leader to Brazil.[10]

One of the first to join the colony ranks was Parson Elijah H. Quillin, a crippled Baptist minister from Hill and Navarro counties who was also trained as a teacher. Like many other Texans, Quillin was bitter about the defeat of the Confederacy and determined that he could not, with clear conscience, remain in the occupied South. The well-known Quillin, his wife Sarah, and their five children represented a notable beginning for the colony rolls, and the minister was undoubtedly influential in the decision of others to follow McMullan.[11]

Another large and important addition to the prospective colony was the Alfred I. Smith family. Smith, Frank McMullan's former teacher from Chestnut Flat, Georgia, came to Texas at Frank's suggestion. Before he knew of the proposed McMullan colony, Smith had already decided to emigrate to Mexico; but when the two men met in a chance encounter, Smith quickly changed his destination to Brazil. One account related that McMullan made the following appeal: "Don't run away . . . until I tell you about the real South—this new land under the Southern Cross where a gentleman is treated like a gentleman and there are thousands of rich acres waiting for us progressive farmers. I tell you we're going to empty the Old South for the Yankees, let them have it if they think they know how to run it better than we did. I'm taking my family to Brazil, the empire of freedom and plenty." The two men were very close friends, for Smith's daughter later recalled that Frank's father, "old Hugh McMullan, had been a father to my dad when he first started in life, and finally gave him a homestead in Texas." She recalled that her father would "follow Frank to the end of the world and die for him if need be, and Frank was truly worthy of [his] affection."[12]

Several other Central Texas families and individuals had little trouble making up their minds to join the Quillins and the Smiths. Two brothers, Cortez and Zeno Fielder from Navarro County, looked upon the Brazilian emigration as a once-in-a-lifetime venture. Both in their early twenties, they joined the colony early in its planning stages. Several other families, including the Wrights, the Weavers, and the McKnights, were seriously considering Brazilian plans by the end of August, 1866. McMullan estimated that as many as thirty families, as well as a number of single men, were planning to go with him as colonists.[13]

In late September 1866, Frank McMullan left Texas for New Orleans. The task of securing a ship was still ahead of him, and he wanted to be sure that he allowed sufficient time to buy or lease a vessel, have it outfitted for the long ocean voyage, and leave Galveston by December 1. This would have been a reasonable number of days under ordinary circumstances, but once in the Crescent City, McMullan encountered a myriad of problems that might have discouraged a less persistent man. The most pressing difficulty for McMullan was his health. Although he managed to endure the six months of travel in Brazil, the problems inherent in tuberculosis began to take their toll. The humid, warm atmosphere in New Orleans compounded his breathing problems and forced him to stay in bed much more than he wished. A photograph of McMullan taken at the time shows a pale, hollow-faced individual who must have been a far cry from the strapping wrestler in Walker's army ten years before. But McMullan continued his plans with the fervor of an evangelist, despite the increasing damage to his physical condition.[14]

Due to McMullan's poor health, he felt that it was critical that he determine whether the agreement that he had negotiated while he was in Brazil was still valid. He was consequently disappointed when, during a visit to the office of the Brazilian vice-consul in New Orleans, McMullan learned of the completion of the June 20 pact between the empire and the United States and Brazil Steamship Company. He immediately wrote to Minister de Azambuja in New York to protest the agreement, arguing that the instructions of the contract were "so restrictive that they do not produce the advantages that the Imperial Government has in sight." In a September 30 letter to Souza Dantas, de Azambuja agreed with McMullan, particularly in regard to the requirement that southerners go to New York in order to board boats for Brazil: "His [McMullan's] provisions do not seem to me entirely without foundation if you consider the antagonism which exists between Northerners and Southerners, the adversity of their voting, and the differences in attracting them to this city, where, according to the last orders of Your Excellency, they [must come] to arrange passage to Brazil."[15]

The logic of McMullan's arguments for an emigrant ship from the South finally began to pay off, and a letter from Souza Dantas to de Azambuja finally confirmed, for the first time, that the imperial government approved of McMullan's plans to contract independently for the passage of his colonists. In his reply to Souza Dantas, de Azambuja noted that he had mailed McMullan authority to do so and gave him written guarantees of payment that he believed were sufficient to convince ship owners of the Brazilian government's strong backing of McMullan. De Azambuja informed Souza Dantas that he had also mailed copies of the letter of support to both Texas and New Orleans, so that they would "without doubt arrive in the hands of that gentleman [McMullan] in time for him to be able to complete, before December, the arrangements he must make in these States." De Azambuja further stated that "McMullan and all of his people are intelligent and industrious, in whose energy and precedents the Imperial Government is able to place confidence."[16]

By October 17 McMullan had heard through the vice-consul in New Orleans of the mailing by Minister de Azambuja of the letter of guarantee that was needed in order to lease a ship. A month later, however, McMullan began to worry that it had been lost. He sent an urgent telegram explaining his situation to de Azambuja, then followed it with a detailed letter the following day:

> Your excellency will pardon me for writing again, but I begin to be apprehensive, that your answer [may] have miscarried; and as my position just now is a very responsible one, so many people looking to, and depending upon me, I feel constrained to request of Your Excellency that a duplicate of your letter be sent to me by return mail, to the care of the Consulate here. Be kind enough to send it in such official form as will enable me to use it in chartering vessels—such form as to be considered a guarantee, that the promises of the Brazilian Government to me will be fulfilled immediately on the landing of the emigrants to Brazil. I would respectfully *urge* this matter as the people expect me to have everything ready for them to sail about 1st. December.[17]

Continuing, McMullan noted that the amount of time remaining to complete the business at hand was growing shorter and shorter. He explained to the minister that he had gone to a "great deal of trouble about this matter, and all to accommodate my friends and encourage the cause of emigration, and without the hope, promise, or desire of remuneration." McMullan said that he hoped those reasons would be a sufficient apology for his firmness. In case the minister had any doubts as to whether McMullan could really find enough emigrants to fill a ship, the Texan offered to secure "a certificate from any County Court in Texas, with the County seal to it, to this effect." If he only had the minister's endorsement, he added, he had the promise of a vessel. As to the quality of the persons who planned to join the colony, McMullan informed de Azambuja that they would be "first class citizens, the most of whom possessed fortunes before the war." Finally, McMullan repeated his conviction that he regarded it as a great pity that the Brazilian government did not have a line of steamers from New Orleans to Rio de Janeiro. "If they had," stated the Texan colonizer, "a stream of emigration would carry with it the energy, intelligence, and chivalry of this country."[18]

After receiving McMullan's telegram, Minister de Azambuja wrote Souza Dantas to inform him of the problem. He reported to his superior that he had answered McMullan the same day and repeated his previous guarantees. De Azambuja also informed Souza Dantas that he had offered Reverend Ballard S. Dunn the same assurances that he had sent to McMullan. De Azambuja reiterated his confidence in McMullan and Dunn, remarking that "these empresarios to whom I refer seem to have extensive relations with important and respectable people of the South and I believe that their diligence in attracting emigrants to the Empire will compensate for the imposters Wood, Waley, and other speculators who so badly repaid the benevolent treatment which was given to them by the Imperial Government and all Brazilians."[19]

McMullan received the long-awaited letter of guarantee on October 19, the day after he had written to de Azambuja asking for assistance. Delighted, he went immediately to several maritime brokerage houses with which he was negotiating and attempted to finalize the charter of a suitable vessel. Without exception, however, the firms refused to honor the assurances given by de Azambuja. They declared that the paper, by itself, was insufficient and that they could honor the warranty only if adequate security in the United States was pledged in their favor. Moreover, they all insisted that the passage for the emigrants be paid to them immediately upon landing in Brazil. The brokers declared that they did not know how well the Brazilian government paid its bills and that they could not afford to risk the large sums of money required in such an undertaking.

When McMullan realized that his efforts to convince ship owners were useless, he returned to the Brazilian vice-consul in New Orleans and asked for assistance. Not wishing to place himself in a precarious position, however, the agent declined to help, with the excuse that he could not assume this responsibility. In a quandary, McMullan wrote another letter to de Azambuja, pleading for answers to his questions and reviewing the multitude of problems he would face if a solution to his transportation dilemma was not found quickly:

My situation is awkward and embarrassing. I am in New Orleans, and my friends are in middle Texas, depending upon me to furnish transportation. They have sold their lands and expect to sail with me from Galveston, Texas, about 1st December. I feel the weight of responsibility resting on me. The people are ready to go at the appointed time; but now the means of conveyance. I have acted in good faith, and have promised them, on the faith of promises made to me by the government that their passage should be paid, and they should have 3 or 4 years to refund the money. The small amount of funds we have on hand, we wish to lay out in machinery, implements of agriculture, etc. etc., before leaving, so as to take these with us *now*. On the faith of promises 30 families will be at Galveston, Texas, on the 1st. of December, ready to sail.[20]

Almost desperate, McMullan told the consul that he knew that he understood the problem but asked for action. "What is to be done?" McMullan queried. "I have never failed in anything in my life that energy and perseverance would accomplish and I can not think of failing now. Should I not receive the necessary assistance from Your Excellency I can only do the best I can. I must get off to Brazil soon, and I must, if possible, take my friends with me."[21]

McMullan then reviewed, once again, his plea that the Brazilian government institute a steamship service from southern ports. "I repeat what I have before said," McMullan remarked, "if the Brazilian Government intends to turn this emigration matter to account, there must be some system adopted instead of from New York; we want a line of steamers from the South; this is the only course that will ever effect anything." No change in policy was in sight, however, and on October 22 Quintino de Souza Bocayuva, a Brazilian who had been appointed special agent to assist the New York and Brazil Steamship Company, arrived in New York. Southern ship service for emigrants seemed more and more remote.[22]

While Frank McMullan searched for a way to get out of the country, at least one Texan proclaimed his strong opposition to emigration in a long letter to the *Galveston Tri-Weekly News*. John Cardwell of Columbia, Texas, considered taking a group of Texans to Brazil, but after a short trip to South America, decided against the project. The anti-emigration *News* devoted four front-page columns to Cardwell's reasons against leaving the United States. Cardwell argued principally that emigrating Texans would be subservient to "an inferior Africanized race, and at the same time become their pliant tools." He pointed to what he termed an "alarming increase" in the number of slaves in Brazil and predicted that the trend would lead to the "utter annihilation of the institution in very few years." In Brazil, he said, "there is no other prospect but that of a thoroughly Africanized government." He also described physical conditions as being undesirable with thousands of poisonous insects as well as unendurable heat and excessive rainfall. The diseases of leprosy and elephantitus, Cardwell implied, would surely infect any North American who dared to venture to that country. Furthermore, Cardwell had a low opinion of Brazilians in general. They were, he claimed, already a mixed race before leaving the Old World, and the worst on the European continent. "They are the most inferior of the Latin races," said Cardwell, "and during the long occupation of the Iberian peninsula by the Mohammedans their blood was deeply tinged with that of the Moor; this compound settled Brazil, and as neither its moral or intellectual standing was good, as soon as the African came in contact with it, an affinity was created, which has resulted in a thorough amalgamation." Cardwell then warned southerners to beware of colonization agents. "Southern men," said Cardwell, "for the sake of gold, will advise you to sell out your all here, and pursue your way seven thousand miles to live in misery, and to entail upon your children a life of shame." [23]

Frank McMullan, still in New Orleans seeking transportation, read Cardwell's arguments in the newspaper and quickly replied. He wrote a long letter to the *Galveston Tri-Weekly News,* parts of which were published on November 4, 1866. The editor, claiming that McMullan's rebuttal was "not quite just to our correspondent [Cardwell]," nevertheless agreed "in justice to the writer" to "state the points of interest to the public." McMullan was quoted as saying that Cardwell wrote "like one who had never traveled through the country [Brazil], and was too much affected by the change of homes to give this new location an impartial judgment." McMullan maintained that the Brazilian government "never offered a penny to an agent of emigration" and that "agents never advised any one to go to Brazil." He stated that he knew of no antislavery agitation in Brazil and that he foresaw no problems concerning the Negro. McMullan said that some of those southerners who were already in Brazil, including Colonel William Bowen, "an old soldier . . . [who] helped [Texas] in her first struggles . . . , and P. B. Hockaday, formerly a partner of the great Henry Clay," were also happy. Further, argued McMullan, if Cardwell would come to Galveston about the tenth and fifteenth of the next month, he would see between twenty and thirty families who believed as McMullan did. [24]

One month later, on December 16, 1866, the *Tri-Weekly News* published, in full, Cardwell's answer to McMullan's statements. After repeating many of his original arguments, Cardwell charged that McMullan and Bowen were "in a co-partnership in a scheme of some kind." Cardwell then returned to his wrangling about the race situation in Brazil and predicted that eventually the whites would have little or no control over government or their own affairs. Emigrants, said Cardwell, would not escape from what they were fleeing, for soon the Negro would be their social and political equal, if not superior, in Brazil:

I think it is proper that people should be permitted to know that
those very things which they would flee from here as a possible evil of
the future will be found there fully developed, both politically and
socially; that the black, whom some admit will one day be our equal
here, will already be found there occupying the foremost and most
honorable walks in society; that although the white fears he will some
day cast his ballot in the same box with him here, he will find him not
only voting there, but making laws—laws to govern whites who go
there; that he will have to shut his doors against all social intercourse,
or admit the negro to his bed and board.

P. B. Hockaday, Cardwell wrote, was an imbecile, "at one time a smart
man, who was wandering about in an unsettled condition." Cardwell
predicted that "of the 20 or 30 families he [McMullan] speaks of, 15
or 20, and probably all, will return, if able, in less than two years."[25]

No other letters on the subject from Cardwell appear in the *Tri-
Weekly News,* but in the *New Orleans Times* of January 24, 1867, Frank
McMullan had the last word. McMullan's letter, addressed "To my
friends in Texas, and to all good Southerners who think of going to
Brazil," began by cautioning his readers "against the combined op-
position of the press, South as well as North, to emigration to Brazil."
He then struck back at Cardwell:

> Some editors are like the politicians of the day, public parasites, who
> feed upon the vital energies of the honest laboring classes, and whose
> business it is to stir up strife and oppose every enterprise which does
> not advance their private interests. There is another sort of opposi-
> tion—that which comes from designing men, such as John Cadwell
> [*sic*] of Brazoria [County], of this state, who has written much against
> Brazil, and who during the two months he remained out of the coun-
> try, (at Rio) was never out of sight of salt water but once, and then
> only about eight hours, when he rode out on a railroad and back the
> same day. This fact being known, his communication will have no
> effect on sensible men. Now, I ask, if it is our desire to go to Brazil,
> whose business is it? Would it not be more honorable to bid us go in
> God's name, and wish us well in the end? If others do not wish to go,
> we say let them stay, and joy be with them. We persuade no one to go.[26]

There is no doubt but that both Cardwell and McMullan were sincere in their arguments for and against emigration to Brazil. However, Cardwell was a journalist and appears to have received preferen-
tial treatment from his colleagues in the press. McMullan, relatively
unknown, had real reason to be unhappy, as his letters were edited
while Cardwell's were not. It is likely that Cardwell's articles were a de-

terrent to many who might have otherwise considered emigrating to Brazil. In 1871 Cardwell, at the request of the Democratic Executive Committee, became the editor of the new Austin *Statesman,* a position he retained for fifteen years.[27]

But editorial correspondence was of no assistance in helping Frank McMullan lease a ship. The refusals of ship owners to honor the guarantees written by Minister de Azambuja were a severe blow to McMullan's efforts. De Azambuja was also distressed when he received a letter with the news from New Orleans. In a communication to McMullan, the minister complained that "it seems to me very strange that my own signature in the official document I sent to you in triplicate would not be considered as sufficient security for the fulfillment of the concessions made to you and Mr. Bowen by the Government of his Majesty, the Emperor of Brazil." De Azambuja continued by saying, however, that Reverend Ballard S. Dunn "assures me that you may carry out your vues [views] by performing his instructions." In the same letter, De Azambuja implied that a compromise was imminent in negotiating with the United States and Brazil Steamship Company and that soon southerners from the United States would be able "to prevail [avail] themselves of this advantage [ships from southern ports]." He told McMullan that he received this news from agent Bocayuva, "who just arrived from Rio de Janeiro to attend to all business on emigration."[28]

The encouraging news from Minister de Azambuja had not been written, however, when McMullan found a solution to his problems. On November 6 McMullan and Dyer completed a lease agreement in New Orleans with J. M. Oriol, a "commission merchant, ship broker, and importer of Mexican and Havana produce," with offices at 127 Old Levee Street. Oriol, almost bankrupt and desperate for cash, leased the English brig *Derby* to the Texans for $7,500 in U.S. currency. McMullan wrote de Azambuja that the lease had been accomplished by advancing $6,000, "which several of us, by putting our means together, have been able to raise." Obviously pleased with the transaction, McMullan remarked that "no other vessel, carrying 150 passengers, will ever be chartered at these low figures. The owner is very much embarrassed financially and needed this money; besides, he wished to put a line of good sail vessels between New Orleans and Rio de Janeiro and wants to secure my influence here and what little I may have with the Brazilian government."[29]

The *Derby,* rated at 213 tons burden, provided enough space to accommodate at least thirty families as well as baggage and moderate amounts of farm equipment and implements. It normally carried a crew of eight to ten men and was commanded by Captain Alexander

Causse. In order to make the brig capable of sleeping as many as 150 persons, Oriol agreed to construct bunks in the hold to supplement the limited cabin space. The commission agent also promised McMullan that all of the carpenter work would be completed no later than December 5, 1866. McMullan expected the ship to sail between December 10 and 15 for Galveston, where the emigrants would be waiting. He notified de Azambuja that the *Derby* would clear New Orleans for Iguape and asked that the Brazilian government be notified of that arrangement "so that we may not be disappointed on landing there." "I have already suffered so many disappointments," McMullan continued, "that I am half becoming disheartened."[30]

McMullan also expressed concern about the availability of passports for the Texan emigrants as there was no Brazilian consulate in the state. Writing to de Azambuja on November 6, McMullan asked whether anyone in Galveston was authorized to issue them. If not, he queried, "are they absolutely necessary? Could not your Excellency send me something of this kind, which would do as a passport to all those going with me?" McMullan explained that there was no way the entire complement of the colony could go to New Orleans to complete the necessary paperwork for passport credentials. He estimated the cost of doing so at a prohibitive $1,500, money that could not be spared.[31]

Although his lease on the *Derby* was secure, McMullan continued to question de Azambuja about arrangements for ships from southern ports in general and New Orleans in particular. He explained that the Brazilian consul in the Crescent City knew nothing about embarkation from the South. The agent for the New York and Brazil Steamship Company, William Creeny, also claimed that he had no knowledge of any arrangements concerning emigration. In an effort to secure more information, McMullan also wrote directly to owner Cornelius K. Garrison of the New York and Brazil line, although he must have expected that he would receive no reply.[32]

On November 17 de Azambuja drafted an answer to McMullan's letter of November 6, but he remained vague in his approval of the actions that the Texan took to secure a ship. "It is not for me to say anything about this transaction as you know better [than anyone] the concessions made by the Imperial Government to you, Mr. Dunn, and some other gentlemen." De Azambuja worried that the total expense might exceed the dollar amount per person approved in previous agreements and informed McMullan that expenses would "be *provata* the rate of passage per head." He promised to forward McMullan's letter to Rio de Janeiro for evaluation. In regard to McMullan's preference for Iguape as a port of arrival, de Azambuja promised to inform the Brazilian government so that "the necessary order be issued to meet you there." The consul reiterated that he did not know of any plans of the New York and Brazil Steamship Company in regard to beginning service at southern ports and made an effort to wash his hands of the entire controversy. "The Agent Mr. Bocayuva attends to the matter," said de Azambuja coldly.[33]

The new agent for emigration to Brazil, Quintino de Souza Boca-yuva, wasted no time in accelerating efforts to recruit emigrants. Rather than concentrate on colonists from the South, however, Boca-yuva immediately began a drive to enlist men from the streets of New York, including some persons just arrived from Germany and Ireland. The Brazilian Emigration Agency, operated by Bocayuva and located on Broadway opposite the Brazilian Legation, began an intense ad-vertising campaign in mid-November, 1866, offering low steamship rates and other inducements that were superior to those given to McMullan and other southern entrepreneurs. Travel costs from New York to Brazil were pegged at only $50.00, with children to be trans-ported at half-price. Exemption from military service in the regular army, a provision not included in either the McMullan or Dunn con-tracts, was given to New York enrollees. The mortgage on land, ac-cording to the agency's advertisement, was only for $50.00, the cost of steamship fare. The prospective emigrant would be required to pay only a $5.00 deposit, which was refundable by the purser of the ship after the vessel sailed.[34]

On November 25 a letter appeared in the New York Times question-ing the offers being made by the Brazilian Emigration Agency for "free passage to Brazil, a homestead, and Confessional liberty." These inducements, particularly the likelihood of freedom of religion in Ro-man Catholic Brazil, were openly questioned by the press. One re-porter claimed that about 600 men had gone to the emigration agency offices seeking information but that none received "satisfactory" an-swers. Concluding that the claim of confessional liberty was untrue, the reporter then declared that the other promises—free passages and homesteads—were also false. A New York Tribune writer expressed the editorial sentiment that "it is surely a strange thing to see [the emi-grants] leave this country on so doubtful an invitation, for a land where white labor is not appreciated because of the superabundance of slave labor, and consequently where it is ill-paid."[35]

A New Orleans Times editorial, however, enthusiastically supported settlement in Brazil. It heartily denounced the profiteering of steam-ship lines and their promotion of emigration to Brazil by Yankees and European immigrants. It also attacked the Brazilian Emigration Agency in New York, questioning the value of such a bureau in a place where men are "prosperous, victorious, and happy at home." "The whole affair," expostulated the *Times*, "is a smart Yankee trick . . . designed to draw many a poor man to New York, there to find, when his little purse of gold is exhausted, that this free passage is a myth." The *Times* condemned those newspaper editors who denounced the opportunities in South America and stated that it had "no wish to listen longer to the vain bubbling of such as talk 'prodigiously' on subjects they do not understand."[36]

Oblivious to the storm over the emigration of individuals to Brazil from New York, Frank McMullan continued with his plans. On the evening of November 6 he finally left New Orleans for Texas, naively confident that most of the arrangements for transportation to Brazil for his colonists were now complete. Had he known of the trouble still in store for himself and his followers, it is questionable whether he could have mustered the physical strength and endurance to continue.

Lack of planning, a confused bureaucracy, and a severe lack of communication by Brazilian consular officials did not completely abort plans for emigration from the South, but there is no question that the movement was severely damaged by the end of 1866. The worst blunder was Brazil's refusal to provide inexpensive transportation from southern ports. Had it done so at the correct time, it is likely that thousands of people would have availed themselves of the opportunity to sail for South America. In the case of McMullan's colony, the failure of the Brazilians was almost fatal. Had Frank McMullan not made arrangements for the lease of the *Derby* at the precise time that he did, it is probable that he would have had to cancel his plans completely. The lack of success by the Brazilians no doubt was an educational experience, but by the time the lessons were learned, it was too late to put them to use in the South.

CHAPTER 4

Gathering at Galveston

ECISIONS MADE UNDER the pressure of time and desperation are seldom wise, and the hurried rental of the *Derby* was no exception. Frank McMullan was to regret his association with J. M. Oriol, the owner of the brig, and deception prompted delays and expenses that McMullan and the Texan colonists could ill afford. Veiled extortion both in New Orleans and Galveston delayed the departure for Brazil for nearly eight weeks beyond the planned date of December 1, 1866. But ignorance is bliss, declared the poet, and knowledge of the problems that were to come would have aborted the entire colonial adventure.

But in Texas there was no hint of the uncertainty, and by late November scores of prospective colonists began to make their way to Galveston. In some cases they sold their land and possessions at distress prices to accumulate the money to purchase supplies, clothing, farm implements, and seed for use in Brazil. After a preliminary get-together, many of the would-be emigrants made plans to assemble at the town of Millican, the northernmost station of the Houston and Texas Central Railway, in Brazos County, Texas. In order to conserve passage money during the trip to Galveston, the central Texans (none of whom had ever ridden on a train) made an arrangement to rent a baggage car. Although such a means of transportation would be less than comfortable, it could easily carry several families as well as trunks and large bulky items.[1]

The Alfred Iverson Smith family, including forty-eight-year-old Alfred, his wife Sarah, and their seven children, left the little village of Spring Hill, Navarro County, Texas, on November 19. Smith, according to his daughter, was "a staunch secessionist and of Southern principles to the back bone. He never owned a slave in his life, but believed in States Rights, therefore he could not make up his mind to submit to Yankee rule." Smith, it will be remembered, was Frank McMullan's childhood teacher in Chestnut Flat, Georgia, before both families

came to Texas in the early 1850s. The Smiths loaded all of their possessions into an ox-drawn wagon and began a two-week journey to the
railroad head at Millican. In preparation for the trip to Brazil, the
Smiths constructed tents of heavy canvas to use as lodging, both in
transit to South America and as a temporary shelter after they arrived. The tents received their first use, however, as the family camped
on the prairie on the way to Millican. The Smith children, Eugene,
Preston, Penny, Marsene, Sarah Bellona, Virgil, and Fully, saw the trip
to Millican as a lark, "a jolly pic-nic, an exciting adventure." From
oldest to youngest, however, they sensed that they were a part of a
very unusual and wonderful excursion that would significantly change
their lives.[2]

Before the Smith family reached Millican, they were overtaken by
widower A. J. Green, his two daughters, and three sons. Driving horses
rather than oxen, the Green family moved significantly faster than the
Smiths. "Old Man" Green and his brood traveled in a carryall, a lighter
and less bulky means of conveyance. The amiable Green's oldest son,
Lewis, was nineteen years old, followed by daughters Jurilla, fifteen,
and Angeletta, twelve. B. H. Green was ten years old, and young
Joseph was only eight.[3]

When the Greens and the Smiths arrived at Millican, they joined
several other families who had agreed to the rendezvous. Saddlemaker Jesse R. Wright, his wife Sarah, children Ambrose, William,
and Boregard, and two coon dogs were already camped and waiting.
Accompanying the Wright family was Thomas Wright, Jesse's uncle
from Cook County, Texas. Also ready to continue to Galveston was
Thomas Garner, his widowed daughter Rachel Russell, and their relative Napoleon Bonaparte ("Bony") McAlpine. The three teamed together as a family group.[4]

The brothers Calvin and Thomas Steret McKnight and their families also gathered at Millican for the trip to the coast. Calvin, his wife
Isabel, and their two sons and five daughters were from Hill County.
During the Civil War Calvin served as captain of a volunteer company
of mounted men in the Nineteenth Texas Brigade. Like the other
would-be emigrants, Calvin and his wife determined to leave the country rather than face the real and imagined terrors of Reconstruction.
Calvin's brother, Thomas, lived in adjoining Navarro County with his
wife, America. Like his brother, Thomas had served as a Confederate
officer.[5]

Two other large groups who also met the colony members at Millican were the S. F. Haynie family and the Thomas Cook family. Haynie
and his wife Mary had six children, four sons and two daughters, who
ranged from Hugh, nineteen years old, to little Mary, only one year

old. Thomas and Ann Cook also had a large contingent, with seven children ranging in age from three-year-old Pet to eighteen-year-old Mary. Susan, Samuel, Nancy, Lilly, and Edward followed the eldest by age.[6]

By the time the train prepared to leave, fifty-two persons were camped in Millican sharing their hopes, their worries, and their dreams of a new life in Brazil. Not knowing what they should take to their new home, they loaded the baggage car with what later would be called a "heterogenous mass of old boxes, grindstones, pieces of mills, old feather beds, boxes with scraps of iron, old horse-shoes, old chairs . . . and stools." They tried to take all that they possibly could because it seemed likely that the commonplace articles to which they were accustomed might be scarce. By the time the baggage car was filled with luggage and freight, little space remained for people. "There was scarcely room for the folks," said one account, "except for a very uncomfortable mix-up, on such places as could be found on the baggage."[7]

As the train got away, the travelers foresaw a long ride to Houston, the train's first stop. The wind was cold, and with little heat the November air created a chill that was difficult to overcome. With the large number of people, including young children, in the car, meals and sanitation were chaotic, noise was nerve-rending, and usually placid dispositions became sour. To alleviate the situation, widow Rachel Russell led the group in singing "some old Methodist hallelujah hymns, which relieved the strain somewhat." The train arrived in Houston late in the evening and stopped for about an hour, providing a welcome relief to the would-be emigrants who had been confined since noon. The trip to Galveston lasted the rest of the night. The final leg of the journey, made in bitter cold, allowed little sleep, although all were near exhaustion.[8]

As the sun rose, the port of Galveston came into view, and the prospective colonists were delighted at the sight of the beautiful bay with its scores of ships at anchor, "looking like a denuded forest." Announcing their arrival, the engineer noisily clanged the bell as the train pulled into the station. When the baggage door opened, the bewildered emigrants dropped to the ground, completely out of their element in the busy depot. As the young ones cried for their breakfast, parents asked questions as to where a restaurant could be found. They were directed to "a shabby little eating place" where they obtained hot coffee and bread for the women and children. Meanwhile, the men made inquiries as to the location of the emigrant camp. Within hours, the new arrivals joined those already in Galveston at a tent city across the island on the beach. Trails of smoke rose from the camp fires as a vigil began for other emigrants, including the McMullan and Dyer families.[9]

The colonists were still in a good mood by mid-December. The Houston *Daily Telegraph* reported that the Brazilian emigrants were "in fine health and spirits" and while camped on the beach were "perfectly independent of hotels and boarding houses." A December 16 news item in the *Telegraph* commented that fifty-five persons already had arrived in Galveston and that a hundred more were "expected in a day or so. These emigrants . . . [are] among the best citizens of Brazos, Milam, Navarro, and the adjacent counties."[10]

The editor of the Houston *Daily Telegraph* did not agree with the idea of leaving the United States to go to another country, but, unlike some anti-emigration journalists, he did not condemn them for their actions. He blamed the emigration sentiment on those in Washington whose actions created unrest: "We are sorry to part with any of our true-hearted citizens of Texas, and we still insist that this is a better country than any other. But the course of Radical disunionists in Congress is having the effect to wean many a noble spirit entirely from his native land, and to drive them to other countries, like the Huguenots of France. We are sorry to part with them, but we wish God's blessing upon them wherever they go."[11]

The *Galveston Daily News* also commented on the emigration movement and attempted to convey the philosophy behind it, stating that it was "a prevailing apprehension that the radical programme of depriving the people of the South of the last vestige of liberty is about to be carried out, and that our unhappy country is to be made the theatre of the most despotic rule the world has ever witnessed in modern times." Yet, the editor declared that he did not think leaving the country was the intelligent thing to do. "We cannot predict the future, but we cannot approve the policy of flying from anticipated evils to those we know not of."[12]

Those who would go to Brazil, however, remained unaffected by editorial rhetoric. McMullan, in fact, was so sure of his colonists that he had established strong criteria for the persons who would settle on his Brazilian grant. They will be required, he said, to "give satisfactory references that they are Southern in feeling, pro-slavery in sentiment, and that they have maintained the reputation of honorable men." Continuing, McMullan said that "every one must come prepared to establish this evidence, before he can gain admittance to the lands which have been set apart to us and our friends." Those who come prepared to offer the required credentials, stated McMullan, "will receive a hearty welcome from friends of their own 'sort' and a Christian prayer for their future welfare."[13]

By January 1, 1867, it is probable that all of the persons who planned to sail on the *Derby* for Brazil were in Galveston awaiting the brig's arrival. The camp on the beach boasted a total of 154 persons who were prepared to leave on the little ship when it arrived from New Orleans. Writing about the diverse character of the crowd nearly fifty years after the event, one emigrant still hesitated to make a full description of them: "Too little time has elapsed since the occurrence of these events portrayed, to allow a description of the varied character that composed this composite hive—suffice to say that it is doubtful if since the crusades there ever was such a jumble of men and women so different in origin, custom, and habits."[14]

Two of the arrivals, George and Lucian Barnsley from Georgia, doubtless learned of the McMullan colony from the Brazilian consul. George had long contemplated emigrating to South America and wrote letters to the legation requesting information. In them he asked for data concerning climate, soil, means of transportation of emigrants, and other advantages that might be offered. Apparently satisfied with his first reply, Barnsley wrote another letter twelve days later indicating that he was organizing a colony of one thousand persons who wanted to locate in the valley of the Amazon River. He asked about the aid and protection given by the Brazilian government in general and about soil and climate in the Amazon Valley in particular. It is likely that the Brazilian consul wrote to Barnsley suggesting that he contact McMullan for some of the answers he sought and that the Georgian then decided it would be easier and more efficient to join an established group.[15]

George Barnsley attended Oglethorpe University before the Civil War as a medical student. He rose from the rank of private in Company A, Rome Light Guard, Eighth Georgia Regiment, to the position of assistant surgeon. His experience and training enabled him to pass the examinations of a medical doctor. After his discharge, Barnsley incurred a number of debts because of bad investments and dreamed of a way to recoup the fortune his family had possessed before the war. His father, Godfrey Barnsley, was an English subject whose sentiments during the conflict were with the South. Godfrey, who owned a large estate called Woodlands in northwest Georgia, was a cotton broker with offices in both Savannah and New Orleans.[16]

George Barnsley had another reason for wishing to "hit it rich." He hoped to marry Jennie Fairfax of Richmond, Virginia, and he knew that he must have considerable money in the bank before her aristocratic parents would agree to a union. Deciding that the affluence he needed might come his way in Brazil, he joined the McMullan colony as its official doctor with a promise of $2.50 per day for his services.

Barnsley did not gain wealth quickly enough for Miss Fairfax, however, as he later wrote to his sister, Julia Baltzelle, that Jennie had rejected his offer.[17] George's younger brother, Lucian, did not have the confidence of his brother and probably felt overshadowed by him most of his life. Lucian served in the Civil War in the same unit as his brother and imitated George's plans to go to Brazil.

When Frank McMullan was in New Orleans making arrangements for the *Derby*, he visited George and Lucian's father, Godfrey Barnsley, at his offices on Camp Street. McMullan explained the plans for the colony and reassured the elder Barnsley about the future for his sons, stating that they "would do well, with industry and economy." In a letter to George, Godfrey Barnsley worried about the companionship his sons would experience and urged them to remember their heritage. "In going you will I expect have rough associates, but [I] have no doubt you will retain that self-respect which belongs to gentlemen by position and education." In another note, the boys' father worried about their lack of first-class accommodations on the *Derby* and offered to provide extra money for them if necessary. "I do not like the idea of your being put in steerage with the class of people that will probably be going and would sooner pay $70 each in currency for you to go in the cabin." For supplies that the two young men would need, Godfrey Barnsley authorized them to draw on a Mr. Davis in Galveston for $50.00 in gold.[18]

Soon after December 1 Frank McMullan's family arrived at Galveston. With Frank still in New Orleans, the natural leader of the clan was Judge James H. Dyer. With his wife Amanda, sons Wiley and James, and daughter Harriet, Dyer had few doubts as to his future in Brazil. He had been successful as a pioneer on the frontier of Texas and saw no obstacle in doing the same in South America. Vowing to accompany the family to Brazil was the judge's former personal slave, a Negro named Steve. The freedman who had been a part of the Dyer family since it left Georgia before 1850 determined to stay with them in the move to another land. Like the judge, Steve was a deeply religious man who was never known to swear. Steve and Judge Dyer probably had much in common despite their racial and cultural differences and for that reason were very close. Both realized that Steve might not be able to enter the country when they landed in Brazil; laws there prevented blacks from emigrating, but both believed that the chance was worth the risk.[19]

William Turner Moore, a dentist, was married to Frank McMullan's sister, Victoria. Billy and Vic, as they were called, became a lively addition to the group—a welcome contrast to the sternness of the judge and the quiet demeanor of his wife, Amanda. Born in North Carolina,

Moore came to Texas from Mississippi with his family after the Civil War and settled at Bosqueville, McLennan County, where he met Victoria McMullan. Romance bloomed quickly for the two, and they were married on June 27, 1865. About a year later, the Moores had a child who was afflicted with hydrocephalus. The baby was never normal, but the couple apparently overcame their grief and maintained an active life.[20]

Troubles seemed to plague the Moores, however, and Billy accidently fired his pistol as he was cleaning it, causing a serious wound in his knee. The damage was so bad and the risk of infection so great that physicians recommended that the limb be removed. Moore agreed and submitted to surgery on January 7, 1867. Moore's condition remained critical, and until the time of sailing, his wife remained unsure whether he would live, much less be able to leave Texas.[21]

Another of McMullan's sisters, Louise, was married to a former Hill County neighbor, John Odell. The couple had no children and probably went with the rest of the family because of the adventure and excitement the trip offered. Little is known of the Odells before they decided to join her brother's colony.[22]

Nancy McMullan, Frank's mother, had been a pioneer twice before in Mississippi and in Texas and saw no insurmountable problems in going to Brazil. It is likely that her biggest regret was leaving two daughters in Texas. Virginia (Jennie) lived in Johnson County with her husband George L. Clark, and Martha Ann (Matt) was married to merchant John B. Williams and lived in the Hill County village of Towash. Nancy's youngest son, thirteen-year-old Ney, stayed constantly at his mother's side and would not have considered remaining in Texas.

Traveling with the McMullans were the children of Colonel William Bowen. Leonidas Sanders Bowen, affectionately called Lon by his friends, was the colonel's oldest child. Along with his sisters Mary, Susan, and Elizabeth and brothers Adam and William, he came to Galveston to board the *Derby*. Nancy McMullan agreed to take care of the brood until they could join their father in Brazil.[23]

Several other persons also reached Galveston by mid-December. They included Othniel Weaver, at seventy-two the oldest of the emigrants, and his family of three. Widow Sarah Garlington and her thirteen-year-old son, Allen, were present, as were Mrs. Garlington's good friends, the William A. (Billy) Gill family. W. E. Parks, Sarah Quillin's father, accompanied preacher Elijah Quillin and the rest of the family. Jacob Wingutter, his wife Susan, and ten-year-old Amy also joined the campers on Galveston beach. Nelson Tarver, his wife Sarah, and their four children, all formerly of Hill County, were early arrivals.[24]

Altogether there were twenty-four families in the emigrant group.

The colony included twenty-seven women and sixty children under the age of eighteen, and the ages of all persons ranged from one-year-old Mary Haynie to seventy-two-year-old Othniel Weaver. The average age of all adults was thirty-three. All of the emigrants except two, the Barnsley brothers of Georgia, were Texans. Apparently all of the colonists except two were of southern birth. Calvin and Thomas McKnight were born in Pennsylvania but had moved to Texas long before the Civil War. Both served in the Confederate army. One former slave, Steve, went to Brazil with the McMullan colony.[25]

Although a majority of those who waited at Galveston for the brig *Derby* were small farmers, there were a considerable number of professional men in the group. Of those persons whose occupations can be determined, there were three ministers, two judges, a teacher, an engineer, a physician, a pharmacist, and a saddlemaker. In addition, the emigrant ranks included a miner, a former Texas Ranger, and a gambler. There were at least two stock raisers. It is likely that most of the men were Confederate veterans, although military records have been located for only about fifteen of the emigrants. Of the sixty-seven men, twenty-seven were bachelors, including several young men who still lived with their families. As far as may be determined, only four of the colonists had received any college-level education.[26]

Regardless of their occupations, the fact that most of the would-be emigrants were from the frontier of Texas must have been evident to the Galvestonians who viewed them as they settled in their tent city. The anti-emigration editor of the *Galveston Daily News* commented on their rural appearance and expressed the fear that the colonists did not realize the trials and hardships they were to suffer:

> We noticed a number of persons on the street yesterday destined for Brazil. The party consisted of women and children, convoyed by several men with guns on their shoulders. All were evidently from the country, and as we gazed upon them, could not help experiencing a feeling of sadness, partly from thinking of the causes that induced them to leave the land of their nativity, and partly because they were about entering upon a life new to them; and we fear, little think of the dangers, trials, and hardships incident to being a stranger in a strange land.[27]

The journalist's observations were, of course, correct. But many more months were to pass before the emigrants themselves would realize the wisdom of his words.

Frank McMullan left central Texas in time to arrive in New Orleans by December 6, one day after J. M. Oriol promised that the *Derby* would be ready to sail. Locating the ship, McMullan found that none of the promised work had been completed. Worse, he learned of the seizure of the ship for an alleged debt of $1,257.23 against Oriol. McMullan was forced to make bond for the claimed indebtedness before the brig could even be moved. On December 9, however, he ordered the ship towed to a dock "up town" where work could be performed by John Robinson, a ship's carpenter hired by McMullan.[28]

It is certain that the Texan confronted Oriol and asked him to explain the circumstances behind the attachment of the *Derby*. Although no record of the conversation has been found, it is probable that the ship owner convinced McMullan that his financial condition was indeed precarious and that he could not have prevented the problem that occurred. Without the means to lease another ship, McMullan was forced to make the best of a bad situation. The longer the *Derby* remained in New Orleans for fitting up, however, the worse the situation became. The brig was seized four more times before it could leave port, and each legal action necessitated the payment of additional fines by McMullan.[29]

The real reason for the detention of the *Derby* is unclear, but recollections of some of the participants indicate that the brig's commander, Captain Causse, the owner, J. M. Oriol, and the sheriff, Harry Hays, conspired against the hapless Texans in an attempt to keep them from leaving the United States. The schemers also sought to enrich their own purses as much as possible in the process. No advertisements of a lien or sheriff's sale concerning the *Derby* appear in New Orleans newspapers of December, 1866, although it was common practice to publish such notices. Frank McMullan's brother, Ney, recalled in later years that Captain Causse "was implicated in these seizures and shared in the money accruing from them." "The authorities . . . did everything possible to prevent our sailing," Ney stated, "seizing the ship four times for false debts, which we were forced to pay." Bellona Smith also recalled the circumstances under which the troubles occurred and remarked that "some say he [Causse] was bribed by the Yanks." McMullan's own comments, although less positive, indicated questionable acts by Oriol. "Besides being irresponsible, insolvent, and entirely devoid of principle, [Oriol] is incapable of fulfilling his contracts."[30]

Although all of the necessary work on the *Derby* was incomplete by mid-December, McMullan resolved to get the ship underway as soon as it could be cleared from New Orleans. This opportunity came on December 22 when the *Derby*, under Captain Causse, "sailed for Rio de Janeiro under the British flag, 214 tons, crew of ten." No one doubted that the brig's first stop would be Galveston.[31]

In order to reach Galveston before the *Derby* and thus allow his colonists to be ready to board as soon as the ship arrived, McMullan caught a fast steamer for Texas as soon as he was positive that the brig had cleared port in New Orleans. He arrived in Galveston soon after January 1, 1867, and provided the occasion for relief and guarded optimism among the persons who were camped on the beach. McMullan told them that the *Derby* was en route and that it should arrive in Texas about January 7. McMullan also discussed the problems that he had faced with Oriol. He apologized to the emigrants but stated that the delay and inconvenience were "not attributable to any fault or neglect of mine . . . [and] the difficulties arose from dealing with an irresponsible party." Writing from Galveston to the *New Orleans Times,* McMullan stated that he was "willing to submit to these little inconveniences looking forward to the great good. I have no fears for the future. I know the country I am going to." If any of the colonists had misgivings, the heavy investment already spent made it too late to turn back. An amount in excess of $7,500 had been spent on leasing the ship, including the fraudulent fines, and another $23,000 had been expended for machinery, agricultural implements, seed, and other supplies. The entire sum was furnished by the colonists—a large percentage by McMullan and Dyer.[32]

The huge amounts of money already spent also necessitated another sacrifice by the emigrants. Meeting with them, McMullan painfully announced that everyone would have to pay their passage in advance, to be returned upon arrival in Brazil. As everyone had believed the promises of the Brazilian government that passage could be repaid over a four-year period, they were extremely disappointed. They did not blame McMullan as they realized his critical cash problem, but nevertheless "discontent and grumbling abounded in the camp."[33]

In order to bring the Brazilian government up to date with his problems and successes, McMullan wrote a letter on January 26 to Minister de Azambuja in New York. He notified the minister that the *Derby* had finally sailed from New Orleans "after many perplexities and disappointments" and was expected hourly in Galveston. "One hundred fifty four persons are here," said McMullan, "and have been here more than five weeks on heavy expenses, awaiting the happy moment when they could set sail for our new 'land of promise.'" Continuing, the Texan leader talked of his brother-in-law's firearms accident. "In his debilitated condition, the chances are against his recovery. His heart is set on Brazil, and he says he will go with us, even if he has to be buried in the ocean a day after we leave shore. This man fought four years for the South, and received no injury. How hard it is to be stricken down thus." McMullan asked pardon for speaking "of domestic affairs" but remarked that "troubles of all kinds have weighted heavily on me, and my health is fast failing me. I am hardly able to be up." The mental stresses clearly added an additional burden to Mc-Mullan's deteriorating physical condition.[34]

Continuing his letter to de Azambuja, McMullan made an effort to prevent possible future problems by asking for assurances that promises would be fulfilled. "I hope to find our lands surveyed as agreed on," said McMullan, "with 640 acre tracts, on arriving at them; also, that I hope to find shelter for my people, as agreed on. I have promised them these things, on the strength of the promises made to me by the Government. Their detention here has caused them so many disappointments, and such heavy expenses, that I hope that they meet none on arriving at Brazil."[35]

On January 8 the watch for the *Derby* ended. The small ship sailed into Galveston harbor and was anchored "in the stream," the area north of the island proper near the docks. McMullan and the other colonists were delighted and immediately began making arrangements to get on board. A committee of the older men purchased supplies, including bacon, flour, hard tack, corn meal, beans, and vinegar. In addition, they bought two barrels of kraut to help tide the party over until they reached Brazil. The emigrants checked their baggage one last time, then began to dismantle the little tent city prior to boarding ship.[36]

None of the colonists were prepared for the events that were to delay them once more. The captain's steward, probably at the instigation of Captain Causse, went almost immediately after arrival to General Loreh Kent, the Collector of the Port, with the charge that the brig leaked badly and generally was unfit for sea. In view of a November announcement in which Kent declared that ships must be "provided with the requirements of the law, for insuring the comfort and safety of those on board," the inspector immediately declared that the *Derby* could not sail until those requirements were met.[37]

McMullan could not believe that he was to be faced, once again, with problems in leaving port for Brazil. He immediately went to Kent and demanded to know the real reasons behind the restrictions on the *Derby*. When the general did not give what McMullan considered to be a satisfactory answer, the Texan demanded an inspection of the ship by an impartial team of experts. His hand called, Kent reluctantly agreed to appoint such a survey board.

The inspection team consisted of three men. Peter Norris was the representative of the United States government. M. W. Danton was appointed in his capacity as a master ship carpenter, and James E. Haviland represented the interests of the marine underwriters. The three men consumed nearly three weeks of precious time in their survey of the *Derby*, an inspection that revealed few problems on board and confirmed the accusations that the prohibition against sailing had been fabricated by Kent and others. Declaring that they had no part in the controversy regarding the seaworthiness of the vessel, the three inspectors issued the following statement:

> We find her tight, and after boring her [the *Derby*] many places find her comparatively sound, strong, and staunch, and has good spore and rigging, one good suit of sales [sails]—require extra mainsail and topsails. We find the upper rudder pintle requires to be repaired secure and will have to be put in good condition; anchors and chains good; we find one boat and recommend that her master procure two more; we find no ventilators in the deck and recommend one to be put in, to ventilate the after portion of the berth deck; we find that she has an ample number of water casks on board, part filled, balance required to be filled; also has an ample stock of provisions, a physician and stock of medicine; good sanitary and police regulations, well arranged for the comfort and safety and comfort of the passengers on board bound for Brazil.[38]

The report of Norris, Danton, and Haviland did not change the opposition of General Kent to the departure of the *Derby*. As a result of the inspection, however, McMullan attempted to repair what reasonably could be done without the expenditure of huge sums of money. Additional ventilators in the decks, for instance, would have been a prohibitive cost. Although it is not known whether an additional set of sails was added, they probably were not. One additional life boat was added. Despite the emigrants' inability to act on all of the recommendations of the inspection team, the *Derby* finally received clearance to leave on January 26. One colonist later wrote that the release was achieved after the payment of "a big sum that impoverished our people very much."[39]

In order to leave before another problem arose, the mass of baggage, equipment, implements, and personal belongings was loaded into the *Derby* as quickly as possible. It soon became apparent that space was at a premium and that if storage was not handled more efficiently there would not be sufficient room for passengers. McMullan pleaded that the emigrants leave behind those items that served no real purpose, but they ignored the appeal, and the abundance of miscellaneous baggage was moved to the rear of the ship's hold. An adequate amount of room was made, and everyone finally boarded the ship as preparations were made to cast off for Brazil.[40]

At last the colonists were in a position to contemplate the words of

an unreconstructed rebel who, tongue in cheek, wrote the following
lines to the *Galveston Daily News:*

> How sweet all day, on diamond reefs to lie;
> While 'long the wanton waves, sweet mermaids lie;
> While far above, the condor (bird most rare!)
> > Proud breathes his native air,
> > Sweeping in circles there!
> Oh, give me a ship with sail, and with wheel,
> And let me be off to happy Brazil!
> Home of the sunbeam—great kingdom of Heat,
> With woods ever green—and snakes forty feet!
> Land of the diamond—bright nation of Pearls,
> With monkeys plenty, the Portuguese girls!
>
> How sweet all night, on a hammock to swing,
> While grief and woe to the devil are fling;
> Up, 'mong the leaves of a lofty cocoa
> > Unceasingly to go
> > To and fro, to and fro!
> Oh, give me a ship, with sail and with wheel,
> And let me be off to happy Brazil!
> I long to rest 'neath her broad-spreading palm,—
> Gaze at her rivers, so placid and calm,—
> Pluck her gold fruits, so delicious and sweet,
> And try a taste of her guanaco meat!
>
> How sweet in death, in dismal swamps to sleep!
> While 'bove you, buzzards sad vigils keep!
> While o'er your bones, slimy reptiles crawl—
> > Eating—devouring all;
> > Till you in pieces fall!
> Oh, give me a ship, with sail and with wheel,
> And let me be off to happy Brazil!
> I yearn to feel her "perpetual spring,"
> And shake by the hand, Don Pedro, her King;
> Kneel at his feet—call him "My Royal Boss!"
> And receive in return, "Welcome, Old Hoss!"[41]

CHAPTER 5

The Isles of the Lotus Eaters

O N JANUARY 25, 1867, the *Derby* was ready to sail. Food and water were on board, repairs were complete, and most baggage, equipment, and supplies were securely stored in the hold. Construction of bunks in steerage was finished and, for those who could afford them, cabins were assigned. The only impediment was the reluctance of General Kent, the Galveston Collector of the Port, to give final permission for the emigrants to leave. This he grudgingly issued late in the afternoon. Although the day was too nearly spent for clearing port that day, McMullan gave orders to the colonists that they should be ready to sail as soon as possible on the twenty-sixth. Before the sun rose, breakfast camp fires already were burning as the Texans made final preparations to leave. They said goodbyes to the friends that they had made on the island, and by mid-morning families were making their way to the pier.[1]

Loading delays and final adjustments on board kept the *Derby* at the pier until mid-afternoon when the crew at last raised the anchor, cast off the ropes, and unfurled the sails. The little brig slowly navigated through the narrow channel in the bay and crossed the bar into the open sea. Although the anticipation for leaving had been building for weeks, there were few persons on board "whose heart did not grow sad as the land faded in the dim distance as the sun's last rays glitter[ed] on the sandy beach and lingered on the far off prairies." The reality of actually going away seemed different somehow than the talk that had consumed them for months, and was "as chilling as the icy hour of death."[2]

In order to thwart any further attempts by port authorities to keep the *Derby* from leaving, Frank McMullan, Judge Dyer, and others did not publicly discuss the implication of Captain Causse in the scheme that had caused the payment of final fines in New Orleans. If such accusations had been made, it would no doubt have been difficult, if not impossible, for McMullan to have obtained permission for the ship to leave for Brazil. Once away from U.S. shores, however, the leaders felt no qualms about bringing the entire affair to light. The ship had been away from the port only a matter of hours when McMullan called a caucus of the emigrants to discuss the matter.[3]

The saloon of the *Derby* was the only area on board large enough to hold a meeting of the entire contingent. Located in the middle of the ship, the room contained a long wooden table nailed to the floor; a row of trunks surrounded it in lieu of chairs. The room had no windows, and ventilation was obtained by opening the fore and main hatches. Narrow halls, too tiny for two persons to pass each other easily, linked the saloon with the "staterooms"—accommodations one writer described as "nothing else but boxes with shelves for human bundles."[4]

It seemed obvious that the colonists would discuss serious business as they filed into the saloon. Neither the captain nor the crew attended at first as the entire sequence of events had to be explained in detail to everyone so that a consensus could be reached. Everyone present soon came to the same verdict; the evidence seemed clear that Causse had been behind most of the problems both in New Orleans and in Galveston. It was obvious to the colonists that the captain was not to be trusted further.[5]

The emigrants dispatched a message to Captain Causse ordering him to the saloon so that they might discuss the charges against him. Leaving his cabin with the messenger, Causse no doubt knew the reason for the summons and was determined to contest the charge. The colonists carefully explained the case to the shipmaster and pointed out to him that they distrusted his intentions. They forbade him to enter any U.S. port, an action already planned by Causse "to take on water." In plain words, they told the captain that they considered the officers of the United States "inimical to their emigration" and that they suspected that he planned to wreck the ship rather than continue to Brazil. They told Causse that they were aware that the ship's owner was deeply in debt and that the vessel was heavily insured. This represented one more reason, they said, for their distrust of him. As Causse continued to deny the charges against him, the emigrants made more and more speeches, "some angry and violent," as the weeks of frustration finally found an outlet for relief. One passenger finally suggested that the problem could be solved easily by dumping the captain overboard, a cry some quickly seconded. Others suggested that he be shot or hung.[6]

Realizing the deepening seriousness of the situation, Captain Causse finally began to show signs of repentance. Tearfully, he asked how the ship would be operated if he were done away with. No one else on board, he pleaded, knew how to navigate, a necessary skill if the *Derby* were ever to reach Brazil. George Barnsley was detailed to question the balance of the crew on the subject. Surely someone else on board was a competent navigator and could assume the captain's duties. After questioning the first mate and the cook, Barnsley reported back to the emigrants that Causse's claim was correct. Obviously the captain had to be retained. Barnsley later said that he had studied navigation while in college, but evidently for Causse's sake he did not admit the skill at the time.[7]

In order to impress upon Causse the seriousness and resolve of the emigrants, McMullan told the captain that he would be closely watched and that any deviation from the wishes of the colonists, especially in regard to docking at a U.S. port, "would be severely dealt with." Causse, according to one account, "took the matter philosophically, made a little speech to the passengers in which he bowed to the inevitable and promised to plumb the straight and narrow path for the rest of the trip." Causse's later actions were to prove, however, that he still was not to be trusted. One colonist commented that the decision to retain Causse was an unfortunate one, and "from that hour the vessel was doomed, if chance occurred."[8]

The problem of adequate water to make the trip became evident when the colonists discovered that only two casks had been filled before the ship sailed from Galveston. Because such a small quantity meant severe problems, the emigrants decided that the *Derby* should proceed to the mouth of the Mississippi River opposite New Orleans where fresh water could be obtained. A lingering worry about the problems that Captain Causse could create if the ship were boarded by U.S. officials, however, soon caused a change of heart. When, after one week at sea, the *Derby* approached the delta, the Texans gave orders to proceed as quickly as possible for Havana. With careful use, they reasoned, the water on board could be stretched for five days. In addition to the drinking water dilemma, a leak that had developed in the hull of the *Derby* on its trip from New Orleans to Galveston began to increase slightly and added to the concern of those on board. The colonists decided that the ship should be put in the Havana dry dock for repair before proceeding to Brazil.[9]

The first day after the *Derby* left "the yellow waters of the delta" at New Orleans, it sailed a southeast course. A fair wind was blowing, which boded well for a quick trip; within five days the ship would be in Havana. The second day out from the Crescent City the winds became "baffling and variable" and continued in that manner until February 8, when they became calm. The sails "flopped lazily against the mast," and the little brig was virtually adrift, moving only as fast as the waters of the Gulf Stream could take it. The "ominous cry for water arose on all sides," and rations became "scarcer and scarcer." If it had not been for a light rain, when a hogshead of water was caught, the situation would have become serious.[10]

As the *Derby* sailed closer and closer to Cuba, the colonists felt gentle warm breezes, a sharp contrast to the mild winter weather they had experienced in their camp at Galveston. Time passed slowly, and the emigrants searched for activities with which to fill the long hours on board ship. Some lounged on deck, taking advantage of the tropical sunshine. A few of the women and children, probably led by teacher Alfred I. Smith or widow Rachel Russell, sang songs. Some of the Texans, uninterested in the company of others, snoozed between decks. A few, wishing to be better prepared for their arrival in Brazil, took lessons in Portuguese from Frank McMullan. The older members of the party "conversed on the hopes of seeing the land yet uncursed by misrule."[11]

George Barnsley preferred a more dramatic spot to spend his time and climbed into the chains that graced the ship's bowsprit. From this vantage point he "watched the scintillations of the sun-fish down deep in the clear gulf-stream." Barnsley's eloquent description of the scene bears retelling. "The air was soft," he recalled, "a delicious langour pervaded the body; dreamy thoughts of the isles of the Lotus Eaters came, chanting their melodies in unison with the gentle whispers of the zephyrs; minute waves lazily lifted up their voices as they beat against the vessel's side or danced in wild delight of eddying whirls in the rear."[12]

In another, less poetic mood Barnsley described the scene in a more realistic tone. "Away to the home of summer we scude for seven days and nights amusing ourselves in the meantime with the mental occupation of idle talks and quarrels, besides in the physical digestion of balls of fat and toughest of stuff worthy of patent by the New York Guttapercha Co. The last gentle and wholesome occupation produced diarrhea and other ills."[13]

On February 9 there was no inkling that any problems might be encountered. The day was still and beautiful. In the distance two sailing ships could be seen, and "a great whale lay in full view, basking on the great waters." Most of the passengers had "passed the initial stages of sea sickness, and the youngsters were having the time of their lives." Early in the afternoon, however, the wind began to quicken and "the vessel ploughed along gallantly." The breeze was welcomed, as it would only hasten their trip. Tomorrow they would be in Havana. By 3:00 P.M., however, the breeze had turned into a high wind as a squall line bore down on the *Derby* from the northwest. As the norther hit, the sea quickly assumed the proportions of a tropical storm. Even with the sails reefed, Captain Causse could hold the wheel only with great difficulty.[14]

After dark the fury of the storm increased. The waves became "mountains high," and huge quantities of water poured over the decks of the *Derby* and spilled into the hatchways, filling the lower decks to ankle depth. "The good ship Derby," recalled Dr. Barnsley, "danced over and through the angry waste of waters." All at once Captain Causse began to move quickly, ordering the brig's sails unfurled. This was highly unusual in that other ships in the area had furled all sails and "seemed to be trying to get away from some point to which . . . [the *Derby*] was headed." By 9:00 P.M. the "yardarms were touching the water, and the sails, except for the flying jib, had to be furled once more." The wind became steadily more furious and "the chant of the Norseman's song was howled and screeched through the rigging." Parson Quillin walked the swaying deck, shaking his head and saying, "O we are gave up, we are gave up!" "Scared?" said Bellona Smith, "There's no name for it." Captain Causse expressed much distress and told those who would hear that all "would be in Heaven or Hell within twenty-four hours."[15]

The leak in the hull of the *Derby*, suffering because of the intense battering of the waves, continued to worsen. Water poured from a crack, adding depth to that which had spilled below deck from the open hatches. Because of the increasing threat, some of the passengers began to take turns on the hand pumps, as there were not enough sailors aboard to man them. Eugene Smith and Cortez Fielder took the first shift from 8:00 to 10:00 P.M. When the time came for relief, none was found. Smith cautiously crawled toward the back of the cabin to look for help. He located no assistance but did discover that the helm had been tied down and abandoned by the captain and that everyone had gone below to go to sleep. The only person on deck was Smith's friend and bunk mate, Walter Schofield. When Smith asked whether he was not going to join the others and go below to bed, Schofield replied that he was "going to stay right there till the day or something else happened." Smith declared that he was too sleepy for fear to have any influence on him and, after trying unsuccessfully to rouse his and Fielder's replacements for the pumps, headed for his bunk. Smith later recalled that he took off no clothes except his hat and was soon asleep.[16]

Lucian Barnsley, George's younger brother, was unable to sleep and ventured onto the deck during the height of the storm. He saw that no one was manning the pumps and realized that the problem of leakage had become grave. Moreover, he found the tied ship's wheel and realized that the captain had deserted his post. About 1:00 or 2:00 A.M. Lucian called his brother to inform him of the situation and then went below to rouse others to assist in manning the pumps, "an exercise," said Barnsley, "which was attended with waste of time and curses." Two men did volunteer to help, however, and "a desultory pumping was kept up" until about 3:30 A.M.[17]

The storm continued to roar into the night, and many of those who found sleep earlier could no longer stay in their bunks. Young Ney McMullan, one of those awake, later described the scene: "The waves towered in maddening heights; their summits were torn away by the force of the wind and scattered and driven like blinding rain over the face of the deep, making it impossible to see but a short distance beyond the ship. The night was made hideous by the incessant roll and plunge of the ship, its creaking timbers, which seemed to groan under the strain of the mighty waves; and the intermittent shrieks of the wind through the rigging grated on our nerves like a death dirge portending our impending doom."[18]

The fury of the storm also awakened Frank McMullan and Judge Dyer, and the two ventured on deck to view the effects of the high seas and wind. When they found that the helm had been tied and that the captain had deserted his post, they tried to correct the situation. With drawn pistols they and several other men went to Causse's cabin, called him out, and forced him to untie the ship's wheel and try to guide the *Derby* through the tempest.[19]

About 4:00 A.M. one of the passengers on deck saw the rocks of Cuba no more than one thousand yards away. "Land! land!" he cried, in an attempt to rouse the passengers and crew. McMullan, realizing that the situation was critical and that the *Derby* would probably strike the rocks within minutes, returned to his cabin to wake his sister Vic and his brother-in-law, Billy Moore. He informed them of the dangerous situation, then went toward his mother's cabin, intending to give the dire news to her and other members of his family. About the time he reached the cabin door, the *Derby* struck a reef. "The awful crash— such a one as I never heard or felt before—came, driven by the breakers of the angry ocean." Continuing, McMullan recounted that he was "knocked down with a force which seemed to jar every bone in me— my whole person badly bruised—it seemed that an ocean of flood and spray swept over me—and I caught at random some of the rigging to keep from going overboard. I thought the vessel was crushed and dashed in a thousand pieces, and that all were lost. These impressions rushed through my mind in less than a second of time."[20]

After assuring himself that his mother and the rest of his family were safe, McMullan rushed back to the deck just in time to find that the crew was in the process of lowering one of two lifeboats. As there were more women and children on board than could be carried in the little emergency crafts, McMullan, joined by Judge Dyer, demanded that they stop immediately. They reinforced their orders with drawn revolvers, and the crew watched as the waves dashed the boat to splinters against the hull of the ship.[21]

The women and children rushed to the saloon, the only room on board large enough to hold them all at one time. There was little panic "outside of a few women who screamed and clung to their husbands." Ney McMullan described the scene and recalled the heroics of all on board:

> Every man, so far as I know or ever heard, proved himself a hero. Among the most conspicuous was Judge J. H. Dyer, who lectured the women on their behavior, making them take the most advantageous positions possible, and bidding them to be perfectly calm, telling them if they were saved it must come from the efforts of the men, and that these must be free to use both body and mind to the best advantage possible, which they could not do if excited by the cries of their wives and children. After this lecture every woman became a heroine, and stood her post like a stoic.[22]

The huge waves continued to pound the *Derby* against the rocks. She was taking on water rapidly and seemed to be sinking fast. The "flood of water was so overwhelming and the shock so terrific that many . . . believed that the ship had gone to pieces and [that they] were adrift among the timbers." In a last-ditch effort to save the ship, Captain Causse "shouted to the crew above the roar of the storm, 'Cut away the mast!' repeating it time and time again, with a long string of wild, reckless oaths; but the axe could not be found in time to avail anything. Crash after crash came, as the long rolls of angry, white-crested waves broke in rapid succession over us, dashing the vessel against the stubborn rocks." "The Derby," said Frank McMullan, "would soon be no more."[23]

The crewmen and passengers remained remarkably quiet. Some prayed, asking the "Work of Waves and Creation to take them . . . to his care." Others, veterans of the Civil War, "were amused, accustomed as they had been to the dangers and deaths of a hundred battles." But none had long to ponder his fate, for another gigantic wave carried the *Derby* pell-mell toward the rocky shore. Dropping the ship as if it were a toy, the wave left it almost on the beach, solidly wedged between boulders. Despite repeated onslaughts by the sea, the ship held together, although its timbers groaned under the pressure of the waves. Its rigging crashed against the masts, and the cargo, loose from its moorings, thudded against the shattered hull.[24]

George Barnsley, after checking to be sure that his brother Lucian had not been washed overboard, rushed to the cabin of Billy Moore to check on his patient's condition. On entering the room, he found Moore, his wife, and their child calmly sitting on a mattress. The three were covered, however, with the contents of the captain's pantry, which had been driven aft by the impact of the wreck. Describing the scene, Barnsley said that it was a compound mess "of macaroni, pickles, flour, molasses, etc., which mingled with contents of a part of my medicine chest; a box of chloride of lime burst open; the floor being smooth with oil carpeting, at every lurch of the ship a general race on the steeplechase principle would commence; and I must say that my patient generally came out victorious although the chloride of lime did well, the molasses jug always coming in last, while the pickles performed sundry fine leaps." One other passenger, however, was not so fortunate. When the *Derby* struck the rocks, C. A. Crawley, formerly of Fairfield, Texas, fell off the table where he was sleeping and broke his collarbone. Although Crawley was in pain, his injury was not extremely serious. Barnsley treated the man as best he could and tried to make him comfortable.[25]

Frank McMullan was extremely proud of the conduct of the passengers of the *Derby* during the storm and wreck. In a letter to the New Orleans *Daily Picayune,* he stated that it was

> with particular pride that I can say I do not believe a single man
> among the passengers was excited. Everyone was calm, and in full
> exercise of his reason. There was no confusion or rush any where.
> And God bless our ladies. I venture that, in the whole history of ship-
> wrecks, their conduct has no parallel. They had been told to stay be-
> low until called upon, and they did it in every instance. They were
> calm, resigned, and confiding. Who, that was not present, can realize
> that, when experiencing a shipwreck, such perfect order could pre-
> vail! Will not such people be an acquisition to Brazil or any other
> country?[26]

Another step was completed in the odyssey to Brazil. In this case, unfortunately, the step was backward. The *Derby* was irretrievably wrecked. Fortunately, no one died. The conduct of Captain Causse in abandoning his post during the height of the storm justified the fears of many of the colonists who, in the general meeting in the ship's saloon, did not believe the shipmaster's promise that he would cause no more problems. Be that as it may, the wreck of the *Derby* necessitated a new assessment by all as to the future course of action.

CHAPTER 6

A Hankering for Brazil

A S THE SUN'S RAYS streaked the horizon on the morning of February 10, the remnant of the storm lingered, and the breakers that crashed in a deafening roar over the rocks of Bahia Honda were a sight to behold. The waves were ten to fifteen feet high and a brilliant blue color, their crests topped with bright foam. "It was a grand scene," declared one of the McMullan colonists, "old ocean in its grandest phase." Where the sand met the sea, rocks and coral ominously threatened the intruders, providing no welcome or easy passage from the wreck of the ship to the shore.[1]

The *Derby* ended its journey at a fortuitous location, lodged between boulders that held the brig in an upright position and prevented the waves from dashing the little ship and its cargo to bits. Had the storm beached the ship a quarter of a mile east or west, it likely would have sunk in twenty fathoms of water. As it was, the green shores beckoned the "shipwrecked crowd," taunting them with a short but threatening stretch of swirling water and sharp rocks. With every breaker, the ship rocked to and fro, making the task of reaching land more and more difficult.[2]

Captain Causse, his aspect almost completely changed from his previously scowling appearance at 4:00 A.M., buoyed the scared and hopeless-feeling Texans with smiles and cheering words. He called to his crew and summoned a sailor to his side. Then he nimbly tied a line around the man's waist and, with the help of Second Mate Ables, lowered the seaman over the railing. After the first crewman was safely on the rocks, Causse let down several more men, making sure that there would be plenty of assistance as the women and children left the ship in the same manner. Reaching the boulders below the deck of the wrecked craft, however, was only the first part of the journey to the shore. To reach land, the passengers had to leap into the surf at just the right minute, then ride the waves onto the beach. This was an extremely difficult maneuver even for a strong man, much less the already exhausted women and children. Two colonists, eager to reach land, were almost killed as the tide swept them into jagged rocks.[3]

Transporting small children to the beach proved even more difficult. Once again Captain Causse showed the unlikely colors of a hero. Taking the sleeves of a child's coat in his teeth, Causse climbed down the rope and, on reaching the rocks, handed the babe to its father. The first child safe, he took another, then another, until all were off of the ship and into the cautious hands of parents and crew members. Second Mate Ables also performed laudably, taking many women and children in his arms and "bearing them safely ashore against the heavy surf."[4]

Wet, tired, and frightened, the colonists stood on the shore looking almost unbelievingly toward the *Derby* as their few treasured possessions washed out of a gaping hole in the ship's bow into the sea. Without waiting for orders, several men waded back into the surf in an effort to save as much of the cargo and baggage as they could. Luckily the old oak-sided English vessel remained intact and consequently remained salvageable after the storm began to fade. The long process of dragging personal effects to the shore continued, and anxious hands spread water-soaked belongings on the sunny sand to dry.[5]

Although the wreck had occurred on a desolate shore with no dwellings in sight, persons who lived nearby soon appeared and spread word to the nearby settlement of Plaza de Banes of the fate of the *Derby* and two other ships that had been wrecked in the storm. One vessel, carrying 500 Chinese laborers, miraculously suffered the loss of only one life.[6]

Don Juan Vermay, a wealthy brick and tile manufacturer and plantation owner, heard of the tragedy of the *Derby* and moved quickly to provide assistance. Vermay's carts, pulled by oxen and driven by coolie employees, were soon creaking their way to the beach to begin the task of moving the colonists to his hacienda three miles away. The Cuban ordered a beef killed for the Texans and soon made available generous stores of rice and potatoes. Until tents could be recovered from the *Derby*, Vermay moved the women and children into his commodious home, where they occupied "his saloon, sleeping compartments, and varied other rooms." Mrs. Vermay, a gentle lady of French ancestry, was particularly helpful in soothing the sorrow of the women as she offered an island of civilization in a strange and foreign land. Soon a degree of order was established.[7]

The rigors of the shipwreck and the exertion of salvage and transfer of their belongings from the *Derby* left the colonists physically exhausted at the end of the day on February 10. Most of the baggage remained on the beach, however, and many of the colonists elected to remain on the site to work at retrieval and to guard what already had been salvaged. Vermay, as well as other Cubans who lived nearby, warned McMullan of possible thievery and suggested that a guard be posted at all times. Jesse Wright, an expert shot with his Colt revolver, took the first watch. Before long the shore was dark and still, with only the rhythmic sounds of the now calm surf to break the silence.[8]

When it looked as if the entire company was fast asleep, two stealthy figures appeared from the brush at the edge of the beach and slowly and carefully began to inspect the salvaged baggage from the *Derby*. One of the men donned clothing and even a hat before the two turned to a full trunk, which they hoisted and started to carry into the underbrush. Wright watched the entire incident and, when confident that the two men were strangers rather than passengers of the *Derby*, yelled for them to stop. The thieves ignored the command and rapidly continued on their way with the stolen articles. Wright, described in one account as a very "passionate" man, leveled his pistol and fired, killing one of the Cubans instantly. The other thief, spurred by the deadly turn of events, fled empty-handed at top speed. The entire camp awoke in an immediate uproar, and there was little sleep for the balance of the night. Early in the morning of February 11 McMullan sent for the authorities at Plaza de Banes to reconcile the problem before it became other than a legal issue. The Cubans were not altogether pleased with Wright's explanation, translated to them by McMullan, but McMullan's language facility enabled him to settle the incident without criminal charges.[9]

After convincing the Cuban police that Jesse Wright was blameless in the death of the thief, Frank McMullan left the colonists in the hands of Judge Dyer and headed for Havana to request assistance from the Brazilian consul. With almost no money, the situation looked more desperate than ever for the young leader. When McMullan began the thirty-mile journey at 12:00 noon on February 11, he had a heavy heart and marginal hope for ultimate success. Of one thing he could be sure, however: he would never appeal for aid to U.S. authorities. On the morning of February 12 McMullan arrived at the Brazilian embassy in Havana. Although received courteously, he learned that no assistance was available because of the death of the Brazilian consul several days before. The staff suggested that McMullan go instead to the Portuguese embassy and confer with Consul-General Fernando Gávez e Fínaz, who was the appointed manager of Brazilian affairs until a new consul could arrive from Rio de Janeiro. On his arrival, McMullan was at once directed to the ambassador's chambers, where he told his pathetic story in detail.[10]

Gávez e Fínaz expressed sympathy for McMullan's appeal for assistance but was reluctant to act because of the large costs involved in transporting over 150 persons. Too, the Portuguese consul expressed concern that none of the passengers of the *Derby* were Brazilian citizens. In a letter of February 13 to the Interior Secretary of the Brazilian Legation in New York, Gávez e Fínaz said that he was directing McMullan there by steamship, "with the end of talking to Your Excellency for whom he has high resolve and respect." He concluded by expressing the hope that his failure to assist the Americans would not be interpreted unfavorably and that he desired always to be of service to the subjects of Brazil.[11]

McMullan was very disappointed at his inability to make direct arrangements for continuation of the voyage to Brazil with the imperial government while he was in Havana. A trip to New York would take time and money, both scarce commodities. After all the fines, advances, and bribes had been paid in New Orleans and in Galveston, he had only $130 remaining. This he had given to his mother for safekeeping on board ship, but even it was now lost in the wreck. Fortunately, Gávez e Fínaz advanced the steamship fare from Havana to New York, and Judge Dyer and others gave McMullan small amounts of cash before he left the scene of the shipwreck.[12]

Frank McMullan arrived in New York City on February 18 aboard the steamship *Eagle* and immediately contacted Quintino de Souza Bocayuva, the agent of emigration for Brazil. After a conference between the two men, Bocayuva drafted a pleading letter to his superior, Henrique Cavalcanti de Albuquerque, director of Brazilian trade with the United States. He decried the condition of the would-be emigrants and pointed out that they were being sustained only by the inhabitants of Cuba. "Citizen McMullan," said Bocayuva, "is at a critical juncture . . . for himself and his companions. He traveled to this city to invoke the assistance and protection of the functionaries of the Empire, and unquestionably should receive help." Bocayuva continued by making an emotional appeal for the Brazilian colonists: "I intreat you to take the liberty of thinking whether or not the Imperial Government promotes and aids emigration from this country to the Empire . . . . Must they go to reclaim the protection of the country which they abandoned? It is sad that these emigrants lack the equality and protection of the new country they search for and prefer."[13] Bocayuva also reminded Cavalcanti that there was precedent for extending aid to the shipwrecked Texans. An identical case had occurred before, he said,

and free transportation had been furnished to Brazilian shores. Bocayuva asked that the director "transmit . . . the results of his delibera-
tions in order to soothe the minds of the emigrants."[14]

Cavalcanti received the communication on February 20 and immediately replied to Bocayuva that he, too, was restricted in what he
could do for McMullan's colonists. He declared that he would draft a
letter at once to the minister of foreign relations for "the necessary
orders to proceed under these circumstances." He also gave implied
permission to Bocayuva to provide assistance without official orders.
"With the intelligence, patriotism, and good offices that Your Excellency has expressed in performing your commission, that was con-
ferred on you by the Imperial Government, I hope that you will take
measures by which these unfortunate ones are to be saved."[15]

Two days later, on February 22, Cavalcanti wrote the minister of
foreign affairs in Rio de Janeiro, Antonio Aoelho de Sá e Albuquerque. In the correspondence Cavalcanti expressed the opinion that the
legation did not have the authority to make a decision in the case. Neither were they able to satisfactorily explain to McMullan why they
were unable to act. "We cannot take the responsibility," the consul
wrote, "of making dispensations without the express orders of the Imperial Government." The cost, which likely would total sixteen *contos*,
also became a factor in the delays in furnishing assistance and alter-
nate ship passage to Brazil.[16]

Despite the procrastination, the Brazilian consul in New York, in cooperation with Bocayuva, finally decided to provide help, knowing
that waiting for official word from Rio de Janeiro could take weeks or
months and still might not be decisive. They called in McMullan and
informed him that they had decided to authorize passage for the shipwrecked Americans to New York, then Brazil, at no cost to the colonists. Exultant at receiving the good news, McMullan wrote a long
letter to the editor of the New Orleans *Daily Picayune*. McMullan titled
the document "For the information of the public generally, but more
particularly for that of the relatives and friends of the shipwrecked of
the South." He described the wreck in detail, told of the series of
events that delayed the departure from New Orleans and Galveston,
and then discussed the extremely human assets of the colonists:

> Perhaps so large an expedition of emigrants never set sale [sail] before
> under more favorable prospects, if we except the thousand difficulties
> under which we labored in getting off, and the many impediments
> thrown in our way by designing parties of whom I will speak in the
> proper place. We formed all the elements of an independent, self-
> sustaining settlement. We had farmers and stock-raisers, mechanics of
> every branch, prepared to build a steamboat or a steam engine, civil

engineers, ministers of the Gospel, school teachers, capable of found-
ing a university, a physician, quite a number of ex-Confederate officers and soldiers who wish to till the soil and live in peace, but when
needed, can fight the battles of their adopted country—no politician.
We can edit a newspaper or work a gold mine.[17]

George Barnsley, ever the writer with a flair for news, also took pen
and paper in hand and addressed a letter to the editor of the *New Orleans Times*. Seated next to Vermay's brick kiln, Barnsley entitled his
epistle "Camp near Guaneyay [Guanajay] Cuba, 15th February, 1867."
He traced the misfortunes of the *Derby* from the time it left New Orleans until the date of the writing and then placed the account with a
letter to Godfrey Barnsley in Georgia. Barnsley asked his father to
forward it to the *New Orleans Times* and any other newspapers that he
thought might be favorable to their cause.[18]

The friends and family of the Barnsley brothers in Bartow County,
Georgia, although sympathetic to the idea of emigration, did not see it
as a practical solution to the problems faced by former Confederates.
George's sister, Julia Baltzelle, had not learned of the shipwreck by
February 16 when she expressed concern for the well-being of George
and Lucian. In a letter to her father, she said that she hoped that the
pair would arrive safely in Iguape and that she would be "very anxious until further intelligence from them." Commenting on an expression of concern from one of George's friends, Julia noted that it
would have been wrong for her brother to have remained in the United
States. "He had a hankering for Brazil," she philosophized, "and
maybe its for the best."[19]

The Texas colonists continued to depend on Vermay's generosity
while McMullan arranged for passage to Brazil. They had no other
choice. Some were almost penniless and others might have faced starvation without assistance. Vermay, who was described by one colonist
as "the noblest of men," offered two substantial meals every day, without expectation of reimbursement, as well as most of the other neces-
sities of life. But the concern of Vermay for the would-be Brazilians
went even farther. On the morning of February 19 he announced that
he was leaving for Havana, where he planned to raise money to purchase a ship so that the American travelers might continue on their
way. On his arrival there, accompanied by Judge Dyer and other
colony leaders, he learned that McMullan had already tentatively
booked passage on the *Merrimac*, scheduled to sail from New York on
April 22, and that another steamer, the *Mariposa*, would be routed to
Havana from its New Orleans–New York run to pick up the stranded
colonists. His charity presumably unneeded, Vermay returned to

Plaza de Banes. The emigrant leaders remained in the capital, determined to sell the remains of the *Derby* to the highest bidder for salvage and, in doing so, recoup what they could of the thousands of dollars that were invested. There was little market for wrecked ships, however, and they returned to Vermay's plantation with only $350 from the sale.[20]

The Texans resolved to make the best of their stay in Cuba and spent time in exploring the countryside around Plaza de Banes. For the first time, some observed the processing of raw sugar. Others enjoyed looking at the natural wonders of the countryside and "becoming acquainted with the queer customs of the people." They described the February climate as "delicious" for sightseeing; however, the sun was much hotter than that to which they were accustomed. "The nights are cool," one man wrote, "making it pleasant to sleep under a blanket."[21]

George Barnsley, who because of his background was very conscious of the cultural differences between himself and his fellow colonists, began to question his choice of companions. "Many are very rough in their ways," he stated in a letter to his father, "and partake of the wildness of a former life in Texas; with all they are very pretentious toward being polished people." The communication was forwarded to Barnsley's sister and brother-in-law, who, like George, were mindful of social considerations. Captain J. P. Baltzelle, commenting on the situation in a note to Godfrey Barnsley, said that he would recommend that if George and Lucian were going to Brazil, "not to wait for that motley crew that they have gotten in with. . . . By remaining on the island they will not only spend their money but most likely get sick exposed in their kind of camp life."[22]

Baltzelle believed that the decision of George and Lucian to leave the United States was a wise one, although he did not personally feel that it would have been dangerous for his brothers-in-law to have stayed. "I doubt if such small fry as the boys or myself would be troubled," he said. Baltzelle welcomed the advent of a military regime in Georgia as an alternative to anarchy. "It is the only kind of government that will keep a certain class of bush-whackers, marauders, and envious scamps in the country in order. If we can get a good commander, I doubt if the law-abiding and quiet men of the South will be molested."[23]

Although Captain Baltzelle believed that the decision of the Barnsleys to go to Brazil was wise, some in Texas remained extremely dubious of the move. The editor of *Flake's Bulletin* in Galveston could not resist the temptation to comment unfavorably on the fate of the former Texans:

The brig Derby, with emigrants from Galveston to Brazil, has been lost on the reefs off Cuba, as will appear from the telegraphic dispatches. It will be remembered that there was no little talk about the unseaworthiness of the vessel at the time she sailed, and that Gen. Kent, the Collector of the Port, detained her until surveyors certified as to her seaworthiness. There has been too much misfortune attending the Brazilian emigration scheme not to cause thought. We all recollect how the misguided emigrants were detained week after week, while the vessel was detained in New Orleans, and subsequently at this port. How she attempted to put to sea when unseaworthy and without water, and the circumstances of her detention by the Collector of the Port. There has been some chronic bad luck attending this scheme that is not understood.[24]

Despite the seemingly endless succession of perplexing and frustrating problems that confronted the Texans, they expressed little desire to return to the United States. Only two persons elected to quit the colonial venture after the shipwreck in Cuba. One Major Penn decided to go home to Texas after the tragedy, and Thomas Wright, Jesse Wright's uncle, determined he had made a mistake and returned to Comanche County, Texas. Of course, Captain Causse and his crew went back to the United States as soon as possible after the passengers of the *Derby* were safely ashore. Causse himself returned to New Orleans on the schooner *Mischief,* a ship with a fitting name for the questionable captain. But even injured C. A. Crawley elected to continue to South America. His collarbone was mending satisfactorily, and his enthusiasm for Brazil was as high as ever.[25]

The amount of baggage that the colonists saved seemed miraculous in view of the difficulty of its retrieval from the ship and the severity of the damage to the ship's bow. Approximately three-fourths of the cargo was salvaged, in various states of condition. Most was soaked with salt water, but a thorough scrubbing made it usable again. The expensive monogrammed linens that belonged to the Martin Felix Demaret family, although thoroughly impregnated with brine, were saved after being carefully unfolded and spread to dry. Even a feather bed belonging to the Alfred I. Smith family was rescued to continue the trip to Brazil. George Barnsley found his supply of medicine to be intact although badly scattered.[26]

One lost item, however, created a controversy that caused hard feelings and bitter accusations. When the *Derby* left Galveston, Albert G. McMahon approached Nancy McMullan and asked if she would consider packing a small buckskin bag filled with gold with her baggage. He reasoned that if anyone should consider stealing it, the gold would be safer in Nancy's trunk than in his own. She did as he asked, not thinking of the possibility that she might be held responsible if a loss should occur. After the *Derby* hit the rocks, the trunk in which the bag of gold was hidden was located, but McMahon's treasure was missing. McMahon became furious. He would not believe that the gold alone could disappear while the balance of the contents remained in place. He confronted Nancy McMullan and charged her with taking his savings. She was heartbroken at the accusation and at the same time chagrined that a person she considered to be a friend would accuse her of thievery. McMahon himself solved the mystery when he found the pouch wedged between rocks as he searched for other missing items. Apologies were forthcoming, but relations between the two continued to be strained.[27]

Another group of items that were salvaged after having been presumed lost included a large number of "private delicacies, such as oysters, wines, jellies, canned fruits, etc.," which were to be used in the first year in Brazil until a crop could be harvested. With these goods having a value of more than $1,000, their loss would have been demoralizing, especially since little money remained for purchasing replacement foods.[28]

Frank McMullan's February 21 letter to the New Orleans *Daily Picayune* surprisingly did not mention the scandalous conduct of the crew in attempting to desert the ship during the storm or the fact that McMullan and Dyer forced Captain Causse with drawn pistols to return to his post on the bridge. Instead McMullan actually commended the captain and crew. "With regard to the capacity of those in command of our vessels for their respective positions," said McMullan, "I do not know that I am capable of forming that judgment; but, during the scene of the wreck, notwithstanding my utter want of confidence in the captain, as a man, his conduct and that of the other officers and crew, was certainly very becoming, for which they have our sincere thanks." One can only conclude that McMullan wished to speak only of the performance "during the scene of the wreck," and not before or after. Perhaps he wished to say as little as possible of the severe problems that had been encountered, believing them detrimental to the overall position of the colonists should they find it necessary to return to the United States. Too, such a confession of violence against the captain of a ship on the high seas could be interpreted by a court of law as mutiny—a charge that would not be easily disproved.[29]

But McMullan had little apprehension about possible prosecution from U.S. authorities. His worry was in securing additional support for his colonists from the Brazilian consul, and this finally came in more concrete form. With transportation by steamer from Cuba already approved, discussion moved to housing for the Texans when they arrived in New York. The old Collins Hotel, on Canal Street, stood empty and available for use. It was rented for the emigrants by General Domingo de Goicouria, William Walker's old Cuban comrade-in-arms from Nicaraguan days, who in 1867 was an agent for the Brazilian Emigration Agency. Although McMullan and Goicouria were never in Nicaragua at the same time, there is little doubt that the two men reminisced about the days in Central America before the Civil War. When all of the necessary arrangements were complete, McMullan boarded a steamer for Cuba, ready to return to his charges and bring them to New York.[30]

Upon his arrival in Havana, McMullan immediately made inquiries as to the status of the Texans. He contacted Felipe de Goicouria, Domingo de Goicouria's brother, who provided significant assistance by helping McMullan make arrangements for food, clothing, and shelter in the Cuban capital. The two men met with Juan A. Colomie, the manager of the horse-drawn City Railroad, and asked for aid in transporting the colonists when they arrived in Havana. Not only did Colomie agree to furnish free conveyance for the North Americans; he also offered the use of one of his terminals for shelter. This structure, although located out of the city proper near the community of Carmeleo, proved sufficiently large to house the entire party.[31]

Returning to Vermay's plantation, McMullan eagerly told the colonists of the arrangements that he had been able to make for them. He had almost miraculously secured all necessary assistance for the remainder of the stay in Cuba as well as transportation to New York. The Texans expressed delight and relief when they heard the good news. They did not relish the prospect of having to return to their old homes, bankrupt and destitute, but many would have been forced to do so if McMullan had not secured free assistance from Brazilian and Cuban authorities.

Undoubtedly Vermay was glad to hear that the Texans would be leaving. Ever a gentleman, however, he unhesitatingly offered the use of his wagons once again to carry the McMullan colonists and their belongings to Guanajay, where rail transportation connected with Havana. The emigrants accepted his offer but with the hesitancy that accompanies an obligation for which compensation cannot be given. "I could almost defy the world to cite another such instance of generosity and true manliness," wrote Frank McMullan. "But for a debt, which we were unable to pay in gratitude, we should have been happy."[32]

Vermay's carts proved insufficient both in size and in number to carry all of the Americans at one time, so several trips were made, each carrying as much baggage and as many persons as possible. One ten-year-old girl later recalled the unusual circumstances. "Again it was ox-carts and only a few could go at a time—so it was some days before we reached the railroad station. We traveled at night over the worst roads imaginable. Driven by coolies, whose queer call to the oxen was so 'triste' [sad]. And what with the jolts, even a child could not sleep, but just before we were 'kilt entirely,' the day dawned and found us in Jonahai [Guanajay], where, after a day's wait, all took the train to Havana."[33]

Guanajay, a small town with an excellent climate situated in the hills of western Cuba, was used as an acclimatization station for Spanish troops upon their arrival on the island. It also served as the terminus of the United Railway, which ran from Guanajay to Havana, thirty miles to the northeast. When everyone arrived at the small resort town, the problem of food supplies appeared once again. The governor of the city was true to an earlier promise, however, and support came quickly and at no cost. Large supplies of beans, rice, and potatoes were soon unloaded at the colonists' temporary camp in the town square. To prepare the food, the Cubans provided large cooking pots. At first no one in the crowd volunteered to prepare the meal for the large group. But as the food was raw and the emigrants were hungry, a chef soon appeared. Alfred I. Smith stepped forward, rolled up his sleeves, and went to work. Mrs. Smith tried to help, but her husband sent her away; he was determined to do the chore himself. Lewis Green, the nineteen-year-old son of widower A. J. Green, also offered assistance, but he too was refused. Although there had been little enthusiasm about food preparation, everyone appeared when the stew was ready to eat. "Such is human nature," commented Smith's daughter when she recalled the event in later years.[34]

The McMullan colonists eagerly anticipated the last leg of the journey to Havana, the train ride from Guanajay, and only one day was spent in the little town before baggage and supplies were loaded. Then, boarding passenger cars, they were on their way to the capital. The trip was a beautiful one as the train passed through seemingly endless forests of banana trees, a sight that made a particularly strong impression on the children of the group. Upon their arrival in Havana on March 1, they were met by Felipe de Goicouria, who assured them that everything was in order. The ship to New York was on its way, tickets were in hand, and sleeping and eating accommodations in Havana were available. Finally, Frank McMullan must have thought, everything seemed to be progressing satisfactorily.[35]

The horse railroad terminal at Carmeleo where the Americans were to stay was only a short distance from Havana, but transportation from the docks had to be provided in shifts. As it would be nearly two weeks before the *Mariposa* was due to arrive, the colonists also found it necessary to transport all of their baggage and equipment to the terminal. The old building, although allowing little privacy, provided a dry refuge from cool evening winds. George Barnsley, in a March 1 letter to his father, remarked that he was pleased with the situation and called the accommodations "comfortable." Continuing, Barnsley noted that he remained unsure of whether the entire fare for passage to New York and Rio would be borne by the Brazilian government. "Whether or not we have to repay it," he explained, "depends on circumstances." Obviously, Barnsley was referring to the fact that the New York consul acted without official orders from Rio de Janeiro.[36]

When it became general knowledge in Havana that the shipwrecked Texans had few belongings and that some were almost destitute, they received widespread offers of assistance. The Ladies Benevolent Society volunteered food and clothing. The Sisters of Charity "brought gifts of clothing, shoes, and stockings—cloth for dresses, and many other useful articles." A Countess O'Reilly, through the president of the Parish of Monserate, offered aid, as did many others. Portuguese consul Gávez e Fínaz raised money for the purchase of clothing. In addition, several hundred dollars were donated by generous Cubans. At the request of Frank McMullan and others, George Barnsley composed the following letter of thanks to be forwarded to Cuban newspapers:

> We, the emigrants for Brazil, under the guidance of Col. McMullen [*sic*], recently cast away upon the coast of Cuba, having received much kindness and attention from the government and citizens of the Island in supplying our necessities and wants from the occurrence of our misfortune to the time of our departure, so hereby desire to express our warmest gratitude to our benefactors, among whom we have the honor to mention the following: To her Excellency, Countess O'Reilly, through the Lady President of the Parish of Monserate; the Lady President of the Ladies Benevolent Society, for food, necessary clothing to our needy. To Sen. Don Juan A. Colomie, Manager of the City R.R. for commodious shelter at Carmeleo and for transportation through the city; To Sen. Don Fernando de Gavare Toscar, Consul de Portugal, for his varied important services; to the Governor of the city of Guanahay [*sic*]; to Sen. Don Juan Vermay for his noble hospitality in transporting free of cost our entire party and their effects to his mansion from the place of the wreck, where for nearly a month our women and children found shelter; And to all our unwearied friends; To many others and to all our most heartfelt thanks are given. Exiles

from our nation's shores, refugees from political oppression, emigrants to an untried land, Cubans, our souls are too full of gratitude for worthy expression[,] yet at the footstool of our common God we will never cease to beg that you be always the recipients of his blessing and providences.

signed

Emigrants to Brazil[37]

On March 13 the side-wheel steamship *Mariposa* arrived in Havana. Commanded by a Captain Quick, the 1,082-ton ship belonged to the New York and Brazil Steamship Company—"The Star Line." It cleared New Orleans on March 8 with a crew of forty men. It was owned by Cornelius K. Garrison, who aided the filibuster efforts in Nicaragua from 1855 to 1857. Although both men once supported a common cause, McMullan had little use for the shipowner. He believed Garrison was to blame for the Brazilian government's decision not to provide passenger service from southern ports for former Confederates.[38]

The Texan emigrants, eager to resume their frequently interrupted journey to Brazil, gathered at the pier, ready to board the *Mariposa* as soon as the steamer's purser announced that the ship was ready. Only a few cabins were available; the ones who did not receive them had to be content with beds in steerage. George Barnsley wrote that approximately 130 men, women, and children huddled in a small room, "with as little regard to comfort as if we had been so many slaves being brought from Africa." Despite the general discomfort, however, the first night at sea was smooth, warm, and generally pleasant.[39]

But the soft winds of the tropics soon began to shift as a huge arctic front moved into the Atlantic off the east coast of the United States. Within hours, everyone aboard ship severely felt winter's cold blast. With the frigid weather came high winds, turbulent seas, ice, and sleet. Without adequate stoves or blankets, the whole of the company and crew of the *Mariposa* soon felt miserable, particularly the steerage passengers. The rolling of the ship added to the discomfort of those in the party with limited maritime experience. Still, most took the discomfort as philosophically as possible, consoling themselves with the expectation of being in "the land of eternal spring" within six weeks.[40]

About three days out of Havana, the weather became even worse. The wind reached near gale force, and the waves buried the bow of the ship in the water, then raised it from the sea, only to drop it recklessly. One huge wave rolled completely over the steamer, causing it to nearly founder and forcing a large volume of water into the hold and steerage area. Afterward all suffered from cold and wet feet, and some had frostbite. An awful fog then encompassed the vessel and made an unpleasant situation even worse. As the ship plowed through the cloud-like mist, the watchman could hardly see past the bow. The ship's whistle "made the most doleful sounds, ever and anon, all night." To make a dismal situation even more unpleasant, the infant child of Billy and Vic Moore died and was buried at sea. Physician Barnsley attributed the death to hydrocephalus.[41]

As the *Mariposa* passed Cape Hatteras, North Carolina, on the morning of March 19, another steamer hailed it, announced that it was in distress, and asked for assistance. Captain Quick, because of the responsibility for the large number of passengers on board his ship, elected to proceed rather than risk their lives in a rescue attempt. He set the wheel for Norfolk, Virginia, where he planned to take on coal and secure a short respite from the heavy northeast gale, the raging sea, and the fog. Soon after the *Mariposa* arrived at the pier, another steamer, the *Charles W. Lord,* appeared in the harbor towing the disabled ship that had requested aid.[42]

The cold, the water, the disappointment, and the frustration took their toll on the William B. Nettles family at Norfolk. The family of seven concluded that it was no longer worth the effort to be rid of free Negroes and Yankees and decided to return to Texas. The family members could not endure the thought of boarding the *Mariposa* again to face the sea and its storms. It is likely that other emigrants had second thoughts, too, but none elected to quit.[43]

On March 21, even though the storm still raged, Captain Quick decided to attempt to leave port and continue to New York. The extremely severe gale caused the ship's master to change his mind, however, and he returned to land, this time docking at Fortress Monroe, opposite Norfolk. When news of their return was telegraphed to Texas, the *Galveston Daily News* once again seized the opportunity to condemn the ill-fated colonization venture:

Texas Brazilians.—A Fortress Monroe dispatch says the steamship Mariposa, from New Orleans to New York, which had put in there, sailed hence on the 21st, but was forced to return on account of a heavy northeast gale prevailing outside. The Mariposa had on board 150 Texian immigrants for Brazil, who had been wrecked on the coast of Cuba, and had embarked again at Havana. These are the same who left here, some time since, on the brig Derby, under charge of Mr. Frank McMullen [*sic*]. We guess that they will soon begin to imagine that providence objects to their leaving Texas for Brazil. They had better come back to first principles, before something happens.[44]

On March 22 the steamer *Merrimac* sailed for Rio de Janeiro from New York, but without the emigrants from Texas who had looked forward with so much anticipation to being aboard. Instead, the colonists found themselves still stranded at Fortress Monroe with no idea when they would be able to board another ship to Brazil. With little or no money, even the proximity of the town of Hampton Roads offered no appeal. In addition, the real or imagined possibility of intimidation from northern authorities caused most of the Texans to remain on ship. They wished no further obstacles to appear that might delay their trip once more.[45]

Two days later, on March 24, Captain Quick determined once again to attempt to leave port. Although the Atlantic storm still raged, the weather had calmed just enough that the *Mariposa* safely made it into the open sea. Only a few hours out of the bay, however, tragedy once again came alarmingly close. Sailing without lights in dense fog at top speed, the *Mariposa* came near to calamity when it was nearly hit amidships by another large steamer. The crew as well as the passengers were visibly shaken. When would troubles end?[46]

Perhaps good food provided the only saving grace in the life of the passengers on the *Mariposa*. George Barnsley complained to the ship's officers, however, that although palatable, the meals were served "brutally." He objected to the lack of cleanliness but received no response. As the colony's official doctor, Barnsley felt an obligation to the emigrants and was determined to correct the situation. A threat to report the infractions to the Sanitary Commission of New York finally caused some improvement.[47]

The March 26 arrival in New York of the *Mariposa* was announced in a column entitled "Maritime Intelligence" in the *New York Times:* "Steamship Mariposa, Quick, New Orleans March 9, Havana 13th, Norfolk 19th, and Fortress Monroe 24th, with mdse. and passengers to C. K. Garrison. Experienced heavy weather the entire passage; was detained 5 ds. at Fortress Monroe by N. E. gales and thick weather. The Mariposa has on board 150 Brazilian emigrants, wrecked on the brig Derby, off Cuba."[48]

Luck must have played a part in salvaging baggage, equipment, food, and supplies from the hulk of the *Derby* as it lay wedged in the rocks off Cuba's coast. The passengers could have lost everything, including their lives, had good fortune not been with them. The delay in Cuba, although involving the waste of another month, perhaps enabled the Texans to gain a second wind before tackling their second stormy voyage along the Atlantic coast on the way to New York. There they hoped to board another southbound ship that would at last take them to Brazil.

Frank McMullan. The photograph was taken in New Orleans in 1866. Family tradition relates that McMullan was very ill at the time of the photo and that he had to get out of bed to keep his appointment at the studio. Courtesy of Rachel McMullan White, Cumberland, Rhode Island.

George S. Barnsley. Courtesy of Harold Barnsley Holland, Jacareí, São Paulo State, Brazil.

Woodlands, the residence of George and Lucian Barnsley in Bartow County, Georgia, before they resolved to go to Brazil with the McMullan colonists in 1867. Courtesy of Julia Barnsley Macdonell, São Paulo, Brazil.

The Smith House, located at the juncture of the Ariado and the Itariri rivers on the McMullan grant. It was an "American-style" house constructed by Alfred I. Smith and his family in 1868–1869. Photograph by the author, 1983.

American emigrants at the village of Americana, São Paulo, preparing to load watermelons on a train for shipment. From Marie Robinson Wright, The New Brazil *(Philadelphia: George Barrie & Sons, 1907), p. 244.*

*William Bowen, Frank McMullan's part-
ner. Courtesy Dr. Fred Brigance,
Murfreesboro, Tennessee.*

*Edwin Ney McMullan. The photograph was taken
about 1895 at Jackson Studio in Waco, Texas, before
Ney returned to Brazil. Courtesy of Beatrice Hill,
Whitney, Texas.*

Hand-drawn map by George Barnsley, completed in the 1880s during his search for gold and other minerals in the area around the towns of Una, São Roque, and Piedade (Sorocaba). Courtesy of Harold Barnsley Holland, Jacareí, São Paulo State, Brazil.

Official symbol of the Fraternidade Descendencia Americana (Fraternity of Descendants of Americans). In possession of the author.

Monument constructed by descendants of Confederates at the Campo cemetery near Americana, Brazil, to honor the emigrants who came from the South after the Civil War. Photograph by the author, 1983.

Brazil. Box shows location of topographic map (next page) and McMullan colony.

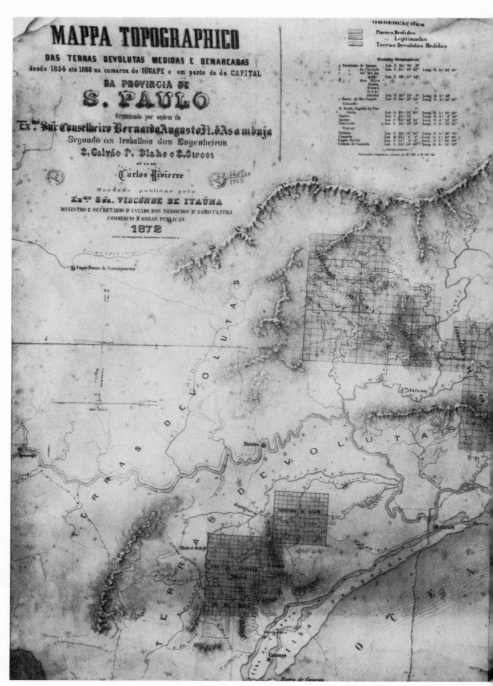

Topographic map of the unoccupied lands measured and surveyed from 1854 to 1868
in the region of Iguape and a part of the capital of the province of São Paulo.
Ministro e Secretario d'Estado dos Negocios d'Agricultura, Comercio e Obras Pu-

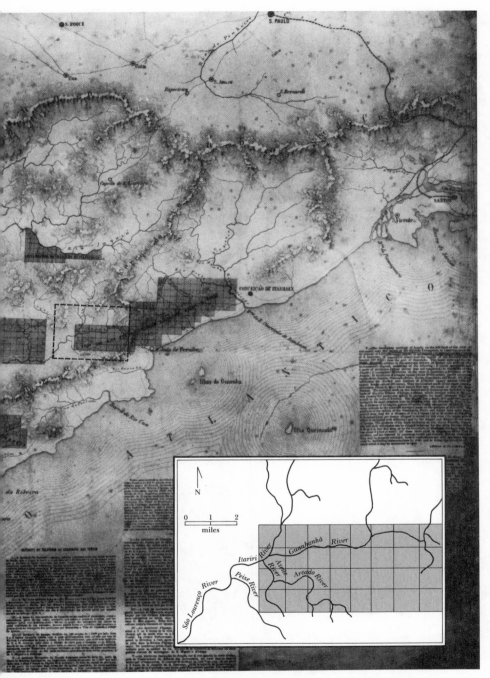

blicas, 1872. Inset shows the main settlement area of the McMullan colony on the São Lourenço River.

Partial map of the highlands of the province of São Paulo. N. Bennaton, November 1868.

CHAPTER 7

The Promised Land

WHEN THE STEAMER *Mariposa* docked in New York harbor on March 26, 1867, a cold, tired, and bedraggled group of former Texans walked down the gangplank. Some of the travelers were virtually in rags and none wore heavy clothing, and a cold wind added to their discomfort. Only the prompt appearance of General Domingo de Goicouria from the Brazilian Emigration Agency gave the colonists encouragement in an otherwise dismal situation. Goicouria cheerfully informed them that transportation would soon arrive to carry their baggage to the Collins Hotel, at the foot of Canal Street, which the agency had rented for the McMullan party.

The hotel was anything but luxurious; in fact, it had been empty and deteriorating for months. It had little to offer but space, and the Texans happily occupied one complete floor. The building had neither fireplaces nor cooking facilities, and its owner long before had stripped it of its furniture. The colonists nevertheless found it a welcome sight—it was away from the ocean, it was dry, and it offered a shelter from the frigid winds. With blankets provided by Goicouria, the emigrants decided that the structure would serve very well as lodging for the twenty-five days before another ship was scheduled to leave for Rio de Janeiro.[1]

Saturday morning, March 27, brought continued cold and snow, an unwelcome contrast to the sunny and humid days in Cuba. In order to stay warm, the colonists donned several sets of clothes as they had no winter apparel. Since they determined to make as good an appearance as possible among their recent enemies, they put their best attire on top. The majority of men proudly donned uniforms of Confederate gray. Those who did not wore good broadcloth suits. The women dressed in clothing described as being of fine texture, "but now sadly worn and frayed—relics of more prosperous times." That afternoon the colonists received a visit from a reporter of the *New York Times*. De-

spite the recent war, the northern journalist's article treated the Texans well. In an article entitled "Wrecked Emigrants," which appeared
on March 28, the writer discussed the problems that had been encountered, including the shipwreck, the stay in Cuba, and the journey to New York. All of the emigrants, stated the reporter, "are native
Americans, and appear to be possessed with more than normal intelligence. They are principally agriculturists, a few being machinists and
mechanics." The article continued with a general description of the
health and physical needs of the southerners:

> Two or three of the men were sick with fever, and one tall youth—an
> unmistakable Southerner—appeared to be dying of consumption. As
> a general thing, however, they looked remarkably well in health for
> people who had undergone the perils and hardships of a protracted
> and stormy voyage. . . . In the meantime the women and children are
> suffering for the comforts, if not the necessities of life, and the chari-
> tably disposed will find a field for the exercise of their philanthropy.
> Contributions addressed to Mr. McMullen [sic], at Collins Hotel, Ca-
> nal Street, or the Brazilian Emigration Agency, No. 26½ Broadway,
> will reach the persons for whom they are intended.[2]

Assistance soon arrived as a result of the appeal in the *Times*.
The Methodist Church proved particularly helpful, donating two
large boxes of religious books, including "song books and old fasion
[sic] question books." No one knew at the time how valuable this gift
would be.[3]

Finally settled in their new quarters, the southerners determined to
take advantage of their stay in the metropolis by wandering around
the city and taking in the sights. The New Yorkers treated them kindly,
calling them "poor shipwrecked creatures." One Texan, however, became the victim of a prank that nearly caused serious trouble. Jesse
Wright kept his coon hounds in his room at the hotel, where they soon
became a topic for general discussion among those New Yorkers who
dropped in on the Texans for polite conversation. Probably in pure
mischief, one visitor decided to steal the dogs, never guessing the per-
sonality and resolve of the animals' owner. When Wright learned of
the theft, he took revolver in hand and started up Canal Street in
search of the pets and the thief. Wright, described as "a very tall, large
man with a booming voice," made an imposing figure. Dressed in
Confederate gray with a heavy shawl streaming from his neck, he cor-
nered every stranger on the street and demanded information. As
Wright wildly pointed his pistol, one may imagine the fearful re-
sponses he received from the innocent pedestrians he encountered.
As he passed a saloon, the hounds heard his curses, and from behind

the bar where their abductors had hidden them, they at once set up a howl. Jesse barged through the door, leaped over the bar, and claimed the dogs; he then triumphantly trooped out of the drinking establishment. His victory was largely unseen, however, as most of the patrons of the saloon had ducked out of sight when the ruckus began.[4]

In an effort to disassociate themselves from Texans such as Jesse Wright, George and Lucian Barnsley chose not to stay in the Collins Hotel. Instead, George borrowed $50 in greenbacks from a New York business associate of his father, and the two brothers moved into the European Hotel, at 163 Hudson and the corner of Laight Street. Barnsley described the place as "a cheap house where we pay $1.50 each per diem." George promised his father in a letter of March 27 to "try to find a cheaper place, if possible."[5]

Probably for the same reason that he chose not to stay at the same lodgings as the Texans, George Barnsley expressed doubts as to whether he should continue to Brazil as a part of the McMullan colony. Instead, he expressed a desire to go first to England to study medicine and then "enter Brazil like a gentleman next year." He wrote his father for advice in making the decision; then he enumerated several reasons that he should continue with the southerners:

> But there are serious considerations which go against absenting myself from this party now; they are: I started with them. I have preserved, with God's help, every life except that of one child; they all desire me to remain with them. I have accepted Brazilian Govm't transportation to New York; I am expected to go on. I have a good deal of influence among the emigrants, and I think they generally look up to me; . . . I have all of McMullan's influence, which separating I may loose [sic]. If I go to London now I [will] get into a manner of life too easy. I am now poor and rough; my hands are hard and muscles tough, and I am by recent and present adversity better prepared than ever to battle with the world. With the first colonists I shall have a foothold, and as they increase in numbers and wealth I will grow too.[6]

It is likely that George and Lucian had already decided to continue with the colonists to Brazil despite the request for advice from their father on the matter. The principal reason, not outlined by George in his letter, was the lack of cash either for an ocean voyage to England or for study. As a practical matter, the brothers had the alternatives of either going to Brazil or returning to Georgia.

While they were in the northeastern United States, however, the Barnsley brothers had the opportunity to visit old friends and acquaintances from school days in Rhode Island before the war. On

April 17 George wrote his father that he had been able to locate a Mrs. Green, his old schoolteacher. Both brothers saw friends in Greenwich, Connecticut, who "would accept no excuse" for their not staying a few days.[7]

Other Texan emigrants also used their time well during the delay in New York. Calvin and Thomas McKnight spent several days visiting relatives and friends in Pennsylvania, including their mother, whom they had not seen since they left for Texas many years before. The Alfred I. Smith family, like many others, took advantage of the interval between ships to tour the city. The Smith's daughter, Bellona, later recalled that the Texans were considered a novelty by their hosts. "Of course we took the opportunity to see the other sights of the great city of which so much has been said—a never failing astonishment to those Greenhorns from Texas. But if New York was a sight to us, we were a ten-cent show to the New Yorkers, and they certainly enjoyed it."[8]

While the southerners were in New York, the news arrived that the mammoth steamship *Great Eastern* was to arrive from Liverpool. This vessel, the wonder of its time, could carry up to 2,500 passengers and cross the North Atlantic in only fourteen days. The Texans all climbed to the roof of the Collins Hotel to watch the huge ship arrive, "towed by little steam crafts that looked like a lot of ants on a grasshopper." From the top of their lodging, the emigrants could also see Central Park, which they later visited with "open-eyed wonder." About the middle of April, however, an event occurred that virtually stopped the pleasant activities and could have become the final tragedy of the McMullan emigrants. One of the colonists became ill and exhibited symptoms that George Barnsley diagnosed as smallpox. No one else became infected, however, and no new cases of illness occurred. To be safe, Barnsley vaccinated the entire party.[9]

As the Texans planned to leave for Rio de Janeiro aboard the steamship *North America* on April 22, another emigrant leader made plans for his group to join them. Like McMullan, James McFadden Gaston had been in contact with the Brazilian consulate in New York. In reply to a query about transportation, Quintino Bocayuva of the Brazilian Emigration Agency offered Gaston's colonists passage with the Texans on the *North America*. In the note, Bocayuva stated that the Brazilian government would "not receive any emigrants but your party and McMullin's [*sic*]. They have only Southerners and people of the same class." Bocayuva also offered accommodations to Gaston "at small cost in the Collier [*sic*] Hotel, opposite Pier 42, North River." Despite Bocayuva's statement that no others could sail with the McMullan and Gaston groups, he did offer to include Dr. H. A. Shaw and his family from South Carolina, who had also been in correspondence with the

Brazilian government about colonization. Bocayuva also told Gaston that any persons who could not be in New York by April 22 could sail with Reverend Ballard S. Dunn's party on May 16 from New Orleans. In a letter to Dr. Shaw, Gaston stated that he and about 100 others planned to accompany McMullan and that they would leave Savannah for New York on April 13. Shaw, who with his partner Robert Meriwether represented the Southern Colonization Society of Edgefield, South Carolina, also decided to sail with the Texas emigrants. By April 20 all were in New York and ready to depart for their new country.[10]

The prospects for a pleasant journey from New York to Rio de Janeiro seemed dim. Although the *North America* was one of the best and largest steamships on the South American run, it did not have a good reputation for courtesy, service, or comfort, even for cabin passengers, much less those in the steerage area, where most of the colonists were assigned. Philosophically George Barnsley predicted "miserable accommodations" and reasoned that it "would not make much difference . . . as it is only for one month." When the time came to board ship, the Texans and their new friends from Georgia, Florida, South Carolina, and Alabama felt exuberant. They were very anxious to leave the Collins Hotel, cold weather, and Yankees in general. The *Dallas Herald* later reported their departure with a brief note: "The Steamship North America of the Brazil line, sailed from New York a few days ago, for Rio, taking about 240 passengers, most of whom are from the Southern States. Included are 138 from Texas, 30 from Florida, and about as many from Georgia and Alabama."[11]

In addition to the Americans, a considerable number of Irish traveled on board the ship. Most had immigrated to New York, but when they failed to find a hoped-for utopia there, they responded to Brazilian promises of happiness in South America. Although none of these former Europeans were asked to join the American colonists, one young man named O'Reilly became a friend of one of the southerners in Gaston's party named Dillard. George Barnsley made the only other meaningful contact with the Irish passengers by providing medical care for them in addition to his assistance to the McMullan, Gaston, and Meriwether and Shaw groups.[12]

The conditions aboard the *North America* proved to be worse than had been predicted. The crew paid no attention whatsoever to cleanliness, even in the steamer's galley. George Barnsley described the food as "execrable," and sickness was common. The purser's time, according to Barnsley, was "altogether occupied in private flirtations," and the officers of the vessel engaged in "constant bickerings and insults" toward the passengers. The only exception among the crew was the chief engineer, who "did all in his power to alleviate the condition of the sick." Fortunately, the weather remained good and there were no delays. The *North America* arrived in the harbor of Rio de Janeiro on May 20 after making the usual stops at St. Thomas, Pará, Pernambuco, and Bahia. The trip lasted only twenty-eight days.[13]

The black cloud that seemed to follow McMullan's Texans, however, still lingered with them. As the *North America* entered the bay outside Rio, it carelessly came too close to a large steamer and a collision occurred, knocking a large hole in the bow of the American ship. To avoid panic among the passengers, the crew minimized the damage until they could lower a large sail as a patch. This maneuver significantly reduced the amount of water that was pouring into the hold. The makeshift repair proved adequate to get the ship to the dock.[14]

Immediately upon arrival, George Barnsley, acting in his official capacity as physician for the American passengers, lodged a strong protest with port authorities, condemning the health conditions on board the ship. After an investigation, the New York and Brazil Steamship Company, the owner of the *North America*, received a fine of five *contos*, although it is not known whether the penalty was collected.[15]

The reaction of various colonists to Rio de Janeiro varied considerably. Bellona Smith Ferguson expressed her feelings in this way:

> My impressions of Brazil when we first entered . . . the bay of Rio was [*sic*] extremely disappointing. The contrast after New York was certainly great. Everything seemed too small. Houses too low, and out of sight behind hills. And way off on a green mountain we saw a toy train winding out of sight, not much like the great thundering American engines we last saw as we sailed away . . . . Then, the streets of Rio—narrow, dirty, and winding up hill and down with no drays, mule carts, or wheeled vehicles of any kind, but great husky Negroes staggering under their heavy loads.[16]

In contrast, George Barnsley expressed pleasure with the capital of his adopted country. He quickly praised the city, its natural surroundings, and its commercial possibilities. "The scenery is too beautiful and grand for description," he said, "such combinations of objects of grandeur and beauty I venture can be found no where else. . . . Rio resembles . . . Havana, and has all the modern improvements of gas, hydrants, sewers, etc. The shops are well filled and very cheap are the contents."[17]

After initial processing by port authorities, the colonists received instructions to proceed to the so-called Emigrant Hotel, also termed Government House or Casa de Saúde, which had been converted into temporary quarters for the expected arrivals from the United States.

Colonel James A. Broome, formerly of the Fourteenth Alabama Infantry, managed the hotel, which was a beautiful and grandiose mansion located on a hill adjacent to a beautiful church.[18]

The generally poor Texans could find no way to get to the government-furnished accommodations other than walking, even though such a strenuous hike was tiring for persons carrying their baggage and just in from a long sea voyage. The hotel was approached by a wide road paved with large white stones. The highway made a broad curve up a mountainside, terminating at a huge iron gate that was the entrance to the grounds of the mansion. Along either side of a walk from the gate to the building stood trim rows of imperial palm trees that lent an almost incomprehensible tropical beauty to the scene. On both sides of the pathway were large marble basins where fountains once played, and marble benches under vine-covered arbors beckoned the weary travelers. Beautiful flowers growing in manicured beds added to the picturesque scene.[19]

Colonel Broome wasted no time in showing the new arrivals to their apartments. Neat and clean, each contained a lightweight iron bed and a washstand, all painted green. There were also enough tables and chairs to make the colonists comfortable in the near elegant surroundings. Many of the rooms, according to one description, "were beautifully papered, some with gilded and frescoed ceilings." Because of the striking contrast to both the living conditions aboard ship and the hotel in New York, the Texans must have felt that they had finally reached the promised land.[20]

The colonists learned that they were not the first to reach Brazil, despite Frank McMullan's sincere wish to have his emigrants become the initial group from the United States. Four days before, the *Marmion,* with Ballard Dunn's colonists as well as those of George Grandioson Gunter, had sailed into port. With the addition of the 240 passengers from the *North America,* the number of guests at the Emigrant Hotel rose to over 500 persons. All were free to stay for thirty days, or until furnished transportation to colony lands, with plain but healthy food furnished at no cost.[21]

On Sunday morning, May 23, the Americans received a message that Dom Pedro II, the Emperor of Brazil, was coming to the hotel to visit the new arrivals from the United States. Excitement swept through the Americans, and a frenzied effort went into making the rooms and kitchen look their very best. Of course, all donned their finest clothing in order to present the best possible appearance to their new ruler. Toward the middle of the afternoon, the children were allowed to stand on the balconies of the old mansion, while the adults began to gather on the porch and grounds. At four o'clock a shout went up as

they saw the royal coach entering the main drive. The imperial pro-
cession stopped short of the building itself, and Dom Pedro ascended
the steps on foot, followed by aides. The emperor was about forty-six
years old. His hair and beard were graying, and he had blue eyes and
a prominent, aquiline nose. He was dressed in a plain black suit, with
only a star on his left breast to denote his royal position. "His countenance," according to one account, "was modest and unostentatious."
The Americans pushed closer, hoping for a good look at a real emperor, until the entire square was jammed with people. From time
to time, a balloon purchased for the occasion would rise into the
air. Other Americans, to celebrate the event properly, fired sky-
rockets. Spontaneously Columbus Wasson threw his hat into the air
and shouted, "McMullan's Colony gives three cheers for the Emperor
of Brazil." Three times three soon turned to "Viva! Viva! Dom Pedro
Segundo!" from all of the new arrivals. More hats went into the air as
a feeling of reckless relief swept through the crowd. For many, this
occasion became the culmination of months of misery, pain, and
worry.[22]

At the end of the demonstration of respect, the emperor began a
tour that took him through all of the lodging facilities. He first walked
around the grounds of the estate; then he went to the kitchen, where
he tasted the bread and declared it well made. Leaving the interior of
the building, Dom Pedro stopped on the front porch where some of
the Americans, probably McMullan, Dunn, Gaston, Shaw, Meriwether,
and Gunter, were waiting. He held a short conversation with them
and said that he was well-pleased with the appearance of the Americans. Seeing a young boy standing nearby, the emperor walked over to
him, placed his hand on the lad's head, and said a few kind words. The
boy was awed by the ruler's action and no doubt remembered it for the
rest of his life. Before the crowd realized it, Dom Pedro was gone,
leaving before many were really conscious that they had been in the
ruler's presence.[23]

The evening of May 23, George Barnsley wrote to his father telling
of the royal visit. Barnsley remarked that Dom Pedro was "a fine looking gentleman" and that the ruler was "especially interested" in Mc-
Mullan's colony. Continuing, Barnsley said that the Texas colony had
received complimentary notice in the newspapers. The favorable welcome given the Texans also gave Barnsley encouragement in his belief
that additional help would be forthcoming. "We have some reasons to
hope that not only will our passage money be remitted by the Govm't,
but also that aid will be extended us." Barnsley concluded his letter
with the request that his father write to him "Care of Col. Frank
McMullen [sic], Iguape, Sao Paulo Province, via Rio de Janeiro."[24]

Five days after their arrival in Rio de Janeiro, the McMullan colonists received word that the steamer *Marmion* was ready to transport them and their baggage and equipment to Iguape. There they were to wait until river transportation was available to carry them to colony lands. Most were anxious to proceed and quickly packed their belongings to make ready for what they hoped would be their last ocean voyage. Others, however, decided for various reasons to go no farther. Gambler McNabb saw no real future for himself in the backwoods of São Paulo Province and elected to stay in Rio with his wife and daughter. Reportedly McNabb relieved a Mexican companion of all of his gold and "got rid" of him after leaving the emigrant party. Presumably using the wealth he extracted from his erstwhile friend, McNabb opened an American-style bar in Rio that was reported to be highly successful. After his death a few years later, McNabb's family left the capital and was not heard from again. Calvin and Isabel McKnight's little daughter, Emma, had become ill on the voyage from New York. Even after several days in Rio, the girl showed no improvement, and the McKnights felt that they had no choice but to remain where good medical facilities were available. Calvin's brother, Thomas, also elected to stay until the crisis was over. William T. McCann, a close friend of the McKnight families, also decided to remain, as he was in no hurry to reach the colony site. The decision of McCann and the McKnights to remain proved of little help, however, as Emma soon died, probably of pneumonia.[25]

One of the McMullan colony bachelors, a Mr. Maston, also determined to remain in Rio de Janeiro. At the Emigrant Hotel he had met and fallen in love with Anna Miller, who, with her parents Irving and Sophie Miller, was set to go to Colonel Gunter's colony on the Rio Doce. Maston proposed to Anna, and she accepted, despite the fact that she had been seeing another young man for quite some time and was generally assumed to be "spoken for." Regardless, the family set a date for the Maston-Miller wedding and made all of the preparations. When the day and hour arrived, however, Maston was nowhere to be found. Guests and family at the event felt mortified, and the bride was hurt and dejected. When a friend went to locate the missing groom, he found that Maston had been murdered. Anna's first lover later admitted the crime with the statement that "if he could not marry Miss Anna, she should not have another man."[26]

Several other former Texans also elected to remain in Rio de Janeiro. There is no record that a Mr. Lee, a bachelor, went on to Iguape or the colony site. Another single man, a Mr. Glen, also presumably stayed in the capital city. It is likely that another young emigrant, a Mr. Johnson, decided to remain in Rio when the others sailed for Iguape. A Mr. Henderson also stayed in Rio, where he adopted a little Brazilian orphan girl. Henderson and his new daughter remained in Brazil only a few months before they returned to Texas. There, the young lady was educated in North American ways and the English language. When grown, she married her foster father.[27]

John "Dad" McMains, a Scotsman who had lived and worked in the California gold fields in 1849, also elected to leave the McMullan group at Rio de Janeiro. Always a loner, McMains wasted neither words nor money. On board ship from New York, George Barnsley, Major Alexander Braxton, and others often solicited McMains' advice, which he usually gave in terse, yet genial phrases. McMains and Braxton went to the Rio Doce, where they formed a partnership for the purpose of exporting fine furniture woods to Rio. The venture proved successful but ended when Braxton failed to return from a trip to the capital where he had sold a quantity of hardwood for a sum of ten *contos*. Braxton had boarded a coastal steamer to return to the Rio Doce, but he never arrived. Most people assumed that he was robbed and murdered. Later McMains traveled alone to Buenos Aires, Argentina, then Paraguay, before trekking across the wilds of Matto Grosso Province to Rio de Janeiro. The trip through the wilderness with no roads took six months. Disappointed at not finding a bonanza mining claim, McMains eventually returned to Texas.[28]

Martin Felix Demaret and his family never officially joined the McMullan colony even though Mrs. Demaret and the children had sailed to Brazil on the same ships as the colonists all the way from Galveston. Demaret, a former resident of Louisiana, lived in Grimes County, Texas, for eleven years prior to his first trip to Brazil in 1866. He traveled all over the empire from the Amazon River to São Paulo Province and finally selected lands near Santa Barbara, northwest of the city of São Paulo. Convinced that he had made the correct decision in going to Brazil, Demaret proclaimed that he was now engaged in "selecting the best from the best." Demaret, his wife, and his children remained in Rio de Janeiro when the time came for their Texas friends to board ship for Iguape. George Barnsley had high praise for Demaret, describing him as a "fine gentleman, of the old, courteous, gallant type, and his family well educated and thoroughly refined in manner, which later merits were very much at discount among most of our American emigrants of that epoch." Like "Dad" McMains, James Monroe Keith sought gold and did not choose to stay with the would-be agriculturalists of the McMullan party. A former Texas Ranger and Confederate soldier, Keith briefly remained in Rio rather than go to Iguape; he then set out on his own into the *sertão* to find his fortune.[29]

On May 25 the *Marmion* lifted anchor from Rio de Janeiro. The ship first stopped at Santos, the port town nearest the city of São Paulo. There some Americans who were not members of the McMullan colony disembarked before the little steamer left once again en route to Iguape, the port at the mouth of the Ribeira de Iguape and the nearest town to the lands selected for settlement. The general bad luck of the Texans continued aboard the *Marmion* when, approaching the city at low tide, the ship struck a sand bar as it neared the docks. Although the steamer was not damaged, it could not move and had to wait until high tide before it could continue to dry land.[30]

Unlike that in Rio de Janeiro, housing in Iguape had not been arranged, as it had been presumed that transportation to take the colonists up the river would be available almost immediately. This was not the case, however. The river steamer would not be ready to sail for nearly a month. Obviously the Texans would have to make do and find shelter wherever they could. A scout of the town soon produced a large empty house, and the colonists obtained permission for many of them to live in it for the duration of their stay. Those who were unable to find room in the old structure were forced to set up camp in the street.[31]

Those who found it necessary to live in a tent included the Alfred I. Smith family. The first day, however, a benevolent Brazilian man approached Mrs. Smith and asked, in Portuguese, if she and her family would like to live in his house. As Mrs. Smith had not yet learned any of the language, she understood nothing of what he said. Fortunately her son Eugene had attended Frank McMullan's language lessons aboard the *Derby* and was able to translate the proposal to his mother. The Smiths thankfully accepted his offer and were soon "domiciled quite comfortably."[32]

Physician George Barnsley and dentist William "Billy" Moore and his wife Vic also found themselves unable to stay in the large house. Rather than camp in the street, however, the three shared what Barnsley described as "a very good house with four rooms, a kitchen, and other rooms for servants (which we have not) all for $3.00 per month." Like many of the other colonists, Moore and Barnsley were virtually penniless. Their families survived on bananas and bread while the men tried unsuccessfully to establish an unlicensed practice in dentistry and medicine, respectively. The situation continued to deteriorate to the point that breakfast consisted of only bananas and water, causing Barnsley to remark that it looked as if they would have to "get enough Portuguese aboard to beg." The versatile Moore cautioned his wife and friend to "hold on awhile" and left for the day, not returning until late in the evening. When he arrived, he held a candle and carried a loaf of bread. He presented his wife with a sack of *denups*—small copper coins—which he said he had won from a party of Brazilians while gambling at a club. "This fortunate luck," stated Barnsley, "started our wheels to grinding, and [we] prospered." Evidently the lack of provisions became widespread, and soon the Brazilian government began furnishing rations, including rice, sugar, pork, *farinha*, *mandioca*, beans, and beef. The donation of food supplies increased speculation among the colonists that before long additional support, including tools and perhaps even money, would be forthcoming.[33]

Despite the tribulations, time passed quickly for the colonists in Iguape, perhaps because for the first time they could see their new country and discuss the home they were going to with a belief that they would actually be there before many more days were to pass. For many, the realization that it would be necessary to speak Portuguese encouraged attempts to learn the scores of nouns, verbs, and adjectives that are essential to understanding. Others busied themselves in meeting merchants, determining markets for crops, and locating sources for seed and equipment. Women attempted to adjust to the new methods of cooking as well as get acquainted with the new foods with which they were unfamiliar. Children were delighted with the forest and the river as well as the wildlife that inhabited both. By the time the steamer was available to begin the shuttle of the colonists up the Ribeira de Iguape, all were ready and anxious to go. Finally the promised land appeared to be a reality.

CHAPTER 8

Under the Southern Cross

T HE SHORT JOURNEY from Rio de Janeiro on the steamer *Marmion* was almost the undoing of Frank McMullan as the stresses of responsibility, tuberculosis, and the long sea voyage took their toll. His health continued to deteriorate, and McMullan sensed that his illness was more critical than he had ever before allowed himself to believe. Forced to bed immediately upon arriving at Iguape, McMullan summoned his physician and friend George Barnsley and his uncle Judge James Dyer to his room. The young man closed the door, opened his small black trunk, and removed the small oilcloth-covered package that he had treasured for over ten years. He took out a yellowed document, unfolded it, and spread it on a small table for Barnsley and Dyer to see. He then narrated the saga of João Aranzel and the Lake of Gold, detailing his forlorn hope of securing both financial security and homes for his friends in the huge land grant where he could "find and secure homes for a brave but unfortunate people." McMullan honestly related to his friends that he did not know whether the directions to the Lake of Gold were real or fantasy, but he expressed the hope that after his death the two would make an effort to locate the treasure in his stead. Tired and weak, McMullan folded the manuscript and returned it to its pouch; then he bid his visitors good night. The prospect for gold was to affect both Dyer and Barnsley profoundly. One would search for it the rest of his life; the other would spend five years in a vain hunt for riches before abandoning the idea forever.[1]

Never having heard the Aranzel legend, however, the rest of the colonists were enthusiastic about land, not gold, and they questioned Judge Dyer about the size of the McMullan grant, the availability of water and transportation, and the completion of the promised surveys. The farmers wished to pick out their acreage as soon as possible, and they hoped that lands would be laid out in 640-acre sections, as McMullan had been promised by the Brazilian government. Dyer could not answer all of their questions, but he promised to find out from the bedridden leader as much as he could and secure their answers.

All would later be surprised to learn that the colony lands were indeed huge—probably larger than either McMullan or the officials in Brazil anticipated. The previously uncharted headwaters of the São Lourenço River and the lands between the towns of Peruibe and Conceição, all provisionally ceded to McMullan, were found to contain over 55 square leagues, or nearly 500 square miles, an area half as large as Rhode Island. The document containing the survey of the McMullan grant consumed 247 pages of field notes, and it outlined detailed measurements and descriptions of the colony lands. It was much more expensive than contemplated, and field work took a year after the execution of the original contract with Inspector-General Ernesto Street. Although still incomplete in June, 1867, the progress was sufficient that the chief surveyor sent word that he would be ready to greet the colonists when they elected to venture upriver to the São Lourenço.[2]

Judge Dyer and Columbus Wasson immediately made plans to take the first contingent of former Texans up the Ribeira de Iguape, and on June 7 about twenty-five persons, including gravely ill Frank McMullan, boarded a dilapidated makeshift river steamer to make the first leg of the trip. The group was on the river shore by daylight, and by 8:00 A.M. they had left Iguape as a damp fog covered the low marshlands along the Ribeira's banks. It was a dismal beginning for a difficult trip. The steamboat was slow, averaging only about four knots, and the Americans stood at the rail, straining to see the countryside. Low trees and capim grass dotted the shoreline, and blue cranes and plover were seen on the frequent sandbars that appeared from nowhere on the surface of the water. Little change in scenery occurred during the long day, and all looked forward to docking and a night's rest. But the misplaced luck of the McMullan colonists was true to form, and by 6:00 P.M. the steamer was grounded, stuck on an unseen sandbar in mid-river. Every attempt was made to free the craft, but the effort was to no avail. The passengers and crew would spend the night on board.[3]

As a dark and gloomy morning appeared on June 8, the situation was unchanged. The bar held the steamboat tight. The craft had to be freed, nevertheless, and to do so, all able-bodied men climbed into the watery sand and pushed time and again on the boat's stern as the little steam engine revved to maximum speed. Finally, the vessel moved, and the men crawled back on board, tired but anxious to continue.

They did not guess that the boat would be aground again two hours later and that the frustrating procedure would have to be repeated.[4]

As the boat chugged farther upstream, changes in geography and scenery began to occur. A group of green-plumed parrots flew near as riverbanks became higher and the trees appeared larger. Small farms began to come into view, and the colonists had their first glimpses of cultivated fields near the McMullan grant. "The bushes of coffee," related Lucian Barnsley, "[were] at least 12 feet high & covered with berries." But the other crops, Barnsley recalled, "were badly cultivated." Rice fields contained masses of bushes, "with trees bedecked with parasites. Shocking agriculture!"[5]

On June 9 the steamboat pulled ashore and its passengers disembarked. They had come as far as was safe by steamer and would continue in two wooden dugout canoes that were expected from settlements upriver. Barnsley continued his inspection during the wait: "Fields of corn but over-run with weeds. The woods perfect jungles. Lands fine; lagoons close to the river." The next morning, the small, thin canoes arrived, and the Texans continued up the Ribeira under misty, cloudy skies. "Mud and water everywhere," Barnsley lamented, "some sick."[6]

Four days the colonists continued—arising early, poling up the waterway all day long, and camping at night on the bank. On June 16 they finally entered the mouth of the Juquiá River, a welcome sign that they were close to the "government house" that William Bowen had constructed at Morro Redondo, the McMullan-owned property on the margin of the river. They arrived on the eighteenth, and Lucian Barnsley noted that the structure was "in very bad condition. A good many [of the colonists] sick with chills and fever. General appearance unfavorable. People don't like it." A weary Frank McMullan nevertheless greeted his old friend William Bowen, who immediately put the colony leader to bed in his own house. Bowen then held a lengthy conference with Dyer, Wasson, and the others, who told him about the problems and unfortunate adventures that the colonists had endured in the year Bowen had been in Brazil.[7]

Late in the morning of June 19, Billy Gill, who had left the rest of the colonists at Iguape to investigate other available lands farther into the interior of Brazil, arrived at Morro Redondo overland from Campinas, a prospering town to the north of the village of São Paulo. Although no detailed findings seem to have been noted, a man named Tully reported that he and Gill investigated properties at Sorocaba, due north of Morro Redondo on the Estrada Real. Gill described the property as mountainous but rich, and stated that he had been offered

18,000 coffee trees and 2,000 acres of land by a Colonel White for $6,000. Upon completion of the report by Gill and Tully, fourteen men including Dyer, Wasson, and Lucian Barnsley left by canoe for the upper São Lourenço.[8]

The men had to travel only six miles up the river before they reached the edge of the McMullan grant, which Barnsley pronounced as "nothing extra, clay & sandy." As they proceeded, the reports became more pessimistic. Properties were described as "very good in spots, but as a general thing not worth much; a large quantity of sand in the bottom strata." One large coffee plantation was decaying, and all of the limbs of the trees were either dead or dying. Lucian dourly concluded his June 24 diary entry by remarking that he had "not seen the sunrise since I arrived at the Govmt House and on my way up the river." It is probable that at this point real questions were developing in the minds of some as to whether a good decision had been made in the selection of lands.[9]

The worst was past, however, and after June 24, when the travelers reached the junction of the main São Lourenço with the Itariri, the prospects quickly improved. Lucian called the waterway "a beautiful river. . . . The lands are high and apparently good—composed mostly of sand and yellow clay." Dyer and Wasson, reconnoitering ahead of the main body, found lands on the Azeite River that were "very fine and heavily timbered." By June 26 Barnsley's previous gloomy outlook had completely changed; he described the region as "a beautiful valley capable of supporting 800 families and all have room. The soil varies from black sandy loam to rich mulatto land." Concluding his entry for June 28, Barnsley noted, "the timber growth I have never seen surpassed for beauty, height, and size. I am well pleased." The stage was set for the balance of the colonists to come to the São Lourenço's tributaries.[10]

By the end of June, the last contingent of Americans prepared to leave Iguape for "El Dorado," as the McMullan colony was by then called. The landing where the steamer docked lay several miles from town, so baggage and supplies were loaded onto two-wheeled Brazilian carts. Early the next morning they boarded the small steam craft and with wide-eyed wonder finally began the next leg of their trip up the jungle-bordered river. The last boatload consisted of only four families. Alfred I. Smith with his nine-person clan joined the equally large group of J. Thomas and Ann Cook. Jacob and Susan Wingutter and their daughter Amy accompanied Parson Richard Ratcliff and his wife Eunice.[11]

After a full day's ride, just at sundown, the steamer came to an abrupt stop in the middle of the river. As none of the colonists could speak Portuguese, they were unable to question the boatmen as to the reason for their halt. The answer came quickly, however, when three canoes pulled alongside the larger craft. In each end of the dugouts stood a native, each with an oar and a pole. Two of the canoes were reserved for women, children, and baggage; the men boarded the third boat. The ladies, recalled one American years later, took the entire experience in fine style. Some of the young women flirted with the young men; others were fearful of the approaching night and storm clouds that began to fill the sky.[12]

The coming of darkness brought a cold, chilling rain that imparted a real sense of helplessness to the Americans and probably made some seriously question their rationale in being there. Bellona Smith was terrified of the combination of night and bad weather. "Imagine us out in open dugouts in the middle of a great river; ignorant of when or where we would land—it was no fun, dark as Egypt except when flashes of lightning showed nothing but water. The rain became heavy and threatening and thunder added to the situation." She recalled that all were quiet and "took the storm with bowed heads, trusting to Providence and the brave camaradas who never slackened their poleing."[13]

About midnight two of the dugouts finally arrived at a small dock where the women and children, joyfully and thankfully, were allowed to disembark. There they met an Englishman, Clement H. Wilmot, as well as several men of the McMullan party who had arrived in an earlier canoe. The men helped the wet and bedraggled emigrants up a long slippery path to the home of a *fazendeiro*—a rice planter—who offered shelter to the travelers. Wilmot took them to a large storage building filled with rice. He told the women to cover their children's heads, especially their ears, then crawl into the rice. All slept soundly and emerged "dry as powder" the next morning.[14]

The canoe carrying the men missed the small pier in the rain and darkness and docked a short distance up the river where they found a small hut. Unlike the women and children, they were wet and cold and had no place to sleep. Fortunately one of the Smith children had a single match in his pocket and the men were able to start a fire. They spent the night huddled around the flames, hoping that their families were enjoying a more favorable evening. The morning of the seventeenth dawned clear and bright, much to the joy of the colonists. When the men made their way down the river to the *fazenda,* they felt tremendous relief to find that their wives and children were safe and well. After a warm meal, all prepared to climb into the canoes once more for the last leg of the trip. The Ratcliffs and the Wingutters left first, followed hours later by the Smith and Cook families.[15]

Few settlers, even Brazilians, lived on the upper Juquiá River near its juncture with the São Lourenço. Only occasionally did the Americans spy small huts built on the steep banks. The few dwellings were covered with palm leaves and "looked more like a poor excuse for a corn crib than a house." As the Smith and Cook families approached one of these small buildings, they were surprised to discover that the two other families, the Ratcliffs and the Wingutters, had taken shelter. Mrs. Ratcliff, long expectant, had given birth to a daughter. The new baby, named Maude, became the first child born in Brazil whose parents were members of the McMullan party. Assured by the Ratcliffs and the Wingutters that no assistance was needed, the Smith and Cook families continued their trip up the Juquiá.[16]

Little Eddie Cook, seven years old, was considered by some to be a "bad boy." He proved to be a continual distraction and throughout the trip his antics created bad feelings among those who believed that children should be seen and not heard. Eddie continued in his undisciplined manner when he boarded the dugout canoe, alternately sitting, then standing, yet receiving no admonition from his parents. Suddenly, without warning, the boy toppled overboard and into the swirling river waters. J. T. Cook, Eddie's father, panicked and stood up in the boat, yelling "Save my child, save my child." The father did not jump into the river himself, but one of the camaradas quickly dived into the water and after a short time safely retrieved the youth. "None but his own family," recalled Bellona Smith, "would have cared had he been drowned but he lived to be a very nice young lad. I saw him years later in Santos and hope his manners have improved as much as his looks."[17]

The next landing the colonists reached stood adjacent to a small settlement "where the river takes a bend to the right." There, once again, a gentle rain fell on the dense forest, but the colonists were by that time so used to the moisture that they paid little attention to it. "There was no room to set up a tent," wrote one American, "so each took such covering as he had [to] spread a kind of shelter from one small sapling to another, crawled under, and slept with the rain dripping all around, too tired and sleepy to fear the 'onças' [leopards]."[18]

Finally the dugout canoes with their passengers reached their destination, the small hut William Bowen had built for himself at Morro Redondo and the roomy structure called "government house" where some of the colonists were to stay. The large building was constructed of palm slats, set up "picket fashion" three inches apart, then covered with palm leaves. The barracks-type dwelling had no inside divisions, no windows, and a door at each end. It hardly represented a welcome sight but was better than no housing at all. The Quillin and Garner

families and others had already filled the building to capacity before
the arrival of the last canoes. Several tents, including one owned by
Bony Green, stood in the clearing. Within days, the colonists believed,
all would be able to continue up the river where they would select
their own plots of land in "El Dorado."[19]

Parson Quillin's personal library, which contained a considerable
number of Sunday-school lesson books and music books, as well as
some story books and books of poetry, received extensive use by many
of the emigrants. Quillin took advantage of the situation and began a
Sunday school. Alfred I. Smith, the former music teacher, led the
singing, and the Americans "woke the echoes with songs never heard
in those valleys before."[20]

The Brazilian government made arrangements for food. A com-
missary was constructed, and each family drew foodstuffs on a regular
basis, "just like soldiers, in camps." Without the support of the Brazilians, the situation would have become dire indeed.[21]

While the colonists waited for Frank McMullan's health to improve,
activity continued at the camp on the Juquiá. Gardens were planted in
areas that did not require extensive clearing of trees. Some of the men
went upriver to explore colony lands and to attempt to locate parcels
that they wished to purchase. For those who lingered behind, the
books acquired from the Methodist Church in New York "helped to
pass a weary life . . . in a weary unknown forest."[22]

In Iguape George Barnsley began studying Portuguese and reading the requirements for certification as a physician in Brazil. From
his home far from the São Lourenço, Barnsley could see the overall
situation of the emigrants better than most of those upriver. He noted
that some of the young men who came to Brazil with the Dunn and
Gaston colonies were returning to the United States dissatisfied. Most
of them, however, were "generally of the class of young men who have
been used to good company and ease or are mere adventurers. Of our
party [McMullan's] every solid man is pleased and all are preparing to
settle on lands."[23]

In a lengthy letter to his father written on July 13, Barnsley commented on the situation of the Americans, and he compared them to
the Brazilians who were native to the South American country. "Some
of the people here are intelligent," he said, "but the mass are a mongrel
set, unhealthy of appearance and of all shades from pure white with
blue eyes to inky inkiness of black negro." Barnsley continued with the
remark that Brazil could progress and "be made a delightful country
to live in provided enough white people came here to settle it and
make society, build roads, and develop the country." The former
Georgian also said that getting a start in Brazil, even for Anglo-

Saxons, was not an easy task. "We have all ranks of officers from the Confederacy here, many . . . making a hand to hand livelihood." At the end of his letter, Barnsley stated that his brother Lucian was "awaiting the arrival of a gentleman from Rio (one of our colonists) who wishes him to distill rum on shares." The prospective partner, Calvin McKnight, had invented a new method of making the rum beverage locally called *pinga*. Although it is not known whether Barnsley entered the partnership, the new distillation method invented by McKnight was unquestionably without peer in Brazil. The little town of Paratý where McKnight established his distillery even today is recognized as the location where the best *pinga* in all of Brazil is made.[24]

At the camp at Morro Redondo, however, the priority was not the distillation of rum but the needs that the colonists would face as they established their farms in the valleys of the São Lourenço. The most important consideration was the construction of a road overland, across the mountains, to the coast. It was obvious that it would be impossible to transport any quantity of agricultural produce in any other way. To solve the problem, McMullan and Bowen wrote to José Tavares Bastos, the president of São Paulo Province, requesting assistance. Composing the message, McMullan explained that he and Bowen asked only for financial help. The actual construction, they said, would be completed by the colonists. It would be a permanent cart road, the letter emphasized, "from the center of the area where we are situated on the headwaters of the São Lourenço River, in the Iguape District, to the city of Santos, a distance of sixty miles." "This road," explained McMullan, "we propose to construct in a[s] straight [a] line as possible, but through the city of Peruibe because of the difficulty of cutting through rugged mountainous areas." Signed by both men, the letter declared the road to be "indispensible . . . for our colony's existence."[25]

On June 17, 1867, McMullan and Bowen wrote to the provincial legislature making a similar appeal and requesting funds to begin construction. The letter began by explaining that both men were naturalized citizens of Brazil; then it underscored the good that the road would do for the area. "It is obvious," the appeal stated, "that great benefit will accrue to the Province of São Paulo . . . from the establishment of routes of communication. It will be of service to the colonists, as well as the rest of the population." Bowen personally carried the letter to São Paulo in hopes of a quick decision, but immediate help was not forthcoming; the request was postponed until the fall session of the legislature.[26]

But the need for the completion of a road to the coast had no influence on the government survey team that still labored to determine the limits of the McMullan colony lands. By the end of June, the chief of the commission for the verification of surveys, Octaviano da Rocha, requested a meeting with McMullan so that the two men could review progress to date and make plans for the completion of the measurement. By July 8, the date on which the meeting was set, McMullan's physical condition was so poor that he was unable to rise from his bed. In a note to da Rocha, he explained the problem and asked for a postponement. "I have your note," said McMullan, "just now arrived from Iguape. I have been sick for a long time, *diseased*, and it is impossible that I can go today to Mr. João Martin's home. I would appreciate it if you could come here. I cannot go there. If you wait," McMullan continued, "I will go there tomorrow to see you." No other correspondence has been found that verifies whether McMullan was able to see da Rocha, but it is likely that some provision was made.[27]

By September 15, two months later, McMullan's health was so bad that Judge Dyer resolved to take his young nephew back to Iguape in hope of some treatment that would at least ease the pain. Nothing could be done, however, and McMullan suffered intensely before the end finally came on September 29. McMullan's family was at his bedside, as was George Barnsley, who perhaps was McMullan's closest friend. Plans were made for a funeral, but when the family attempted to secure a burial plot, they found that the Roman Catholic Church controlled the only cemeteries and emphatically refused burial of the Protestant American. The plight soon became known, and a German immigrant offered as a grave site his *quintál,* or backyard. With no other options available, the family quickly and thankfully accepted the offer. With the solution of one problem, however, another emerged. There were no ministers in Iguape who would perform the service; the funeral would have to be done by a layman.[28]

George Barnsley volunteered to personally take care of the situation. Although he had never led a burial service before, he had seen it performed during the Civil War and believed that he could do a creditable job for his friend. A coffin was secured, and a wagon carried the young man's body to its final resting place. With friends and family present, Barnsley read from the Episcopal prayer book. Obviously moved, he recalled the event in later years: "Over his tomb I read the service of the Episcopal Church, and as I said 'Dust to dust,' we heaped the fresh earth over him—and thus for ever, as far as we were concerned, the light of a noble soul faded into night."[29]

In a eulogy written years later, Barnsley continued to praise his friend Frank McMullan. "He was gifted by talents of no inferior order; of a warm and generous nature, enthusiastic as a poet, and as usual in such characters a shadow of melancholy pervaded his whole action and life." Barnsley always placed Frank in a separate category from the other Texans who went to Brazil. "He was incapable," declared the physician, "of swerving from the path of honor and rectitude; he knew of no guile, and was as far removed from most all that came with him to this country as selfishness and little meanness are from virtues and grandeur of soul. He deceived no one but himself, he worked with unceasing energy for the benefit of those who surrounded him."[30]

The news of Frank McMullan's death traveled quickly. In early November, 1867, the *Anglo-Brazilian Times,* an English-language newspaper in Rio de Janeiro, reported his demise. By November 23 the *Two Republics* in Mexico had picked up the news item. On December 1 Josephine Foster, a member of the Gunter colony on the Rio Doce, wrote of the event in a letter to the editor of the *New Orleans Times.* Like others, she had nothing but praise for the former Texan. "Strictly upright and honest in his dealing, he gained the respect and confidence of all who knew him. May his soul rest in peace, and the blessing of God attend those who cast their lots with him, is our sincere prayer."[31]

After McMullan's funeral, none of the family were eager to return to the lands on the Juquiá or the São Lourenço, at least until the grief over the untimely death subsided. William T. Moore, his wife Victoria, and their new daughter Juanita stayed for a short time in Iguape, then moved to Campinas, a prosperous city north of São Paulo. Louise and John Odell moved to São Paulo, as did Nancy McMullan and her son Ney, before all followed the Moores to Campinas. Although Judge Dyer returned for a time to the colony site, his wife Amanda and their children Hattie, Wiley, and James remained in Iguape. Columbus Wasson, who by that time was engaged to Hattie Dyer, also decided not to return upriver.[32]

But many of the McMullan colonists did go to the headwaters of the São Lourenço, some as early as June, 1867, to locate land within the colony site for their own use. Many difficulties were encountered on the river, particularly waterfalls and snags, which prevented easy access by water. Perhaps the worst of these was at the junction of the São Lourenço and the Itariri, where three huge waterfalls slowed progress. In the main channel, the water fell straight down about twenty feet with terrific force, while a side stream offered a "gradual descent over rocks and boulders, for one hundred yards or more, waters foaming along between, leaving the rock bare." The wooden canoes, too heavy for portage, had to be pushed, pulled, and lifted with poles to get up each fall. The slightest mistake, recalled Bellona Smith, "meant death, for the boat had to be lifted . . . and forced by main strength seemingly beyond human power. The baggage had to be carried from boulder to boulder in jumps."[33]

The main tributaries that fed into the Itariri—the Peixe, the Guanhanhã, the Azeite, and the Ariado—all supplied huge amounts of cold, clear water to the Itariri and the São Lourenço. On these four streams the McMullan colonists settled. In their movement into the region they first encountered the Peixe, so called because of the large number of fish it harbored. The second was the Guanhanhã, or "Land without Evil," and the third was the Azeite, or "River of Oil." The Ariado, like the others, was enveloped by thick, green forests and seemed to be the outer limits to the Texans, who had never seen vegetation so dense.[34]

Alfred I. Smith and his family went all the way to the Ariado, where they were surprised to see a typical Brazilian river dwelling, "a dried mud-daubed house surrounded with orange trees and [a] mandioca patch and other plants." They were even more surprised when they found two American sailors living there, hunting for gold. The men, one named Bob Smith and the other named Crony, had quarreled for some reason and decided that they could not live on the same side of the river. Crony therefore had set up a crude shelter in an area on the other side of the stream, coming back to the hut only for meals. One of the men "soon drifted back [to the coast] and the other followed later on."[35]

On August 11, 1867, Alfred Smith decided that this spot on the Ariado River would serve as an outstanding homestead, and he consequently staked his claim, christening the shore of the waterway the "head of catfish navigation." He returned to Morro Redondo for his family; then he began a survey of the natural resources available. In addition to the already noted orange trees and mandioca, Smith found food crops that included sugar cane, rice, and bananas. The first nights the large family camped on the spot were traumatic, especially for the younger members, as the sounds of the jungle conjured visions of all kinds of ferocious animals. After a few days, however, sleep came easier as they finally realized that most of the chatter came from noisy birds and monkeys.[36]

Also on the Ariado were William Bowen, his children, and his new Brazilian wife, twenty-three-year-old Anna Martins. The Nelson Tarver family also chose a little branch of the Ariado and built a house near its junction with the main river, the Azeite. On the Guanhanhã, the stream west of the Ariado, several American families found homes. Parson E. H. Quillin lived there, as did the Fielder brothers, the Greens, and the Beasleys. Bachelor William Hargrove built a house on the river's bank. Jesse Wright and his family, as well as his infamous hounds, also found a home on the Guanhanhã. The Weavers decided to homestead the Peixe, as did the Garners and the Cooks. Several others also settled on the Peixe River, but no record has been located as to exactly who they were.[37]

Parson Quillin wasted no time in once again starting his Sunday school. For a long time, only those families who lived on the Guanhanhã attended the services, but eventually the word spread up the valleys and the rivers about the religious services, which became the one social event that brought the different families together. Quillin, an eloquent preacher, held the colonists spellbound during the services. There was no church building, only the shade of trees and makeshift seats, but "the lessons were just as interesting and the hymns just as sweet" as if the service had been held in a cathedral. Americans "made the woods ring with 'There is a Happy Land' and many other traditional Baptist hymns." The worshippers were often accompanied by J. Stampley, who, according to one account, "could make a fiddle talk, and when he played the old hymn, 'Show Pity Lord,' he could make tears flow from a rock."[38]

Soon the Alfred Smith family learned of the Sunday services and made their way to them, first up the rivers, then over an old trail over the mountains. They found that they could shorten the distance by cutting a new path, thus having only one mountain to climb rather than three. Even then, however, they had to begin their hike early in the morning or they would not get to services on time. The Smith children all read *Pilgrim's Progress* and thus named landmarks on the route for those in the book. "One was hill 'Difficulty,' then beyond, the 'Valley of Humiliation,' and so was born in our early minds," according to Bellona Smith, "the aspiration to follow Christian to the city of God."[39]

Lon (Leonidas) Bowen was also concerned with paths over the mountains, but in a different way from the Smith children. Lon became the official supervisor of road construction for the colony and, with other emigrants who were willing and able to work, began the difficult chore of cutting trees, bridging rivers and streams, and stabilizing the roadbed with rocks and fill once the route was cleared. Beginning at the Smith house on the Ariado, it wound along the river to the east and toward the low range of mountains that separated the São Lourenço valley from the coastal plain. As the primitive highway progressed, it became a real convenience for the colonists, particularly the Bowens and the Smiths, but the road's obscurity often terrified children. Leopards were often seen in the area, and the young ones consequently imagined that they lurked behind every tree. Monkeys were a common sight, and large bands of them passed overhead. Above the wide pathway through the forest "the branches of the great trees met above, and easily gave the monkeys a chance to cross."[40]

A few Brazilians also lived on the McMullan grant, but as there was almost an unlimited amount of land available, the Americans made no attempt to remove them. One account said that "though few in number, [they were] still kind and ready to help the stranger. They lived mostly on fish, black beans, and mandioca farinha." On the Peixe River, however, lived a tribe of Indians who considered themselves to be the owners of the land, regardless of government surveys, grants, or sales. Resentful of the intrusion of the McMullan colonists, they filed a written protest, through an agent, with the government, but there is no record of any response.[41]

The Brazilian family of one "Old Man Camargo," who lived near the Smiths on the Ariado, became especially close to some of the settlers. Camargo had a large plot of cleared land—a *roça*—planted with all of the necessary staples such as rice, corn, sugar cane, bananas, potatoes, and the "inevitable mandioca." Alfred Smith bought Camargo's entire crop as well as his buildings for $50.00. The old *caboclo* told Smith that the money was the largest amount of cash he had ever owned in his life. Sarah Tarver, in another trade, let Camargo have her precious feather bed, which she had brought from Texas with so much difficulty. The old Brazilian cared nothing for the item as a bed—he wanted only the ticking—and he emptied the contents into the river, which soon "floated white with goose feathers."[42]

The Fielder brothers, not content to live on the land that they had first picked on the Guanhanhã, spent a considerable amount of time exploring the scores of tributaries and rivulets that were found at every turn. "With fool hardy courage [they] went poling up the rivers, each on his own resources, hoping to find the long promised land." Zeno Fielder was unhappy with his situation and longed for home. He wrote to his father in Navarro County, Texas, in December, 1867, and outlined the disadvantages of living in Brazil. He said that the colonists were "nearing starvation" and asked his father for $250 to come home. He noted in his appeal that Brazil was "not a white man's country." Unlike his brother, however, Cortez Fielder was pleased with the situation. He married A. J. Green's daughter Sarah, built a comfortable home, and began clearing land for a farm. On Sundays when rain threatened Parson Quillin's services, the Fielder couple offered their home as a church sanctuary.[43]

But the general sense of well-being that existed on the colony lands camouflaged a power struggle that had been developing since Frank McMullan's death. When McMullan was sick, the authority of the colony logically fell on William Bowen, McMullan's partner in the enterprise. Bowen, however, was not a forceful individual and did not assume control as he should have done. Therefore, Judge Dyer quickly preempted the leadership role. The judge's "hard, overbearing manner," in contrast to the gentle McMullan, soon created problems within the community. Most of the Americans began to gravitate to Bowen, perhaps to spite the judge rather than because of any personal attraction held by McMullan's partner.[44]

Judge Dyer, not understanding the reasons for his lack of support, continued to criticize Bowen's leadership and made an increasingly strong effort to regain consensual control. Dyer's manner, however, continued to rankle most of the colonists, and they thwarted his attempts at every turn. As the former Texans turned against Dyer, the judge's mood became worse, and he caused continuing problems. The judge was later described as "an extraordinary man; . . . a philanthropist, but positive in manner, warmly loving to his friends and equally cold to his enemies." Dyer began to concentrate on legal methods by which he could take over the colony.[45]

After Frank McMullan's death, Judge Dyer discussed with Barnsley his ideas concerning a takeover of the settlement and asked the doctor to be his ally and partner. Both men remembered the legends of gold on the property and realized that without the sanctions of the government they might never be able to exploit either the land or the treasure, if found. Thus, Dyer and Barnsley cemented a pact. Immediately Dyer wrote a letter to the Secretary of Agriculture, Paula e Souza, and asked for an official transfer of leadership to Barnsley, a move calculated to disguise the plot so that it would not be viewed as a continuation of Dyer's earlier attempt to oust William Bowen.[46]

By October 28 Bowen had received notice from Paula e Souza of the request for a transfer of rights to Barnsley. Bowen was outraged and immediately called a meeting of the members of the colony to discuss the situation. All agreed that a change in leadership at that juncture would be fatal. The colony already rested on shaky ground, and its members had no desire to be under the thumb of either the doctor or the judge. They composed an emphatic appeal to Paula e Souza begging for rejection of the request:

> Most excellent Sir, we, the subscribers would represent to y[our] Honor that a certain man at Iguape, an American calling himself a Doctor by the name of G. S. Barnsley, prompted as we believe by (others) designing spekulations [sic], are makeing [sic] by false representations, efforts to get into their or his possession, the management of the affairs and interests of our new settlement on the head waters of the

Sao Lorenso [*sic*] River in the District of Iguape, Known as McMullans and Bowens Collony [*sic*], and to remove William Bowen, the only survivor of the firm as written. He being now our agent we have no disposition to change him for another . . . [for the] management of our affairs will be against our will and interest of the people of this settlement, and will be the means of braking [*sic*] up the Collony [*sic*] which is now promising, and in which we wish to live, if the said G. S. Barnsley is . . . put at the head of affairs here. There is not a man in the Collony [*sic*] who will submit to him. Praying for your Excellency's good health and the prosperity of the Empire, we remain your humble and obliged servants.

A. I. Smith	William A. Gill	L. M. Bryan
Nelson Tarver	John Hickman	J. C. Cobb
Othniel Weaver	S. F. Haynie	Thomas Garner
Daniel Weaver	W. T. Smith	C. A. Crawley
Riley Weaver	N. B. McAlpine	William Davis[47]
	J. R. Wright	

While waiting for an answer from Paula e Souza, Bowen received a request from Joaquim Saldanha Marinha, then president of São Paulo Province, for a census of the colony and a description of the colony's boundaries, with a particular emphasis on rivers and natural boundaries. Bowen prepared an excellent survey of the persons under his control, including a number for each family as well as names, sexes, and ages. As a preface to the document, Bowen noted that he also was including a petition from colony members in his favor. He apologized that some persons were not included, noting that the omission was partly "on account of the scarcity of provisions and also on account of efforts makeing [*sic*] by lies and false statements efforts to get into their possession the interests of this settlement." Bowen also told the president that one of the colonists was writing an exposé of the whole scheme that very soon would "be published to the World, in the Journals of Brazil & also the U.S.A." As an addition to the charges, Bowen also sought sympathy for himself and bitterly denounced the former leadership of the colony, perhaps including but not naming McMullan. "Your Excellency will understand that these people are not paupers but were unmercifully robbed by those who brought them out from the U.S.A. having paid out over twenty thousand dollars. . . ."[48]

Bowen's problems extended far beyond the attempt by Dyer and Barnsley to take over the colony. For an unexplained reason, the government food supply had been unexpectedly cut off. An appeal by Bowen for assistance to Saldanha Marinha resulted in money being sent to the *delgado* (mayor) of Iguape, but the items purchased and sent upriver were of very poor quality. The meat was spoiled and inedible. The *farinha* (flour) proved to be so bad that it was drawn only as food for pigs. No coffee or sugar was supplied.[49]

Despite the resentment expressed by Bowen toward George Barnsley because of the attempt to gain colony leadership, several men went to Iguape and asked the physician for help. Barnsley had no money to buy supplies but was sympathetic to the pleas for assistance. He went to the *camera* (city council) of Iguape with a request for aid, then made a request to the citizens of the seacoast town asking for contributions. Both appeals resulted in help, and Barnsley was able to fill two or three canoes with provisions. He even made out a list of how the food was to be divided upon arrival and appointed men in the colony to see that the equal division was honored. Those who had money, said Barnsley, gave their allotment to the needy.[50]

Then the colonists received some good news. The legislature of São Paulo Province, in response to the request made by McMullan and Bowen on June 13, allocated five *contos de reis* to Bowen for the construction of the road between colony lands and Santos. Work started in earnest on the highway, and Leonidas Bowen moved quickly to purchase the supplies and equipment needed to complete the task. The young superintendent soon determined, however, that the five *contos* given to the road-building project was much too meager an amount to complete the route, even with most of the labor being done by the colonists at no charge. In another letter to Saldanha Marinha on November 10, William Bowen explained that the route proved much more difficult than he had anticipated and that it would "cost at the least calculation 20$000 [twenty *contos de reis*] . . . to make a good road, as there is a great deal of . . . wet land which will have to be cropswayed [filled], and also many bridges to make and hills to cut down, but this must be done as my people have no way to get to market. . . ." Bowen implored the president to lay his request before the next legislature.[51]

As crops matured, Bowen's appeal for a road took on even more meaning. Although some farm produce was of good quality, there were absolutely no buyers. Desperate, the farmers sold for a pittance or gave away the results of several months' labor. For many this setback became the last straw, and they packed their bags and returned to Iguape, Rio, or the United States. On November 7 the four-member George A. Linn family boarded the steamer *Ella S. Thayer* for New Orleans. "Gradually, day after day," said George Barnsley, "men dropped down the river to Iguape seeking some new outlet. My house became sort of a ranch and it was all I could do to keep going, as I never refused to help." Clearly, the colony was close to falling apart.[52]

Thus, the Brazilian adventure took on a new aspect for all concerned. The emigrants attempted to settle on colony lands, but were delayed by the sickness and death of Frank McMullan. The power struggle that developed once the emigrants were on their own farms served to split the colony, and the exhaustion of money and food supplies was a final blow. When the road was not completed and crops found no markets, there was no doubt in the minds of most colonists that, to survive, they would have to leave the São Lourenço and go to a region more suited to their experience. El Dorado no longer seemed enticing to many. Only George Barnsley and Judge Dyer had enthusiastic hopes for real financial success, and that from gold rather than agriculture. Yet, despite the seemingly overwhelming problems, most of the former Texans did not abandon their fervent dreams for an exciting new life in an unexploited new land. Life went on in the valley of the upper São Lourenço River, and as frontiersmen, the colonists persisted and searched for new ways to cope with frustration and change.

CHAPTER 9

Life in El Dorado

B Y EARLY DECEMBER, 1867, George Barnsley and Judge Dyer
still had not received a reply from Secretary of Agriculture
Paula e Souza concerning their request to remove William
Bowen as the head of the McMullan colony. Since most of
the remaining colonists had signed the letter from Bowen
to the secretary in which they affirmed their allegiance, neither Barnsley nor Dyer had illusions concerning their chances. But hope springs
eternal where gold is concerned, and both men anxiously continued
to await a favorable reply.

Unaware of the belief that the grant was to be rich in mineral
wealth, Barnsley's father wrote a letter to his son in which he questioned the effort to gain the colony leadership. "I cannot see what advantage it will be to you to have a transfer of grants which were held
by Major McMullan, of whose death I regretted to learn, as the land
lies I think 150 miles or more above Iguape and the Colony would not
receive your personal attention—but as you have applied for them [I]
infer you considered it desirable to have them and therefore shall be
glad to learn you have been successful." By mid-December, however,
Dyer and Barnsley had received the news that the request had been
denied. In an effort to rationalize the loss, Barnsley wrote a note to his
father in which he remarked that to his "infinite satisfaction" he had
"escaped the agency of the colony—the people refused, and are now
reaping their reward. Most of them are leaving Govm't lands and settling in various localities. I am quite satisfied with helping Americans
and do not wish to have more from the same plate." Emphasizing that
he would have nothing more to do with the other McMullan colonists,
Barnsley wrote that they "acted very meanly after all my trouble in
procuring provisions." Paradoxically, Barnsley wrote his father again
in February, 1868, to say that much of his time was used in assisting
Americans and aiding their projects, despite the fact that their conduct in Brazil had "not been creditable to themselves or the nation

which they represent. There is plenty of bad faith shown, and many persons who in their own land would scorn to stoop to low deeds here swindle when they get a chance. The Brazilians are not a stupid people and are fast learning."[1]

Judge Dyer took a philosophical approach to the rejection of the petition to the Secretary of Agriculture and resolved to continue his search for gold. Because of the opposition to him from the colonists, however, he decided to confine his activities to an area far from the center of the settlement. Logically the most productive area to cover was the region described in the directions to the Lake of Gold written so many years before by João Aranzel. Accordingly, he and Columbus Wasson hired canoes and left Iguape for the Una River, where they camped on the edge of the river at the base of the mountain generally identified as São Lourenço Peak. Following the ancient instructions, they skirted the stream above the fall line for two days. To their disappointment, however, they found no *figueira* (fig tree) and no Lake of Gold.[2]

Convinced that the treasure was probably there but difficult to locate because of the removal or decay of landmarks, the two men resolved to continue the search for as long a time as possible. In order to be able to do so from a financial standpoint, however, they decided to secure land, then operate a sawmill that had been laboriously salvaged from the wreck of the *Derby*. The banks of the Una River abounded with fine furniture woods, and they were confident that a good market was available in Rio de Janeiro. Since the property they selected was still within the bounds of the huge McMullan grant, it was available for purchase, and Dyer and Wasson staked their claim to a large area. They paid cash for the lands selected and filed their deeds in Iguape before the end of 1867.[3]

The speculation in lumber proved to be profitable, and soon profits justified the acquisition of a second mill, which they promptly purchased and set up alongside the first. To carry the large amounts of wood to market, they soon found that additional transportation would be necessary. To solve the problem, Dyer and Wasson borrowed $60,000 from an English firm, bought a steampowered river boat, and began to operate their highly profitable business. As the weeks and months passed, less time was spent in the search for gold, and more days were spent on the successful business venture. In a symbolic sealing of his partnership with the judge, Columbus Wasson married his longtime sweetheart Hattie Dyer on April 30, 1868, in Rio de Janeiro. Everything seemed to go right for a change, and George Barnsley, thinking of Dyer and Wasson, wrote his father that "some of the emigrants are now on the road to vast fortunes."[4]

Romance also bloomed on the headwaters of the São Lourenço as Eugene Smith and Sue Bowen announced their engagement. Eugene went to the far bounds of the colony, over the mountains to a spot near Peruibe where he cleared land, built a hut, and planted a crop. The two asked Parson Quillin to perform the wedding ceremony at the Bowen home on the Ariado, and preparations were made for a two-day *festa*. The wedding was performed in the morning, after which all sat down for a marriage feast in "central Texas" style. About mid-afternoon fellow colonist C. A. Crawley arrived for a visit on the way to Peruibe to purchase supplies. All were delighted to see their companion, especially the parson, who was dissatisfied that no witnesses save family were present to sign the wedding certificate. To correct the situation, he called the newlyweds into a room in Bowen's house, made them pronounce the vows again, then secured Crawley's signature on the official papers.[5]

The other colonists who remained on the Ariado, Azeite, Guanhanhã, and Itariri rivers also settled into the routine of their new life. Alfred I. Smith, Frank McMullan's old teacher from prewar days in Georgia, made more of the wilderness situation than most of the others, and he quickly transformed his little shack at the junction of the Ariado and the Azeite into a real home for his family. The structure had only one room, and the walls were made of palm slats set three inches apart and interwoven with palm leaves. It had a single door, and the floor was dirt. The area set aside for cooking was in one corner where trivets hung over the firepit to hold clay pots. Although usable, the primitive structure offered few amenities, so Smith and his sons began remodeling as soon as time allowed. They constructed two inside walls, which created two rooms with a hall in between. A lean-to was added at one end, and the kitchen was moved to it along with a small cast-iron stove the family had purchased in New York. By driving posts into the ground and then adding palm slats for springs, they improvised beds for the entire family.[6]

After readying the house, the Smiths faced the pressing task of preparing farmlands for planting to ensure a food supply. They felled and removed large trees, then planted crops of rice, sugar cane, sweet potatoes, mandioca, and onions. When the crops were harvested, methods for processing them had to be developed or learned from the natives. A cane press, already on the place when they arrived, enabled the Americans to make molasses. Describing the machinery, Bellona Smith recalled that "the cane knots had to be smashed first with an axe or club. One [person] held the cane while the other turned the . . . [roller]; the juice fell into a wide, wooden tray." Recounting her part in the process, Bellona remembered that it was her task "to boil down the juice to molasses—one tank in the morning, another in the evening." [7]

As soon as possible, the Smiths planted a little hill of coffee trees. A rice house and mill were constructed so that rough grains could be cleaned for market. Next to the road to Bowen's house, they constructed a dam and waterwheel that turned a six-mortar mill. The paddle boards of the wheel were sawed by hand, then covered with "ever ready palm leaves." This mill allowed the children to stop their daily routine of beating rice by hand. [8]

After the first six months in their new home, the Smiths were able to enrich their diet somewhat with chicken, bacon, and ham. These delicacies added immensely to the meals of fish, caught in baskets in a manner learned from the natives, and *tatu,* a type of armadillo cooked in its own shell. Describing the menu in detail, Bellona noted that "of flour we had none and when hungry for chicken pie we made 'canja.' We had sweet potatoes and cara, also vegetables and onions—also mandioca, mansa, and [we] learned to make 'parvilha' cakes and on the whole lived fine." [9]

The Smith children quickly devised ways to amuse themselves when not doing their chores. They made swings of hanging vines. The young ones set traps for small animals on the trails and poled up and down the river in dugout canoes. The huge number of birds in the forest were a special delight, and all enjoyed "watching and hearing the kingfishers call and the sapsuckers tap tapping. Also the great tucanas [toucan's] queer honk-honk away up in the trees, robbing little birds' nests. Then the lone sad notes of the 'perdiz' while the white anvil-birds clanging bell rang out now and then. The cooing wood dove's plaintive note, and at twilight the whippor-will sent thrills along the spine. And when the night birds opened up, the symphony was complete." [10]

After the Smith family had lived on the Ariado for nearly three years, its members decided to begin the difficult task of building a real American-style house. After a long search, a kind of tree was located that could be easily split. Smith, with his sons Penny and Marsene, worked at this task, while Eugene, Preston, and a Brazilian worker sawed the lumber for posts, doors, joists, rafters, and floors. The job of transporting the completed boards back to the building spot was a task for Bellona and Marsene. In later years Bellona described the operation. "To get these boards hauled to the house site was the next question. This was done on the backs of . . . two horses and Marsene and I were the drivers. We would ride bareback to the place, tie a dozen boards together—a dozen for each side, mule pack fashion— scramble on any old way into place, mount again on top of the boards and ride away down the narrow trail, singing as loud as you please, happy as kings."[11]

Real ingenuity was also necessary in making such common items as shoes, unavailable at any price. Smith, described as a "jack of all trades," resolved to make footwear for all of his family. He set out to find a tanning material and located an excellent tanbark in the jungle by tasting samples from dozens of trees. Smith then dug a trough in a log, filled it with his home-concocted tannic acid, and had usable deer-skin within a week. He hand-carved lasts for each member of the family, then stretched and hammered the leather, attaching the tops to the soles with wooden pegs.[12]

By the time the Smith's new house neared completion, the other remnants of the McMullan colony had moved from the headwaters of the São Lourenço. The reasons were varied, but the isolation, wistfulness, and in some cases, homesickness, had begun to tell on many of the families. As the road to Peruibe was incomplete, it re-mained extremely difficult to get crops to market. Stories of the rela-tively successful American settlement at Santa Barbara could not help but lure some who wished to live once more in a town. The Cooks went over the mountains to Santos but had to bury their young son, Pet, beside the trail. Cortez Fielder and his wife Sarah, with two chil-dren, headed for the coastal *serra-sima* (high coastal plain) country. N. B. McAlpine, who married Sue Tarver, headed for the region of the Norris colony near Santa Barbara. William Hargrove married Julia Beasley, and the two returned to the United States. C. A. Crawley and his wife, Rachel Russell Crawley, went to Santos, then Santa Bar-bara. Rachel's father, Thomas Garner, followed the couple to their new home. Parson Quillin moved to a spot on the railroad from São Paulo to Santa Barbara that was locally known as "the station."[13]

The movement of most of the former Texans to the area near Santa Barbara finally began to tell on Alfred I. Smith. Although the new house was virtually complete, crops were beginning to mature, and life was becoming easier, Smith resolved to leave the lonely forest. About the end of the third year at El Dorado, Smith surprised his en-tire family one morning when he abruptly said to his wife, "Sarah, this won't do—we got to get back out of here somehow." His astonished wife and children, although astounded by the sudden declaration, ex-citedly agreed to the proposal.[14]

For several reasons, but principally because they lacked adequate money to pay for ship passage from Iguape to São Paulo, the Smiths elected to follow many of their friends over the mountains to Peruibe, then to Santos, on their way to Santa Barbara. Rather than attempt to take everyone before adequate arrangements could be made, Smith and his son Penny set out on foot to find the other Americans. They traveled to Santos, then boarded a train to the town of Jundiahy, at that time the railroad's terminus. From there the two walked to Campinas, then on to the station of Rebouças. Meeting an American there (whose name also was Smith), Alfred learned how to locate his old friends. Upon arrival at Santa Barbara, Smith rented a *fazenda*, left Penny with an American named "Old Man Perkins," then returned for the rest of the family. The journey of the Smith family, which proved to be a herculean task, was well-described by Bellona in these words:

> All our baggage had to be carried over the mountains by hand and it took many days. Two men were employed to help our boys, two days for each trip and one day to rest before the next. At last the whole of us started, each with a load. I shall never forget that trip, over mountains, down in the valleys, crossing creeks waist deep and small streams galore. My shoes were soon lost, one after the other, first one kicked off, the other left in the next mud hole. We passed the place where the Cooks had camped and their little baby boy died. We saw the grave of the lonely child left, to wait forgotten till God is pleased to call him out of death into his glorious kingdom. Tired and completely exhausted we at last came to a river [then] crossed in boats to Pernibe [Peruibe]. We stayed there a day or two with a kind family with several nice girls, and we would take long walks in the low scattered bushes and white sandy soil. Just beautiful. Then in boats down a long, long river, through a canal to Conceição. There we got a cart and traveled . . . some 40 miles on the beach till we came in sight of Santos, beyond a body of water.[15]

The following day, the family crossed over the inlet to Santos. There, they unexpectedly met the Cook and Haynie families, who were preparing to leave for the United States. The Smiths then boarded the train to Jundiahy and on the way passed São Paulo, "a small town with low scattered houses on a hill, quite a distance from the station of the same name." After they reached the end of the railroad, the Smiths fortunately met an old Brazilian who had two empty carts and was returning to the town of Campinas. A bit of negotiation convinced the cart owner to carry both the Smith family and their luggage directly to the farm that Smith had rented, Fazenda de Bocudo. Recalling the experience, Bellona Smith said that the final leg of the journey consumed a week or more. At first they enjoyed seeing the open country after living in the forest for three years, but the travel soon became tiresome. "There was so much red dust and the squeaking carts and pack mules—camping each night at one or another of the mule shelters along the roadside. The cartman had his wife along to do the cooking, but we cooked for ourselves and afterwards, sat around the camp fires trying to talk to each other and learning new words of Portuguese."[16]

Other McMullan families like the Cooks and Haynies, as previously mentioned, had given up the idea of trying to remain in Brazil and resolved to return to the United States. The three members of the John Baxter family, without money and desperate, were allowed to return to North America on the United States warship *Guerriere* on May 31, 1869. On September 6 of the same year, the Gills, the Weavers, and the Garlingtons boarded the *British Lion* at Rio de Janeiro en route to New Orleans. John Johnson, his wife Molly, and one of their sons died at sea, leaving the only surviving child, a boy, in care of the ship's captain, who shipped the child from New York to relatives in Texas.[17]

Even as some former Confederates were returning to the United States, another colonizer, a relative newcomer named Charles Nathan, brought more Americans to Brazil. Nathan, an English subject who had at one time lived in New Orleans, received a seventeen-condition contract from the Brazilian government on July 23, 1867. In dealing with Nathan, the empire finally discarded its long-standing agreement with the New York and Brazil Steamship Company and provided in the new pact that the American emigrants would be transported on steamships that navigated between New Orleans, Mobile, and other southern ports and Rio de Janeiro. It called for the transportation of one to five thousand persons within the twelve-month period.[18]

In late April, 1868, the *Tartar* sailed with the first contingent of colonists under the Nathan contract. The ship's arrival was noted in a letter from George Barnsley to his father. "The Tartar and her emigrants arrived safely and the people and govrn't have been much pleased with the class of passengers, and it is generally conceded that as a body they are far ahead of any other emigrants which have yet arrived at Rio."[19]

The arrival of Nathan's ship came too late, however, to infuse new life into any of the established coastal colonies. In most cases they had already bloomed and were beginning to wither. Nathan's colonists were just in time, however, to add a new vitality to the upland gathering of Americans at Santa Barbara. It was to this destination that most of those in Nathan's group set their course.

By 1870 all of the original McMullan colonists had moved off the grant on the São Lourenço River. As closely as may be determined, sixty-four of the ninety-six persons who were on colony lands in November, 1867, remained in Brazil; documentation exists that thirty-two of those listed on the Bowen census had returned to the United States. Of the total of 154 persons who boarded the *Derby* in Galveston, ninety-two were probably in Brazil in 1870. Twelve of the total number of colonists are not accounted for, and at least two were dead by that date. Nine of the 154 *Derby* passengers had returned to the United States before the colonists as a whole arrived in Brazil. On the basis of these figures, 63 percent of the Americans who arrived in Brazil in 1867 with the McMullan emigrants were still in the empire in 1870.[20]

The three years after the arrival of the McMullan colonists in Brazil were crucial ones for the emigrants who actually settled on colony lands. They learned, at least to some extent, to overcome the problems of a primitive society. All of the colonists, whether or not they went to the lands on the São Lourenço, continued to search for their own elusive Eden. Some did not find it and returned to the United States. Those who moved to Santa Barbara, however, had a good chance for contentment. The little community of Americans offered excellent lands, good transportation for crops, and, perhaps more important, the opportunity to live among other former Americans.

CHAPTER 10

Straitened Fortunes and
Baptized Souls

HE PATHS TO WEALTH or even solvency for the Americans who emigrated to Brazil were filled with pitfalls, and it soon became evident to many of the McMullan colonists that the likely route to financial security did not lie in the lush river valleys of the São Lourenço River but in upland areas with climates and agricultural conditions similar to those they had left in Texas. The most popular location was the region north of São Paulo near Santa Barbara, the region selected by the Norris colony in 1865. It was here that remnants of all of the American colonies drifted and joined together in a second attempt to recreate a way of life now gone but not forgotten.

At Santa Barbara few grew wealthy, but without question some of the colonists gained fleeting fame and moderate fortunes. McMullan colonist Thomas McKnight and his wife America settled near Santa Barbara at the village of Bom Reteiro, where they bought a farm and built a home before joining fellow Texan John Domm in the manufacture of the moldboard plow—an implement unknown in Brazil until the arrival of the Americans. Although McKnight is credited with owning the first iron plow in Brazil, he soon sold his interest in the factory to Domm. One fellow Confederate noted that Domm's shop was extremely important to the colony, as "nearly every American or Brazilian who uses plows, depends upon him to make and repair them." That evaluation greatly underestimated the value of the implement to Brazil, however, as the agricultural change that was its result continued well into the twentieth century. Commenting on the impact of the introduction of the plow, former American Cicero Jones wrote in 1915 that "the leaven sown by them [the American emigrants] has transformed a country whose area is larger than the U.S. By transformation, I mean agriculture, and that means all." Jones stated that the Americans "introduced the plow for the first time in Brazil . . . which enabled them to buy lands and reclaim them [*sic*] that were lost to the Brazilian except for grazing purposes. At present the Federal Government has twenty of our American boys teaching plowing, one in each state. And one day Brazil will have to send to you [those in the United States] your principal beef supply."[1]

Thomas McKnight's introduction of the moldboard plow was not his only contribution to the economic and social fabric of Brazil. He became interested in the manufacture of rum and its Brazilian complement, *pinga,* and traveled on a regular basis to the colonial town of Paratý, south of Rio de Janeiro. Working with Brazilian distillers, McKnight soon developed advanced production methods that were soon recognized for producing a better quality of *pinga* than had ever been brewed before. In addition, one account notes, McKnight distilled the first whiskey ever made in Brazil.[2]

While one faction of the McMullan colonists was responsible for the production of high-grade alcohol, another more vocal group was the catalyst for the formation of liquor's nemesis, the Baptist Church. On September 10, 1871, McMullan colonist Reverend Richard Ratcliff established the First North American Baptist Missionary Church at Santa Barbara. In a letter to the corresponding secretary of the Foreign Mission Board of the Southern Baptist Convention of the United States, Parson Ratcliff and church secretary Robert Meriwether stated that twenty-three persons, "with letters from various Baptist churches . . . , did unite and organize . . . with a pastor and such other officers as Baptist churches usually have." The letter to the Foreign Mission Board also presented a resolution by the congregation that called for American missionaries to come to Brazil.[3]

In another letter calling for assistance, the members of the new Baptist congregation promised even further support: "If you do come . . . our homes shall be open to you, our progress, our influence and labors will be for and with you. We hope a large Baptist community in this country will be added to the great Baptist family of the world, teaching, preaching and practicing the faith once delivered to the saints." The correspondence continued with a brief statement about Reverend Richard Ratcliff. "The Pastor of this church has been in this country five years or more, hailing from Louisiana, and having been a pupil of the late Rev. Mr. Hartwell. He is well qualified for his position and very acceptable to the members; preaches once a month, with one hundred and fifty dollars salary per annum." Although an attempt had been made before the Civil War to start a Baptist church in Brazil, the Santa Barbara church became the first to be permanently established.[4]

The congregation at Santa Barbara continued to grow through the 1870s but received a severe challenge when its pastor, Richard Ratcliff, decided to return to the United States about a year after the death of his wife. With five young children, Ratcliff believed that he could not give them proper care in Brazil and moved to Mexia, Limestone County, Texas. Parson Elijah H. Quillin took over the church's ministry. Despite Ratcliff's return to the United States, his interest in the establishment of a strong Baptist church in Brazil remained undiminished. On October 1, 1878, he wrote a letter to elder H. A. Tupper, head of foreign missions for the Southern Baptist Convention, in which he encouraged Brazil as a missionary field for North American Baptists. He cited the toleration of Free Masonry and the legality of civil marriage as reasons for increased activity. With an emphasis on Brazil, Ratcliff reasoned, "the [Foreign Mission] Board could accomplish more with the same amount of means than in any other field."[5]

Ratcliff had high praise for the First North American Baptist Missionary Church and stated that the Americans under Parson Quillin's leadership would assist the U.S. church without pay. "Their present pastor authorized me to say to the Board, that he would accept an appointment to the Brazilians, (he is a teacher of their language) and make quarterly reports to the Board, without charging one cent." The 1879 Southern Baptist Convention reviewed correspondence from Quillin assuring them that the Santa Barbara church would be of assistance if the appointment were made. "The members," Quillin stated, "are prosperous in their basket and their store, and are on the highway to wealth." Based on the pleas from Ratcliff and Quillin, the 1879 convention passed twenty-one resolutions in favor of opening South American activity and officially appointed Quillin as its missionary. On Sunday, December 7, 1879, a second Baptist church was opened near Santa Barbara. Named the Station Church, it boasted twelve members and was located on the railroad leading into the interior. Parson Quillin became the church's missionary pastor. In 1880 a report from the church's membership to the North American Baptists lauded Quillin as being "able in the pulpit, exemplary in daily life, sound in doctrine, simple in manners, esteemed by the Americans and popular with the Brazilians; perhaps more conversant with Brazilian affairs than any one known to them, and adapted in every respect to the missions."[6]

The popular parson's physical condition, however, was not good. Always a cripple, Quillin's health began to deteriorate rapidly in the middle of the 1880s, and on March 21, 1886, he died of a liver ailment. Soon after, Reverend R. P. Thomas, an occasional preacher at the Santa Barbara church, wrote to H. A. Tupper in the United States and gave a brief survey of his friend's career. Thomas explained that Quillin's only concern in his illness had been for his family and their future and that Quillin had wished that they could return to Texas after his demise. In his letter to Tupper, Reverend Thomas asked for support for this purpose from the United States. "Will not the Baptists of Texas help Sister Quillin to get back there? She is well educated and a good teacher, and if she was back there she could support her family. She is well-known in Hillsborough [Hillsboro, Texas] as a teacher." Thomas asked the Baptist newspapers in Texas to note his plea, but no evidence is found that such an effort was made. Support was not forthcoming to send Sarah Quillin back to Texas.[7]

Parson Quillin, like most other former southerners who had died in São Paulo Province, was buried south of Santa Barbara at the "Campo," a burial ground established eighteen years before when a pressing need arose for a non–Roman Catholic cemetery. Upon the death of his wife Beatrice, A. T. Oliver had dedicated a part of his farm, approximately 260 feet by 325 feet, for burial purposes. Beatrice Oliver, who died on July 13, 1868, became the first to be interred there. Ten years later, the cemetery was growing rapidly. Even after the death of A. T. Oliver, the new owner of the surrounding property encouraged its use for the burial of Americans and agreed to the construction of a small chapel on the grounds. Baptists, Presbyterians, and Methodists used the little church after its completion.[8]

But nourishment for the soul was not always accompanied by food for the body, and by 1870 agricultural conditions in São Paulo Province appeared grim because of a general slowdown in the economy. By September it was reported that business had come to a standstill. "Cotton has fallen from $2 to 80 [cents] an arroba. Money [is] hard to obtain. Many [mercantile or cotton] houses in Rio have gone by the board. If this state of affairs continues many days," said one colonist, "we can only look for a harder time than we have ever seen before."[9]

By March, 1871, the situation for the American farmers looked no better than it had in September of the previous year. The 1870 cotton and coffee crops remained "mostly unsold." One account listed four principal reasons why the growing season of 1870–1871 was "a year of bitter losses to the farmer. First a killing frost, second the war [with Paraguay]—thirdly low prices and utter stagnation of business, and fourthly, army worms, wet weather, etc. All live in hopes of better changes soon."[10]

But changes did not come soon, and consequently many small farmers, including some former southerners, found themselves in a difficult situation. There is little doubt that some Americans decided to return to the United States during this period. The economic picture certainly provided an excuse if one was needed. Some of the Americans (and those who claimed to be) who did not have the means to return to North America but wanted to do so congregated in Rio de Janeiro in hopes of financial assistance from the U.S. government. It is almost certain that large numbers of those who asked for help were German and Irish immigrants who had sailed from New York without money or the prospects of making it.[11]

The seeming destitution of the "southerners" laid the basis for what appeared to be a journalistic coup for a *New York Times* reporter in Rio de Janeiro. Writing about the problems of the "southern" emigrants to Brazil, he took dead aim at the McMullan colonists, remarking that "extensive sugar planters from the famous Red River district of Louisiana and Middle [central] Texas, dazzled by the brilliant prospect of recuperating their depleted fortunes, emigrated with their families to the provinces of Sao Paulo and Espiritu Santo, in lower Brazil." The newspaper article continued by exaggerating the extent of the disaspora from the former Confederacy, stating that "whole districts of the finest land in the South, from Maryland to Texas, were sacrificed for a mere song. Entire counties were depopulated by the exodus of emigrants and disreputable adventurers who were alike infected with the fever for Brazilian colonization."[12]

Continuing, the *Times* article reported that hundreds of persons who had in years gone by "reveled in luxury and affluence, were actually begging from door to door, and making a poor pitiful effort to drown their miseries in the nearest drinking booth . . . [consuming] aguardiente—the vilest concoction in Christendom." The writer described one American, said to be a graduate of Jefferson Medical College in Philadelphia, who accosted him on the street and implored him, "for God's sake, give me only a vinte (less than a quarter of a cent) to get something to eat." The *Times* reporter devoted considerable space to an American bar in Rio called the Dixie Free and Easy Concert Saloon, operated by a man who was "once a might among his people." There, said the northern writer, lewd women surrounded the customers, and the barkeepers dispensed "the commonest native liquors to as vile a set of scoundrels as ever cut a throat." The bar was probably the one owned by Jimmy Graham of Texas, certainly not a well-known public character. One southerner recalled that "most of us frequented [Graham's bar] not so much on account of the whiskey, but as a rendezvous to compare our impressions. Mr. Graham was a very kind-hearted man, and helped, to his private loss, a great number of stranded Americans."[13]

George Barnsley raged at what he considered to be a malicious Yankee exaggeration in the *New York Times* article. On August 20, 1871, he wrote a long letter to the *New Orleans Times* about the incorrect reporting, stating that a thousand or even ten thousand colonists could not "depopulate entire counties in such densely inhabited states as those in the South." As for the graduate of Jefferson Medical College who was supposedly begging in the streets, Barnsley retorted that he knew every doctor in the American colony and that "no such person existed as he depicts, for all that were there were still living and doing well." Barnsley continued by stating that most of the remnants of the McMullan and Gunter colonies were settled at Santa Barbara. "These persons," said the doctor, "are doing well and some are accumulating riches. That any one can be permitted to die of starvation and misery here, as depicted by the credulous writer to whom reference is made, is simply impossible, unless that person by his besotted habits, or idleness, puts himself beyond the pale of humanity."[14]

George's brother Lucian was also indignant about the *Times* article and wrote his father that "the man who wrote about the Americans in Rio and other parts is a fool." Lucian agreed with his brother about the unlikelihood of any Americans starving in Brazil. He contended that if a "decent man with common sense will only come and see us as we are, I will guarantee him as much hog and hominy, good milk, fresh butter and a corn crib full of corn to feed his horse as he ever saw in the states. If New York had not shipped the meanest cuss[es] that ever left a country we would be better off here. The Yankees and the Irish ruined us for awhile, but we are coming out of the mist now." In another letter Lucian expanded on his previous statement. Explaining that a larger number of those who demanded passage back to the United States were not southerners, he commented that "the [ones] that returned were the scum of New York, drank up all their money in whiskey and then swore the Govm't had fooled them and asked Mr. Yankee . . . consul to ship them back to the best country the world ever saw. All I say [is that] I feel a pity for you all—to have a miserable set of humans let loose on you. But America is now the hell of earth and all good devils go there."[15]

Obviously Lucian Barnsley presented a personal viewpoint in this tirade. However, much of what he said was substantially correct. For persons living in rural areas particularly, the supply of hominy, milk, butter, and corn was probably sufficient to feed any southerners who for any reason were unable to feed themselves. Lucian also knew of a large number of nonsoutherners in Brazil who yearned to return to the United States. It will be remembered that a large number of Irish and Germans sailed with the McMullan colonists from New York on the steamer *North America*.[16]

In the United States anti-emigration newspapers such as the pro-Union *San Antonio Express* had a field day with the news about "destitute former Americans." It published a letter purported to be from a colonist in Brazil that voiced a desperate cry for help, pleading "if the government means to take us home, hurry and do so, or it will have the dying curse of starved Americans." Since no name was given, it is impossible to determine whether the letter was authentic or whether it was in fact even written by a southerner. Another news item in the same newspaper was somewhat more credible. It stated that the Americans in Brazil were "in poverty and distress," and had harsh comments about Ballard S. Dunn's handling of his colony. Unfortunately, no source was supplied for either news item.[17]

Without question, there were some Americans who wanted to return to the United States but were financially unable to do so. In January, 1872, James R. Partridge, chief of the U.S. legation in Brazil, wrote to Secretary of State Hamilton Fish asking for assistance in returning Americans, particularly women and children from São Paulo Province, to the United States. "I venture respectfully to submit to you," the consul suggested, "whether the President would think it expedient to ask of Congress . . . a small sum, say three or four thousand dollars, which would secure relief and passage home, at half rates, to the most pitiable cases, at least, if not all who cry for help." Continuing, Partridge made it clear that he knew he was asking the government "to relieve persons, or rather their widows and children, from the consequences of their deliberate folly in leaving their own country in vain hope of finding a better one; and if men alone were concerned, I would be silent. But if the sad history and present condition of many of these women and children could be known to the President, I feel sure he would most willingly do, in their behalf, whatever, in his judgment, expediency and the proper policy would permit." Secretary Fish's reply was short and unforgiving. "There is no appropriation from which a sum to defray the passage of these persons to the United States can properly be drawn." Over the next few years, nevertheless, many unfortunate Americans "found passage home on the Guerriere, the Kansas, the Portsmouth, the Quinnebaug, and other . . . vessels."[18]

In Brazil many former Confederates who were not in economic distress continued to discuss the reasons for either staying in Brazil or returning to the United States. George Barnsley admitted in 1871 that he believed that a large number of former southerners were contemplating leaving Brazil and were "saving means" to do so. The most convincing arguments, continued the physician, were "dissimilarity of language and customs; difficulties of transportation; low price for skilled labour; differences in religion; inability to vote and be sovereign; disgust for the Brazilian idea that a man who sweats from work is not a gentleman; and finally—the most potent of all, that this country offers and gives nothing for the American, which he cannot get in his own country—nothing worth the sacrifices of exile from his native soil and kindred."[19]

The distance from families and friends in the South became even more critical at the times of crisis for American emigrants to Brazil, and the problems of Judge James H. Dyer were no exception. After the death of his wife Amanda on July 4, 1871, the judge was disheartened and considered giving up everything and returning to the United States. The loss on a sandbar of the expensive and heavily mortgaged riverboat he and his son-in-law Columbus Wasson had bought to haul furniture woods was the last straw, and he decided to dispose of the sawmills and take the speediest ship to the United States.[20]

Dyer's resolution to sell the mills and his ability to actually find a buyer were two different things, however. After failing to find anyone who was willing to pay anywhere near the value of the business, Dyer and Wasson decided to turn one of the buildings and its machinery over to Dyer's ex-slave, Steve. Steve by that time had developed a real liking for Brazil, knew the business well, and had nothing to lose if he failed. The second mill was finally sold to a man from Rhode Island named Crawford Allen, who, as a young man, attended school with the Barnsley brothers. One account concludes that Allen was unsuccessful with the mill and "threw away a lot of money, got disgusted, and went to Rio Grande do Sul to saw pine." George Barnsley recalled that Allen spent $80,000 on the Rio Grande operation, "purchasing the best sawing machines from the United States," before returning to North America.[21]

Dyer's sister, Nancy McMullan, continued to live in Santa Barbara with her son Ney but saw no future for herself there. When her daughter Louise died of typhus, she also decided to return to the United States. The Moores, Vic and Billy, soon made the same decision, and in April, 1872, virtually the entire family sailed for Texas. Columbus Wasson, who was teaching school, chose to remain in Brazil until the expiration of his contract. Sadly, the Moores' little daughter, Juanita, died on the way home and became the second child of the couple to be buried at sea.[22]

At least one McMullan colonist fled Brazil because of legal problems. On October 29, 1877, a seventy-five-year-old settler named Hervey Hall inspected his farm and found that a burro belonging to his neighbor, Jesse Wright, had destroyed a considerable amount of his crop. It was not the first time that the animal had been found trespassing, and Hall, enraged, killed the animal on the spot. Wright was furious over the death of his valuable animal and itched for revenge. Egged on by "Dock" Tarver, one of Nelson Tarver's sons, Wright confronted Hall. In a fit of temper Wright pulled his pistol and fired, finishing his former friend instantly. The murderer ran away toward a nearby farm where Wilber McKnight, Thomas McKnight's son, was plowing. Wright told young McKnight what had happened, informed him that he was leaving the country, and asked Wilber to look after his business and his property. McKnight agreed to do so and consequently incurred the wrath of the Hall family. Jesse Wright left his wife and fled with his son Ambrose to Rio Grande do Sul Province. Later Wright returned to Texas, where it is said he "got religion" and became the sheriff of a central Texas county.[23]

Regardless of the motivation for return, however, not all southerners were sure that a return to the South would be a wise course for the former Americans who went to Brazil. Godfrey Barnsley, writing from Woodlands Plantation in Georgia to his son George, urged the physician to stay in Brazil and "not return to this country. You are in a much better one." The younger Barnsley had no intentions at that time of returning to Georgia, however. He had completed his examinations for a medical license in Brazil and was pleased with his prospects. The problems encountered in dealing with Brazilians were the only factor that gave him cause for second thoughts. "I do truly believe that if there is any earthly paradise, it is here in Brazil, and if this present race of people could be swept away or educated I would not prefer any other place on earth; but my goodness, such moral deprivation, such darkness, such lack of education as exists now!"[24]

George Barnsley's attitude toward the Brazilians was shared by many of the other southerners who had come to South America. Americans were, as a whole, slow to become Brazilians, preferring instead to remain within enclaves of other emigrants from the same cultural background. Even so, almost all of the colonies eventually failed. The reasons for this were varied. George Barnsley intimated that many were unsuccessful because of the lack of integrity of the promoters. "In the precipiency of emigration," said Barnsley, "a number of places were chosen by American speculators as suitable locations for our Southern emigration. I will exculpate only Major McMullan; with regard to the rest simply say that some were more noble than others." In an 1868 letter to his father, Barnsley evaluated the other colonial attempts and outlined the principal reasons for their failure.[25]

Lansford Warren Hastings' colony, commented Barnsley, "attracted much attention and a number of emigrants settled near him, but either through the climate, or rains, or insects, or more probably laziness, his colony came to nothing." Actually the Hastings colony was in fairly good condition at that time, and it survived for many more years. In 1888, twenty years after Barnsley's doleful statement of the colony's condition, Methodist minister H. C. Tucker claimed to have found ninety-two settlers still on the Hastings grant on the Amazon. As late as 1940, one writer found three original emigrants, one man and two women, at the Santarem settlement at the intersection of the Tapejos and the Amazon rivers.[26]

Speaking of George Grandioson Gunter's Rio Doce colony, Barnsley said that it had failed because of an unfavorable climate. Gunter's location, he commented, was "celebrated by the Brazilians for its sickness and fertility of soil." After the first year, Barnsley asserted, "near all the people . . . [returned] to Rio, with injured health and straitened fortunes." Another observer agreed with Barnsley's observations, but added that lack of transportation facilities added to the failure.[27]

Many of the settlers who left New Orleans with the expectation of settling at Ballard Dunn's Lizzieland changed their minds and went instead to other colonies. Some decided on Gunter colony lands on the Doce River. Of those who did settle on the Juquiá River with Dunn, many disliked their new surroundings. George Barnsley described the area as "extremely picturesque, but with the slight defect of being without good lands and in the rainy season half under water." Another source confirms this evaluation of the property, stating that the "top soil was very thinly spread over low-grade sub-soil." Realizing his mistake, Dunn mortgaged his property for $4,000 and returned to the United States, ostensibly to locate additional emigrants. He never again appeared in Brazil. Soon after Dunn's departure, floodwaters inundated Lizzieland and wiped out virtually every permanent improvement as well as the first year's crops. The colonists thereupon scattered in every direction.[28]

The settlement at Santa Barbara, originally colonized by William H. Norris's emigrants, became the most populated North American gathering place. According to one evaluation, it "was the most flourishing place in the Empire. The crops have been good and the health excellent." George Barnsley observed that the Brazilians also liked their American neighbors, no doubt a factor contributing to the settlement's success. "Three Brazilians living near them [the southerners] have recently come to Rio to purchase goods and speak highly of their brisk trade, etc., with the Americans." Among the most attractive features to the former Confederates were the area's good farmlands, which were well adapted to American-style agricultural implements. This, combined with the community atmosphere in which Americans could continue to associate with each other on a daily basis, constituted the main reason for Santa Barbara's success.[29]

On the whole Barnsley believed that most of the emigrants who had come to Brazil were expecting too much and were unprepared for the hard work that was necessary to be successful. "They find that the streets are not paved with gold nor [is] the astute Brazilian ready to open his coffers to every needy stranger." He continued with a condemnation of the Americans who would not make the adjustment to the new life. "I am sometimes sickened at the want of manliness shown by our people. I cannot now recall a single instance of any man who has acted as a man but is doing well. Of course removing from our native land we find trouble, sorrow, and many vexations of spirit; we had these in the States; but there we had no hope and were crushed by the Government; here we are with every hope and are fostered by the Government."[30]

In search of that hope, the southerners who sailed from Texas to Brazil under the leadership of Frank McMullan made a substantial impact on their new country. Extremely important was their introduction and manufacture of the steel moldboard plow, an implement unknown in Brazil before their arrival. This tool made possible a revolution in Brazilian agriculture in that it allowed lands to be utilized that would have remained useless under the old system. Equally important to Brazil was the establishment by McMullan's Texans of the Baptist Church in Brazil. Because of their efforts, an evangelism program was begun and a Texan, Elijah H. Quillin, became the church's first appointed missionary. Despite the accomplishments of the former southerners, however, many yearned for home and Texas. Homesickness, disillusionment, financial problems, and difficulty with language were the most common reasons for the decisions of the colonists to return to the United States. Still, many determined to stay in Brazil; those who did generally vowed to become good citizens of their adopted country.

CHAPTER 11

The End of El Dorado

THE DREAMS OF GOLD, of a new frontier, and another Dixie in Brazil were all but forgotten by most of the former McMullan colonists by the middle of the 1870s. Hardship, loneliness, and homesickness caused many of them to return to North America; most who remained banded together with the remnants of other colonies at the village of Santa Barbara in an attempt to recreate a common culture reminiscent of the Old South. Only two of the Texan colonists who remained in Brazil, George Barnsley and James M. Keith, continued to actively pursue El Dorado, and neither lived near the other Americans. Of those who returned to the United States only one person, Ney McMullan, still nursed a longing to find the hidden treasures of Brazil. Because of his relatively young age, Ney's search was postponed for over two decades.

One person who had come to Brazil with the McMullan colony had little interest in hidden treasure, however, and he searched for his fortune with hard work and the sweat of his brow. Steve, the freedman who had come with his former master Judge Dyer to South America, continued to work the lumber mill given to him when Dyer elected to return to Texas, and he found it to be very profitable. After the return of his "family" to the United States, Steve adopted the surname of Columbus Wasson, Judge Dyer's son-in-law, and settled down on the Rio Una north of Iguape to operate his business. Hard work, patience, and good sense paid off handsomely for the former slave, and he accumulated a considerable fortune. George Barnsley later wrote that Steve had become sort of a figure among the natives of the region. "Steve worked his mill, made money enough to live on, had [as] many wives . . . as a tolerably well off Turkish Pasha, and died highly respected. If he had been educated he might have turned out to be a Barão [baron] of Brazil. At any rate, he ruled all that section and had a good time. He always held that he was a true American." After several generations Steve's descendants are said to be still in the

Rio Una area, although their name has evolved over the years to Vassão.[1]

Unlike Steve, who built his reputation and his estate through hard physical labor, George Barnsley always believed that it was his destiny to achieve greatness and wealth through promotion, skill, and a great deal of luck. He began the search for gold almost from the first days he spent in Brazil, although the quest was intermittent because of the necessity of his returning to medicine to make enough to keep his creditors—those who funded his various schemes—away from his door. Barnsley always considered medicine as secondary, although it is likely that if he had pursued it with the fervor that he did gold, he would have been highly successful and perhaps even wealthy.

Barnsley's marriage on March 4, 1869, to Mary Laniera Emerson, the daughter of former Confederate and Mississippian Reverend William C. Emerson, seemed to promise better things, but Barnsley's financial schemes soon created a financial abyss. The marriage, nevertheless, was a relatively happy one despite Barnsley's inability to remain in one place long enough to establish a lasting medical practice.[2]

When worries about financial difficulties were compounded by the death of members of his family, Barnsley's preoccupation with gold became less intense. The death of his father Godfrey Barnsley in June, 1873, the loss of a little daughter named Julia in August, 1873, and the death of his father-in-law in October of the same year were devastating to Barnsley's morale; he yearned for home, often wondering about the reasons that had taken him to Brazil in the first place. In a letter to his sister on January 20, 1874, George expressed doubt about his original decision to leave the United States. "Whether it was weakness of character, whether it was dictated by spurious ambition, or by that old absorbing longing to see the isle of the lotus eaters—the far off islands of the tropics of eternal summer, I know not." Regardless, the idea of returning to Georgia from that time on dominated his thinking and was spurred by the frustrating fact that he could not accumulate enough money to even consider the trip.[3]

By 1878 Barnsley's desire to return had become intense, and his letters home painted a dreary picture of his life in Brazil. "God only knows," he wrote his sister Julia, "how I could hug those old oaks at the front gate . . . and shake the hand of such as one left [at home]." Later the same year, Barnsley painted a pathetic picture of the situation of his family in Brazil. "Lucian," he said, "went to Rio . . . [and] waited there until he and his family almost starved; his wife is sick. Murray [one of Barnsley's nephews who married his wife's sister], I suppose, is still drinking whiskey in Rio. Times are getting harder and harder." Barnsley seemed to have resigned himself to his fate by 1879 although he still regretted his inability to leave Brazil. He moved continually, going from small towns in São Paulo Province, then to Rio, then back into the interior. His failure to make money in his search for gold prompted him to invest in a drugstore and even to try to promote a transcontinental railroad. None of his enterprises except medicine were successful. Yet Barnsley convinced himself that "get rich quick" schemes were surer than the everyday work of being a physician. Reconciled to the fact that he would likely never again be able to return to Georgia, he wrote his sister and asked her to care for their father's burial plot. "As long as you keep the old gentleman's grave clean it is a matter of no importance to me whether I am here or there—if I never return drive a stick down close to the old gentleman's dust and write on it—G.S.B. Co. A, 8th G[eorgia] . . . C.S.A."[4]

In 1881, however, Barnsley's yearning for home was subdued, at least for a short time, with renewed gold fever. An article entitled "Montanha de Ouro" in the *Almanaque Literario da Provincia de São Paulo,* written by one José Maria Lisboa, indicated that there was yet hope for finding the Aranzel treasure, but in a location different from the one indicated in Aranzel's "directions." Lisboa suggested that the mountain named Dado de Deus (São Lourenço Peak), located in the Itatins Mountains between Conceição and Iguape, might not be the mountain that Aranzel was referring to in his recollections about the Lake of Gold. Lisboa suggested that, according to an article published in the eighteenth century by one Carlos Ilidro da Silva, the fabled peak lay not near the ocean but due west of the city of São Paulo near the village of Una and the town of Piedade, located a few miles south of the city of Sorocaba.[5]

In partnership with his old friend and fellow McMullan colonist James M. Keith, Barnsley formed a new company to make a serious search for the Lake of Gold. In search of financing, the two men secured the backing of a major investor and asked two other Americans, Dr. Horace Manly Lane and Dr. R. Coachman, to purchase shares in the venture. Relying on a previously unknown set of directions discovered in the archives of the city of Itapetininga and said to have been written by Aranzel himself, the Americans requested legal authority to engage in the venture from the governor of São Paulo Province. On February 14, 1881, permission was received.[6]

Like the other mining ventures in which Barnsley and Keith had been involved, however, this one also went awry. Publicly optimistic, Barnsley wrote his sister Julia on July 5, 1882, explaining his investments and predicting profits from the enterprise. The physician said that he continued to be "very hopeful," and stated that he had "made large sacrifices, of time, money, and interests." Barnsley claimed that machinations of other shareholders (unquestionably Lane and Coachman) had caused the breakup of the organization with the result of "a great loss of money to the capitalist." "Both he and I," Barnsley continued, "have suffered from the villainy and intrigue of others interested." Barnsley later claimed that more than forty *contos de reis* were spent in excavation and in construction of roads through the forest in search of the natural treasure.[7]

The impending collapse of the company did not appear as a calamity to Barnsley, however, and he predicted that a new association would soon be formed with European capital. Explaining the extent of his investments to his sister, Barnsley said that he had "15% in two gold mining privileges, 15% in R.R. [railroads] of 53 kilometers or more, and 40% in another R.R. project of 300 kilometers." The larger railroad interest, said the doctor, "will be conceded, it is said, by persons to speak in a few weeks or months." In addition to the mining and railroad investments, Barnsley also wrote his sister about his interest in "three new petitions for the fabrication of sugar from the cane, for which the Gov't will give a privilege with guarantee of 7% on the capital employed." Despite the impressive holdings Barnsley claimed to have, he confessed that they were not yet yielding any results. "At present I am poor as a church rat and involved in some little trouble, out of which I trust soon to be."[8]

Despite the optimistic forecast, Barnsley's fortunes did not improve. Penning a letter from the interior town of Sorocaba on September 12, 1882, a despondent Barnsley wrote that "altho my interests are thoroughly guaranteed, I have hopes soon to have better news to communicate. At any rate if no result comes out of these affairs by March I shall send the whole matter to pot and return to the States to settle down somewhere to clinic." Barnsley complained that he and his wife were "getting very tired of this life out here and she is now anxious to return to the States. Times are getting worse and worse." By 1883 Barnsley's attitude toward his adopted country showed even more despair. In another letter to his sister Barnsley recalled his instability and failure to stay with one profession until it paid off. He lamented that "it was the greatest mistake of my life, except that of coming to Brazil. O! Julia, what a sad mistake Lucian and I made by coming to this country and worse by continuing. I frankly say that after so many years of residence in Brazil and intimate contact with them I am less a Brasilian today than I was a year after my arrival."[9]

Continuing financial problems caused Barnsley to intensify his determination to return to the United States. He wrote letter after letter to Julia and her husband asking for money for passage even if it meant the mortgage or sale of Woodlands. In one appeal, he despaired that "disastrous affairs have reduced me and Lucian to utter poverty; we have no means to return to Woodlands at present. If you can find any way to send out 2 to 5000 dollars to aid us to return it would be well to do so at once. If so much money cannot be raised, make some sort of contract with any of the sailing or steam vessels from N. Orleans to Rio for our passage."[10]

For unknown reasons, the family in Georgia did not send passage money to the brothers. Perhaps it could not be raised. It is possible that, in light of the lack of financial acumen shown by George and Lucian, the family in Georgia did not feel that such an advance would ever be repaid. Four years later George Barnsley and his family remained in Brazil, still insolvent and still begging for help from Julia. In January, 1887, George wrote a vehement letter to his sister in which he declared that he determined to return to the United States with or without her assistance. "It seems impossible," he railed, "that you should have hesitated on raising the money for my expenses. I am here in an interior town and everything amiss for you did not reply. Get back, you better believe I will. . . . I will at last prove that I am not lost on the deserts of Egypt. I am here in Pirrasunga [Piraçununga]." This letter may have had the desired effect, for in the following year, 1888, George finally returned to Georgia and Woodlands, leaving his wife and children in Brazil until adequate funds became available to send for them.[11]

George Barnsley arrived at Woodlands on July 19, 1888, twenty-one years after he had left Georgia for Texas to join the McMullan colony for Brazil. Over a year later, on August 21, 1889, his wife and children followed him to the old family home in Georgia. Barnsley received a lukewarm welcome from his sister Julia, who had little trust in Barnsley's financial or management abilities. Consequently, the doctor spent much of his time, particularly during the first six months he was home, in preparing written narratives about Brazil and the emigration of southerners to that country after the Civil War. The interest in and knowledge of mining Barnsley had acquired in South America also manifested itself again, and the physician began a systematic survey of the plantation grounds, gathering samples of various ores. This was viewed as a worthless activity, however, and someone, probably Adelaide Baltzelle (Julia's daughter), threw the samples in a barrow ditch. Everything Barnsley did, especially concerning any efforts to sell, divide, or settle the Barnsley estate, was viewed suspiciously, and he later claimed that his sister and her daughter conspired against him in an effort to keep Woodlands intact for themselves.[12]

Adelaide was extremely suspicious of her uncle, and she did everything possible to thwart attempts by Barnsley to settle the estate.

Barnsley, in turn, stated that "Addie" was incapable of honesty. "She can not tell the truth about anything; her imagination is so vivid that she clothes the facts in her own images and believes them true. . . . She has been brought up to believe that Woodlands is hers and to that purpose she has devoted herself." Nevertheless, Barnsley continued to try. One sale of the estate for $80,000 to a Tennessee buyer seemed complete then failed at the last minute, probably because of machinations by Addie. In the meantime George began a concerted effort to put the once-beautiful estate back in a semblance of its former condition.[13]

The work on the grounds of Woodlands did not put food on the table for his family, however, and soon Barnsley decided to begin, once again, the practice of medicine. In August, 1891, he printed a circular announcing his clinic, declaring that "having again and again been requested by my neighbors and friends to enter into the practice of my profession, I have acceded to this request, and from this date announce myself." He noted that he would office "at the cottage, (Gardener's House), near the public road. I am ready at any hour day or night." It is not known how successful the practice was for Barnsley, but at least it gave him a degree of independence from his sister and her family.[14]

But the intrigues of Addie Baltzelle, who soon married a questionable mining engineer named B. F. Armington Saylor, whom Barnsley himself had brought to Woodlands to work with him on analyzing mineral deposits on the estate, were too much for the doctor to countenance. Barnsley was "hooted at" when he made suggestions for making Woodlands self-sufficient, and he viewed the life there as becoming unbearable. Consequently, when it was suggested that he return to Brazil to review the prospects for his gold mines, Barnsley eagerly accepted, not realizing that the offer was really a ruse to get rid of him. Accompanied by two mining professionals named Lydick and Glasgow, he left for South America on August 29, 1895, probably planning to return to the United States.[15]

Once in Brazil, however, Barnsley realized that his real home was not in Georgia but in the country where he had lived for twenty-one years before returning to the United States. He once again began the practice of medicine and began saving and planning to bring his family back to South America. He would not have guessed that it would take so long, for it was January 9, 1899—over three years—before Mary and the children could leave Woodlands for Brazil.[16]

Despite the problems, George always maintained that he loved Julia. "I was devotedly attached to my sister Mrs. V. Schwartz and my desire was always for her good, even though the thunder of Jove rolled around me and the Furies lashed. To outside persons my actions seemed queer, and in the family I am blamed for every disaster. I worked as long for my object as consistent with a continuance of a sound mind. I welcomed the S.A. mining project, as a relief from terrestrial Hades."[17]

While the Barnsleys were in the United States, political events in Brazil were causing changes in the government and Brazilian society that made the country very different from the one the physician had left seven years before. A strong feeling of republicanism was sweeping the country, led in part by Quintino Bocayuva, Frank McMullan's old contact at the Brazilian Emigration Agency in New York in 1867. By 1889 the movement was so strong that it appeared that it might both topple the government of Dom Pedro II and, simultaneously, eliminate slavery. Conveniently for the antimonarchists, three major problems developed sufficient momentum to keep the controversy alive. One was a religious dispute, a conflict concerning Free Masonry and the Emperor's control over secular affairs of the Roman Catholic Church. Another was a military question about whether officers could discuss political affairs in public, especially with the press. The third and perhaps most important conflict concerned the abolition of slavery. By the mid-1880s the spirit of abolition was so strong that it seemed that Dom Pedro would have to take action toward emancipation. The Rio Branco law of 1871, which made some provisions for future freedom for some slaves, had been a stopgap measure, and radical abolitionists were never satisfied with it.[18]

In 1884 Dom Pedro asked abolitionist Manoel Pinto de Souza Dantas (who had been one of the persons most involved with the problems of Frank McMullan) to form a new cabinet and propose a plan for emancipation at some future date. Souza Dantas devised an approach that called for the prohibition of the sale of slaves, agricultural implements for freedmen, and an increase in the emancipation fund that had been created in 1871. When the House of Deputies defeated a test vote on the issue, Souza Dantas resigned. Although another plan was passed in 1885, slaves were still years from actual freedom in most cases. By 1887 many had fled from their masters, and some slave owners had voluntarily freed their slaves. In 1888 sentiment in favor of the abolition of slavery reached a crest. On May 19, the House of Deputies passed a bill by an overwhelming majority outlawing the practice. Princess Isabel, acting as regent while Dom Pedro was in Europe, signed the legislation.[19]

But the movement toward revolution and a republic could not be stalled by the abolition of slavery. Indeed, the manumission encouraged the movement. Unhappiness of former slave owners about lack of compensation for freed slaves, distrust of a possible future regime headed by Princess Isabel, and, most important, dissatisfaction of the military because of its treatment by the monarchy, led to a coup d'etat that deposed Dom Pedro II and led to the establishment, five years later, of a republic. Among the principals in the overthrow were Lieutenant Colonel Benjamin Constant Coelho de Magalhaes, Ruy Barbosa, Manoel Deodoro da Fonseca, and Quintino de Souza Bocayuva.[20]

For the former Confederates in Brazil, the change in government had important consequences, including the renunciation of land grants made by the empire. George Barnsley claimed to have lost mining privileges of an area the size of Rhode Island. James M. Keith, the former Texas Ranger who spent years in the *sertão* searching for minerals, also lost a considerable amount of land. Unlike Barnsley, however, Keith decided to try to recover his lost properties. He went to the new government, applied for another grant, and reportedly received fifty square leagues of land south of Sorocaba, São Paulo Province, including the properties in which Keith and Barnsley had invested in the abortive 1882 mining scheme. The titles to Keith's properties were "all registered and perfectly good in law and possession." After years of exploring his grant, Keith located numerous mineral deposits including gold, tin, silver, copper, quicksilver, and graphite. All of the necessary requirements for mining, including large amounts of water power and timber, were readily available. Despite Keith's claims of possible riches on his property, he could not convince "men of means" that they should invest in mining ventures there. George Barnsley, however, purchased a tract of about 2,000 acres of wooded land from Keith. The doctor claimed that a gold mine was on this property, but "the land is hard to get at, and nobody believes in the gold, and the mine, except Mr. Keith and myself." Writing about it twenty years later, Barnsley hoped that some of his grandchildren might "take a notion to look at my mines, and then be so pleased to remember me."[21]

In 1908 George Barnsley made one last effort to secure financial support for the development of his mines. On December 30 of that year he wrote a long letter to B. F. Armington Saylor, Addie's husband, in which he asked for help in selling his and J. M. Keith's land or acquiring capital to exploit the property. After a long explanation of the steps that both he and Keith had taken to be sure that title to the land was secure, Barnsley pointed out that North American companies had already shown interest in the mines. He reported that a Mr. Lydick of Pittsburgh (almost certainly the man who had accompanied Barnsley back to Brazil over ten years before) "came on his

own account to examine the mines of my old privileges, which are
contiguous with mine now." Barnsley said that Lydick "reported fa-
vorably, and collected samples to be analyzed in Pittsburgh." Continuing his sales presentation, Barnsley said that the property was fertile
and would be "especially adapted to colonize." He then completed
his letter to Saylor with an assessment of the costs of a professional
evaluation. "As to expense of examination, under Mr. Keith's guid-
ance, a look over for general appreciation, I presume would not cost
over $1,000.00. The time best selected to explore is from May to No-
vember which is the dry and cold season. No option or other contract
exists with Mr. Lydick, if you are the man you once were there is
a million or more in it for you." There is no record of a reply to
Barnsley from Saylor.[22]

George Barnsley never gave up on his belief that somewhere in Brazil there truly was a huge amount of gold just waiting for the right
time and the right person. He never realized that his happiness (as
well as his misery) had from the beginning been in the search for the
elusive Eden, and not in its discovery.

CHAPTER 12

The Last Exile

NEY MCMULLAN WAS eighteen years old when he returned to the United States with the rest of his family in 1872. He had adored his older brother, Frank, and if it had not been for the fact that he believed that he needed to stay with his mother, he would have preferred to remain in Brazil. However, because of the recent death of his sister Lou, of typhus, he believed that it was his responsibility to stay with the family until all were back in the United States, secure and at home once more. So it was with a heavy heart and considerable regret that he left the country where he had grown up. Having lived in Brazil for five years, since he was thirteen, most of his ideas of life had been shaped in the mode of the huge South American country.

But return he did, and when the ship docked in New Orleans, he was as excited and as enthusiastic about returning "home" as the others. The former exiles were met at the dock by Virginia and George L. Clark, Ney's sister and brother-in-law, who suggested that Ney and his mother share the Clarks' Mississippi home until they could readjust to the life they had left behind years before. The offer was graciously and quickly accepted as Nancy McMullan had mixed feelings about returning to her former home in Hillsboro, at least for a while, even though Judge Dyer and the other members of the family had returned to Hill County. And so it was that Ney and his mother settled in Attala County, Mississippi, where they resumed their life in the nation which they had abandoned in the wake of the uncertain Reconstruction after the Civil War.[1]

Having traveled the world and confident that he would soon do so again, however, Ney was restless in the Mississippi farm community of Kosciusko. Consequently, it was not long before he left for Memphis, Tennessee, to learn the skills that would be necessary to make his mark, whether it be in the United States or in Brazil. By October, 1873, he had completed the requirements for a diploma for Leddin's

Business College; he then returned to Mississippi and told his mother that he wanted to go back to Texas. Nancy McMullan was not surprised by the request; in fact, by that time she believed that she too was ready to return to the spot where her husband and three sons were buried. In October the mother and son, accompanied by the Clarks, were back in Hillsboro.[2]

It is said that one can never go home again, and this is true to the extent that things are never the way they were when one left, whether it be one year or five, as in the case of the McMullans. While they were in Brazil, the small village that Hugh McMullan had helped found had grown into a thriving town. Business activity was at a high pitch, and hundreds of new settlers vied for choice farms and city properties in the county seat. Many believed that the McMullans would never return from South America, and consequently they had no qualms about squatting on the square mile of land that Hugh McMullan had purchased ten years before from John Carothers. As a result, the news that Nancy McMullan would be returning to Hillsboro created quite a stir among those who claimed but had no deed to land in the controversial section of property.[3]

It was reasoned by some squatters that the land was theirs by default, and they were loath to give it up, especially those who had constructed homes or built other improvements. Therefore, it was no surprise to some when, on September 3, 1872, a fire broke out in the Hill County courthouse, destroying most of the records of the Probate Court showing the transactions that had occurred before the McMullans left for Brazil. According to one publication describing the loss, the fire succeeded in "destroying a few of the public records, namely, all of the records of the District Court excepting the minutes of 1857, one record book (Book L) of the County Court and all of the records of the Surveyor's office . . . . Five years records of the Probate Court were burned. The fire was supposed to be the work of an incendiary." If no records existed, at least one person reasoned, no one could judge whether the administrator of the Hugh McMullan estate had sold the specific tracts of property. The fact that former executor Frank McMullan was dead added to the belief that the destruction of the records would make a legal fight very difficult to win.[4]

The last thing that Nancy McMullan wanted to do as she returned to Hill County was become involved in a lawsuit. She believed that she had had enough grief in the past few years, and she looked for no more. After all, the land was not too valuable, and she knew that it was her word against that of the squatters as to who had title. As a result of Nancy's reluctance to pursue the matter, the ownership of the property was to remain in limbo for years to come.

Despite Nancy's decision not to seek legal relief in the question of the McMullan property in Hillsboro, however, her life continued in a course of tragedy. In 1873 her daughter Vic Moore died soon after the birth of a daughter. Before too many years passed, she learned that her daughter Virginia Clark—Jennie—was suffering with cancer. The young woman died in 1882, and the remnant of the family followed her hearse in the rain to her burial. Nancy herself died four years later, leaving only Ney and Martha Ann (Mattie) remaining out of the large and happy McMullan family that had moved to Texas less than twenty years before.[5]

Judge Dyer, Nancy's brother, quickly returned to a familiar way of life in Hill County after his return from Brazil in 1872. As a former county chief justice, he was comfortable in the profession of a peace officer. Because of his proficiency, he was appointed first a U.S. marshal and then to the influential job as the superintendent of the Steiner Valley Prison Farm. He also farmed and ranched, and he was said to be one of the best Durham cattle breeders in the region. Dyer soon remarried, and he lived a good and prosperous life until his death in 1901. His epitaph in the *Waco Times-Herald,* although praiseworthy of the venerable pioneer, unfortunately made no mention of the judge's saga in Brazil. Dyer's son-in-law, Columbus Wasson, after losing by a large margin to Indian Wars hero Lawrence Sullivan Ross in a race for election to the Texas Senate, moved to the little West Texas town of Gail where he and his wife Hattie became relatively wealthy.[6]

The death of Nancy McMullan set the stage, in 1887, for an attempt to legalize the title of squatters to the McMullan land on the Carothers grant in south Hillsboro. Attorney William L. Booth, a native of New York who had lived in Iowa, Indiana, and Michigan before moving to Texas in 1853, represented some of those who claimed title to lots within the 640 acres. Although Booth had been a Democrat before the war and had served in the Confederate army, he later became a Republican and was bitterly resented by many Hill County residents. One account relates that during Reconstruction Booth's life was "several times exposed."[7]

The probate records of the Hugh McMullan estate were not the only ones lost in the 1872 courthouse fire, although the McMullan land probably formed, by far, the largest tract in question within the Hillsboro city limits. Another block of land administered by one James Wornell had essentially the same legal elements of that of the McMullans. The property owner had died over twenty-five years before suit was filed; the probate records had been destroyed; the records in the administrator's deeds were insufficient to show an order for the sale of land for the estate. In the Wornell case, styled *White and others v. Jones,* Booth argued before the Texas Supreme Court that title should be given to those who claimed to have made the purchase of land. The court agreed, saying that "after twenty-five years, the presumption *Omnia recte acta* must apply; and the records having been destroyed by fire, every intendment must be presumed in favor of the validity of the proceedings." Using *White v. Jones* as a precedent, Booth claimed that the decision also could be legally applied to the McMullan estate lands, a presumption that evidently was never tried in court. The heavy expense in opposing those who claimed title, coupled with the relatively low price of land at the time, kept the McMullan heirs from pursuing the matter. A cloud remained and perhaps continues to hang over the property. McMullan descendants recall that quit-claim deeds were still being signed for a fee as late as the 1930s. An inquiry about McMullan lands in 1873 brought an anxious and belligerent response from an abstractor in Hillsboro who snapped, "If you are planning to sue, forget it, you can't win." The same year, another property owner recalled that his attorney had removed "something with the McMullan name" from his land abstract with the comment that it "might cause trouble someday."[8]

But in the last quarter of the nineteenth century, Ney McMullan showed little interest in recovering the Hill County lands. Ever since his return from Brazil, Ney had been unsure as to the direction of his life. Although born to a farming and ranching family, his interests turned to literature and research, qualities neither highly appreciated nor especially needed on the Texas frontier. He had a way with words, and he wrote extensively even after his marriage to Mabe Oldham of Iredell, Bosque County. The couple moved often, and this frequent change was no doubt a reflection of Ney's failure to set and pursue long-term goals. The lure of Brazil never went away, and the young man made up his mind to return there when he could afford to do so.[9]

In 1895, at the age of forty-one, Ney was financially able and mentally ready to return to South America. At first, he told his wife, he wished to survey the country alone to see if his recollections of Brazil matched reality. Then, if the situation looked favorable, the two Texans and their children would go there to make their home. After spending eight months looking at properties and discussing prospects with both Brazilians and former Americans, he returned to his wife with a renewed fervor for emigration. Mabe was less than enthusiastic, but she agreed to follow her husband. She knew that there would be no living with Ney if he was not allowed to follow his star.[10]

As in the years just after the Civil War, the Brazil fever was catching for other members of the McMullan family. The children of Ney's sister Mattie Williams, Monk and Ileita, were eager to follow their uncle. Ileita's husband, Swan Hudzeitz, and their children, Lucia, Rie, and Coon, were also enthusiastic about the proposed adventure and yearned to go to the land about which they had heard all of their lives. Counting all of those listed above, plus Ney and Mabe's three sons, ten members of the extended McMullan family were ready to follow Ney back to Brazil.[11]

As the ship left for Brazil, Ney no doubt remembered the day twenty-eight years before when he, as a youth of thirteen, had left from the same docks. Instead of the anxiety he felt at his first sailing, however, Ney felt as if he were continuing the reason for his life. He excitedly awaited the ocean voyage and looked forward to showing his family the Brazil he and his brother had loved so much.

Upon arrival, the new Texan colonists went directly to Santa Barbara, where the majority of former Confederates made their home. The ten were welcomed enthusiastically, particularly so because they were the family of the beloved Frank McMullan, whom many of the former Americans had known so well years before as the leader of the Texas colony. Homes were opened to the new arrivals so that they would feel welcome and comfortable, and the McMullan, Williams, and Hudzeitz families made plans to find their place in the Brazilian-American community.

Of those who were new to the country, only Monk Williams expressed real enthusiasm. He immediately loved Brazil and saw it as a mecca for entrepreneurs in which he could make his fortune. Like others who knew of the legends of gold mines, Monk quickly caught the "fever" of prospecting and in short order located several claims that he believed to be worth further examination. He filled a trunk with ore—each piece logged as to location and type—and prepared to pursue the mining business with vigor.[12]

But Monk Williams' enthusiasm for the country contrasted with a genuine unhappiness on the part of his sister and her husband Swan. They missed the family in Texas and wrote pleading letters to her brother Coon, then a dealer for the Waters-Pierce Oil Company in Cleburne, Texas, and her younger sister Nanneita to join them in Brazil. Although he hesitated to forfeit a profitable business in Texas, Coon agreed to move to Brazil and bring his fourteen-year-old sister with him. Bags were packed when Coon fell dead of a heart attack. The news of their brother's death convinced the Hudzeitz family that they should return to Texas. They waited only for the birth of their fourth child, Swan, Jr., before sailing for home to "take care of Nanneita." Monk Williams did not want to leave, but felt it necessary to do so for the sake of his family. He no doubt planned to return to Brazil, for at his death years later, his possessions included the trunk of ore—promptly styled as only "a bunch of old rocks" by family members who did not know the history of the collection.[13]

It goes without saying that Ney and Mabe McMullan remained in Brazil when the other family members returned to Texas. Ney had not yet begun to explore possibilities in Brazil and would not have considered leaving. Most important was his desire to inspect the fifty-five league McMullan grant on the headwaters of the São Lourenço that his brother had literally died trying to secure so many years before. He criss-crossed the huge property soon after the departure of the Williams and Hudzeitz families, pondering the prospects of the land and wondering about the possibility of gaining the grant for himself.

Ney consequently made inquiries of the Brazilian government about the procedures for applying for a new title for the property, and he was pleasantly surprised at the response he received. The mountainous, relatively inaccessible land was not considered to be of great value, and Ney was reportedly offered clear title to it if he agreed to pay back taxes, estimated at $5,000. Despite the fact that Ney had sufficient cash to complete the transaction, he declined to do so. No real reason is known for his decision, but without question he was to regret it within a short time.[14]

About 1915 electric power was brought to the region, making inaccessible timberland and fertile valleys extremely valuable almost overnight. Settlers flocked to areas such as the upper São Lourenço, and prices rose steadily. Ney soon heard of the activity, and he resolved to take up the government's earlier offer. One real problem, however, was the fact that he no longer had the $5,000 that was needed to request transfer of the title. Consequently, he immediately began writing letters to all of the family in Texas, asking for participation in the venture. One of Ney's nieces, Ileita Williams Peacock, recalled receiving a letter that implored her to "contact all the family . . . and get $200.00 from each one and send it." Ney said that he was making an effort to "do something about our land in South America and could make millionaires out of all of us if he just had a little money." Ney's reputation precluded most of the family from forwarding cash, for, as one descendant remarked, Ney was "something of a dreamer." Another said that she "knew Uncle Ney too well."[15]

Despite Ney McMullan's lack of vision in failing to secure the lands included in his brother's huge land grant, he continued to look for his own El Dorado until his death. Not only did he seek legal means to obtain the fifty-five leagues that had been set aside for Frank McMullan, he also endeavored to gain title to the Una River properties that had

been purchased by Judge Dyer and others. He engaged a law firm in
São Paulo in which the son of one of the American emigrants was a
partner and began to make inquiries. According to one account, however, the attorney made little effort to solve the problem. Instead, he
continued year after year to tell the former Texan that "only a little
more time" and a "little more money" were necessary before they
could make him rich. Ney spent a substantial part of his income for
decades on lawyers, never doubting that in the end he would achieve
his goal.[16]

Time went by, however, with no results. In an effort to build a
stronger legal claim, Ney again wrote to all of his family in the United
States requesting a power of attorney as well as cash. Although Judge
Dyer had died in 1901, McMullan secured such a document from
Dyer's son, Wiley Simpson Dyer, from Columbus Wasson, and from
Helen Domm Curry, John Domm's daughter. In the document, each
of the three persons authorized Ney McMullan to act as "My true and
faithful attorney, for me and in my name, my place and stead, to re-
cover and sell all my rights, titles, and interests situated on the Rio
Una de Prelado, in the State of São Paulo, Republic of Brazil, which
I . . . acquired by direct purchase in the year 1867, the same being
registered in the City of Iguape."[17]

About the same time, Montie Moore, the daughter of Victoria and
William T. Moore, also received a letter from Ney asking for a power
of attorney, claiming that a diamond strike had been made adjacent to
the original McMullan colony lands. Although Montie planned to forward the document, her lawyer was murdered only days after the receipt of the appeal, and Montie's intentions of helping her uncle were
abandoned.[18]

Ney continued to write to his relatives in Texas about the happen-
ings in Brazil. He owned a farm and may have done some farming
himself, although his granddaughter does not remember him doing
so. McMullan was also said to have written articles for such well-
known periodicals as *Review of Reviews* and *World's Work*, but if he did,
his name was not included in the by-line. One intense study was of the
habits of Brazilian monkeys, but no record of publication has been
found.[19]

Ney McMullan was without question one of the original Confederate emigrants to Brazil; he spent his formative years in Brazil, yet he
always considered himself to be a true unreconstructed Rebel—almost
imagining that he had never left the country, then returned. He sent a
photograph of himself to his nephew, Hugh Clark, on May 31, 1918,
in which he emphasized his position as he saw it: "In the city of São

Paulo, Brazil. As I look today: aged 64 years, 3 mos., and 8 days. See how inexorable time has bleached my forehead and around my eyes scribbled in hieroglyphics, the story of my long exile from friends and native land."[20]

Another former American who lived in Santa Barbara, Cicero Jones, made an assessment of those who remained at the little town in the back country of São Paulo State. Writing in response to a letter from the United States in 1915, Jones stated that "some have prospered; some have not. Many have died and left their families here. All are more or less content and would fight for the Stars and Stripes as we would for the Stars and Bars." This statement was confirmed within three years when at least one Brazilian-American died with U.S. troops in France during World War I.[21]

Cicero Jones' statement that many of the older citizens had died by 1915 was indeed accurate insofar as the McMullan colonists were concerned. Alfred I. Smith, Frank McMullan's old friend and teacher, suffered a stroke in 1889, then passed away in 1892. Thomas McKnight died in 1890, and blacksmith John Domm in 1900. Sarah Parks Quillin, never able to return to Texas, died on December 9, 1902. By 1921 Napoleon Bonaparte McAlpine was also gone.[22]

In 1921 James M. Keith, George Barnsley's old friend and partner in a score of mining ventures, also died in the home of one Antonio Exel in Sorocaba. Keith passed away at about eighty-five years of age, with the cause of death officially listed as "la grippe, cardio-pulmonary form." His only relative was listed as Edward Currie, a nephew from Meridien, Mississippi. The U.S. consul who signed Keith's death certificate stated that "Keith was poor, but had a large grant of land from the Brazilian government worth possibly $5,000. He was possibly a naturalized citizen. Has no relatives in Brazil. Died intestate." The civil code of Brazil stated that when heirs of an intestate decedent were unknown, the property could not be disposed of for two years. After that time, the property could be sold and the proceeds placed in the state treasury. The money received could be claimed by relatives for a period of up to thirty years. Despite the law, Keith's land was disposed of immediately after his death. Despite inquiries by E. M. Lawton, the American consul, Brazilians would not disclose the amount for which the Keith property was sold.[23]

Several of Keith's heirs, through attorneys and individually, carried on an extensive correspondence with U.S. consular authorities for about two years after Keith's death. Their inquiries produced no results, however, as U.S. authorities did not believe that the value of the property was sufficient to pay attorneys' fees. In one letter, Consul

Lawton pointed out that there was not even a lawyer in Sorocaba, the place of Keith's death, and that he could not employ one in São Paulo without advance guarantees of fees and costs. "Frankly," he stated to an American attorney, "I question very much if it is worth while for your client to take further action." Thus, the estate of James Monroe Keith, which he had labored so many years to create, was dissolved within days.[24]

In the case of George Barnsley, Keith's constant partner, very few things remained to be distributed when he died in 1918 at the age of eighty-one. Unlike Keith, however, Barnsley did have a will outlining his wishes regarding the few possessions that the physician had saved and treasured through his life. "My land," Barnsley decreed, "should not be neglected, or *sold*, before it is examined for its minerals. I am convinced that it may be of great value." Barnsley spent his life in search of elusive fortune and, in the process, probably acquired and spent enough money to have had a considerable estate if it had been wisely invested. Fortunately, his children proved to be smarter or luckier, for most were at least financially comfortable at the time of their father's death. Like his friend James Keith, Barnsley never found the monetary success he had searched for all of his life. It is of interest that the two old men often visited in their declining years, sitting in Barnsley's attic room and discussing the land, the gold, and the past.[25]

Although George Barnsley remained a Brazilian after his visit to the United States, his niece Adelaide Saylor believed that he returned to Georgia one last time. On a rainy evening in April, 1918, Adelaide's young son Harry answered a knock at the door of the house at Woodlands. He ran to his mother with the cry, "It's Uncle George! It's Uncle George!" Adelaide ran to the door, all the while admonishing her son that Uncle George was in Brazil. When she reached the front door, no one was there. Everyone treated the incident as a boy's hallucination until word came that George Barnsley had died at exactly the time he supposedly knocked on the door at Woodlands.[26]

Ney McMullan, the last exile, continued to search for El Dorado as Barnsley, Keith, Dyer, McMains, and other McMullan colonists had done for over fifty years. But the pot of gold at the end of the rainbow remained elusive, even for the descendant of an Irish baron, and he died in the early 1930s with little money and diminished hopes. His wife Mabe would have liked to have returned to the United States at least for a visit, but the dollars to do so were nonexistent. She enjoyed her family of five sons and enjoyed seeing them prosper as the years went by. The youngest, named Frank after his famous uncle, spent his career with U.S.-owned tire companies in Brazil. Wylie Dyer McMullan became a dentist and perhaps did better financially than any in the family. The others, Dana, Lorin, and Caskey, moved to the city of Rio Verde, Goias, where all were moderately successful.[27]

The North American settlement at Santa Barbara continued to grow and progress, although by 1900 its population included a large number of Brazilians and Italians. The tradition of the emigrants from the United States was so strong, however, that the native population decided that the name of the city should be changed to reflect the influence of its founders. On July 30, 1904, the legislature of São Paulo officially recorded the creation of the Distrito de Paz de Vila Americana. The entire name was never used, however, as the town's citizens preferred simply Vila Americana.[28]

As the years passed, Vila Americana continued to prosper. Upland cotton, grown with seed imported from the United States, became one of the area's principal crops. The machinery for a gin was purchased and set up nearby, although it did not prove to be extremely profitable. Watermelons, raised from seeds brought to Brazil by "Uncle Joe" Whitaker of Georgia, soon replaced cotton in dollar volume. Due to the economic success, the North American emigrants at Vila Americana at one time numbered "near one hundred families," wrote William F. Pyles in 1915, but "has diminished at least half in these forty-odd years." Ney McMullan, in a letter of October 20, 1915, declared that the Americans in Vila Americana "are scattered over considerable territory and all are farmers or stock growers. And are mostly remnants of two Colonies; that of my brother, and the Rev. Ballard S. Dunn. . . ."[29]

Old ideas die slowly, however, and in the case of the southern tradition in Brazil, it still lingers. Less than thirty years ago, Mabe McMullan admonished her granddaughter Kelly to "marry an American; don't marry a Brazilian." Other descendants of Americans felt the need for continuity so much that they organized the Fraternity of American Descendants, a loosely knit organization that meets several times each year near the chapel at the old Campo cemetery to renew friendships and to keep alive the common bond that ties them together. At an October, 1983, meeting of the organization, English with a Texas accent wa. still heard in conversation with all but the younger generation, and fried chicken, watermelon, baking-powder biscuits, and other southern staples adorned the table.[30]

And yet the tide of change is finally going out. Fourth-generation Brazilian-Americans in most cases no longer speak English and are thus losing a significant part of their heritage. Letters and documents treasured by their families for over a century can no longer be read by some and consequently have lost much of their meaning to this newest group of descendants of Confederates. For better or for worse, the new generation of Brazilian-Americans are becoming Brazilians in the truest sense, but it took over 120 years for the change to occur.

But older descendants of McMullan colonists still live in a dual world of both nations. Two of George Barnsley's grandchildren admitted that they still nourish the ties to North America that their grandfather grasped until his death. Julia Barnsley Holland Mac-Donell and Harold Barnsley Holland declared that when they speak English, they still feel like real Americans. When they speak Portuguese to Brazilians, however, they seldom think of their North American heritage and consider themselves completely Brazilian. "It is a strange feeling," Julia said; "it is as though we were a composite of two cultures."[31]

Harold Barnsley Holland, a respected citizen and manufacturer who lives in the small town of Jacareí north of São Paulo, also feels deep ties with the past, and he serves as the keeper of many of the letters, photographs, and mementos of his notable grandfather. But perhaps the most interesting remnant of the past in the trunk that George Barnsley treasured is a carefully drawn pattern that provides instructions for making a Confederate battle flag. In this case, at least, a relic of the Old South seems to take on even more significance in Brazil than in the United States.[32]

Another item once thought to be long lost—the little trunk in which Frank McMullan kept those things that he considered to be most valuable—may still be in the possession of one of the descendants of the American emigrants. Ney McMullan's granddaughter recalls that an old man—one of the Smiths, she thinks—used to visit in her father's home when she was a young child. The little trunk was always with the visitor, and he declared it to be Frank's. Smith considered the possession priceless and declared that he would kill anyone who tried to take it. One day perhaps the little oilcloth pouch that contains a yellowed parchment written by João Aranzel will once again be discovered and another generation of descendants of Texans will become obsessed with the burning ambition to find the Lake of Gold.[33]

Although each succeeding generation of "the shipwrecked crowd" of the brig *Derby* remember less about their past and thus are growing away from their heritage of Texas and the South, there is no question that it will be many more decades before the tradition of the event completely fades away. Thus it is fitting that, as this narrative closes, it should do so with a poem of exultation written by a southerner soon after arrival in Brazil, a verse that expressed joy, hope, and thanks for the country that welcomed them at a time when they felt a dire need for help and friendship:

With what joy our hearts were burning
    As we gazed upon the Bay,
On a bright and glorious morning,
    Just two years ago today!

Round us lay a scene more charming
    Than our dreams of Fairyland,
And our breasts with rapture warming
    Throbbed with feelings deep and grand.

Thought we of the cause we cherished,
    Of its short but glorious reign,
How our heroes fought & perished,
    Died for us, alas, in vain!

Then we thought how foul submission
    Stained a once untarnished name,
Of our sad oppressed condition,
    Of our bitterness and shame.

Then we fondly blessed the nation
    Which with pity 'cross the sea
Looked upon our abject station,
    Welcomed us and made us free.

Many changes have come o'er us,
    Weeks & months have passed away,
Toils & hardships are before us,
    But we'll n'er forget that day.

Still its thrill magnetic feeling,
    Onward we our course pursue;
Thus ourselves for action steeling,
    We will build our homes anew.

And we bless the glorious nation,
    That unto our rescue came,
Saved us from humiliation,
    From oppression and from shame.

For the kindness she extended,
    In our days of direst ill,
To a people unbefriended,
    May God ever bless Brazil!

                    Confederate
          Rio de Janeiro, May 17, 1869[34]

Appendix A.

Census of the McMullan-Bowen Colony, As Taken by William Bowen, November 9, 1867[1]

Family 1	J. C. Cobb	male	age	47
	Malinda Cobb	female	do [ditto]	44
	Mary P. Cobb	do	do	16
	Bell C. Cobb	do	do	6
	L. M. Bryan	do	do	28
Second 2	W. H. T. Beasley	do	do	40
	Julia Beasley	female	do	17
	Cary Beasley	male	do	15
	Mr. R. Smith	do	do	60
3	J. J. Green	male	age	45
	Lewis Green	male	do	19
	Jurilla Green	female	do	15
	Angeletta Green	female	do	12
	B. H. Green	male	do	10
	Joseph Green	male	do	8
Family 4	Cortes S. Fielder	male	age	24
	Sarah Fielder	female	do	21
	Zeno R. Fielder	male	do	21
5th	Thomas Cook	male	age	50
	Ann Cook	female	do	45
	Mary Cook	do	do	18
	Susan Cook	do	do	16
	Samuel Cook	male	do	14
	Nancy Cook	female	do	12
	Lilly Cook	do	do	9
	Edward Cook	male	do	7

	Pet Cook	do	do	3
	William Hargrove	do	do	28
	William Boyles	do	do	45
6th	S. F. Haynie	male	do	43
	Mary L. Haynie	female	do	36
	Hugh H. Haynie	male	do	19
	C. B. Haynie	male	do	14
	J. H. Haynie	male	do	11
	S. Travis Haynie	do	do	9
	W. Boothe Haynie		do	6
	Mary A. Haynie	female	do	1
7th	W. A. Gill	male	do	24
	Frances R. Gill	female	do	17
	One infant son [unnamed]	male		2 mos.
8th	Othniel Weaver	male	do	72
	Rebecca Weaver	female	do	20
	Daniel Weaver	male	do	19
	Riley Weaver	male	do	17
9th	Mrs. Sarah Garlington	female	age	35
	Allen Garlington	male	do	13
10th	J. R. Wright	male	do	36
	Sarah J. Wright	female	do	28
	Ambrose Wright	male	do	9
	William Wright	do	do	7
	Boregard Wright	do	do	5
11th	Thomas Garner	male	age	55
	Rachel C. Russell	female	do	31
	N. B. McAlpine	male	do	24
12th	C. A. Crawley	male	do	41
	James Davis	male	do	40

13th	William Bowen	male	do	45
	Anna Bowen	female	do	23
	L. S. Bowen	male	do	23
	Mary H. Bowen	female	do	18
	Adam L. Bowen	male	do	17
	Susan S. Bowen	female	do	16
	Elizabeth B. Bowen	female	do	13
	William R. Bowen	male	do	11
14th	E. H. Quillan	male	do	40
	Sarah Quillan	female	do	35
	Leroy Quillan	male	do	19
	Leona Quillan	female	do	17
	Aulina Quillan	do	do	15
	Leonidas Quillan	male	do	13
	Parks Quillan	male	do	2
	W. E. Parks	male	do	50
15th	John Baxter	male	do	40
	Catharine Baxter	female	do	25
	Oscar Baxter	male	do	5
	John Johnson	male	do	22
	John H. Hickman	male	do	35
16th	Jacob Wingutter	male	do	30
	Susan Wingutter	female	do	25
	Amy Wingutter	female	do	10
17th	A. I. Smith	male	do	35
	Sarah Smith	female	do	28
	Eugine Smith	male	do	19
	Preston Smith	male	do	17
	Pennington Smith	male	do	16
	Masserly Smith	male	do	16
	Sarah B. Smith	female	do	11

	Virgil C. Smith	male	do	9
	Fulton Smith	male	do	7
18th	Nelson Tarver	male	age	50
	Sarah Tarver	female	do	35
	Abner Tarver	male	do	15
	James Tarver	male	do	13
	Ben F. Tarver	male	do	11
	Luisa [Tarver]	female	do	8

Appendix B.

Sarah Bellona Ferguson List, May 29, 1935[2]

Frank McMullan	7 persons	Frank, his mother, and Ney
		His sisters Vic. and Lue [Louise]
Dyre [Dyer], wife		Their husbands Dr. Moore and Mr. Odell
daughter and 2		
sons	5	
Lon Bowen	6	Lon, Mary, Sue, Berry, Bill, Bettie
Old Man Green	7	3 sons and three girls
Mr. Haynie	8	self, wife, 2 girls and 4 boys
Mr. Cook	9	self, wife, 4 girls and 3 boys
Calvin McKnight	9	self, wife, 2 sons, 5 girls
Sterit McKnight	2	self and wife
A. I. Smith	9	self, wife, 6 sons 1 girl
Parson Weaver	3	Old man and 2 sons
Mrs. Garlingtin		
widow	1	his daughter and her daughter. married to
Mr. Gill, Mrs. Gill	2	
Judge Tarver	6	self, wife, 3 sons, 1 girl
Old Man Garner	1	with son in law Wright
Mr. Wright	6	self, wife and 4 sons
Mrs. Russell (widow)	1	daughter of Garner
Mr. Linn	3	self, wife and sister
Mr. Cobb	4	self, wife and 2 girls
Wingetter	3	wife, self and 1 girl
Parson Quillin	7	self, wife 5 children and father in law—
		Parks
Parson Ratcliff	2	self and wife
Mr. Nettles	7	self, wife, 2 sons 2 girls 1 nephew

Of the Bachelors. Major Penn. McAlpin. 2 Mr Johnsons (no kin) 2 Fielder brothers
2 Barnsley brothers, Mr Warson, Mr. Glen, Mr Lee, Mr Henderson, Parson Carter,
Mr Mason, Mr Stampley, Mr. Schofield, Mr McCann. McMains and Mr Hargrove and
Hickman and a man named Crawley and Maston. Since writing this I remember three
more names. Sailor Smith and Mr. Croney and an old maid. forget her name but
[s]he had a sewing machine the first I ever saw. she was with the Linns I think.

Appendix C.

List of the Names and Families of the American Emigrants on the River Juquiá, by George Scarborough Barnsley, March 4, 1915 [3]

nomes / names	Solitarios / Unmarried	Casados / married	Homen / Men	Mulhers / Women	Criancas girls	Criancas boys	Total Criancas	Total Persons
J. T. Cook		casado	1	1	3	4	7	9
J. D. Hargrove	single							
J. Wright		do [ditto]	1	1		3		6
W. O. Weaver		widower	1	2		3		6
W. Gill		casado	1	1	1	1		3
L. F. Haynes		do	1	1	2	4	6	8
A. J. Green		widower	1		3	2	5	6
C. Fielder		casado	1	1				2
Z. Fielder	single							1
F. Cobb		casado	1	1	2		2	4
A. F. Smith		do	1	1	6	1	7	9
B. F. Tarver		do	1	1	3	1	4	6
E. H. Quillin		do	1	1	2	3	5	7
J. Winguter		do	1	1	1		1	3
L. Bowen	single							1
W. Bowen		casado	1	0	3	2	5	6
W. T. Smith	single							1
Beasley		widower	1		1	1	2	3
Braxton		casado	1	1	1		1	3
J. Hickman	single		1					1
Johnson	do		1					1
McAlpine	do							1
Russell	do							1
Boyd	do							1
Bryant	do							1
Smith	do							1

Notes

PREFACE

1. Rebecca Minis, Savannah, Georgia, to Godfrey Barnsley, Bartow County, Georgia, July 27, 1865, in Godfrey Barnsley Papers, Robert W. Woodruff Library for Advanced Studies, Emory University.

2. Alfred Steinberg, "Fire-Eating Farmer of the Confederacy," *American Heritage: The Magazine of History* 9 (December 1957): 22–25.

3. George Barnsley, Bartow County, Georgia, to the editor of the *Rome Courier* (Rome, Georgia), November 6, 1866, as quoted in Douglas Grier, "Confederate Emigration to Brazil, 1865–1870" (Ph.D. diss., University of Michigan, 1968), 19; *Galveston Daily News*, January 8, 1867, 2.

4. Lawrence F. Hill, *Diplomatic Relations between the United States and Brazil*, 149–159.

5. *Diario de São Paulo*, September 26, 1865, as quoted in James McFadden Gaston, *Hunting a Home in Brazil: The Agricultural Resources and Other Characteristics of the Country*, 60; Blanche Henry Clark Weaver, "Confederate Emigration to Brazil," *Journal of Southern History* 27 (February 1961): 34.

6. Gaston, *Hunting a Home in Brazil*; Ballard Smith Dunn, *Brazil, The Home for Southerners, or, A Practical Account of What the Author, and Others, Who Visited That Country For the Same Objects, Saw and Did While in That Empire.*

7. Sarah Bellona Smith Ferguson, "The American Colonies Emigrating to Brazil," *Times of Brazil* (São Paulo), December 18, 1936, 18–41; December 24, 1936, 14–15; December 31, 1936, 20–21.

8. "Correspondencia Diplomatica," *Revista de Imigração e Colonização* 4 (June 1943): 268–333.

1. DESIGN AND DESTINY

1. Legends of El Dorado have persisted since the discovery of the New World. The most persistent myth deals with a remote tribe of Amazonian Indians who lived on the borders of a lake, the beaches of which were lined with gold. The Indians, as a daily routine, coated their chief with a thin film of gold dust that, at the end of the day, he would wash off into the waters of the lake. Hence, the chief was El Dorado—the gilded one. The best discussion of

the legend may be found in Adolf Bandelier, *The Gilded Man* (New York: n.p., 1893).

2. Callender Irvine Fayssoux, Notebook kept by C. I. Fayssoux aboard the steamship *Fashion* from Mobile, Alabama, to San Juan del Norte, Nicaragua, November 14, 1857, to January 12, 1858, ms. no. 136, Callender I. Fayssoux Collection of William Walker Papers, Latin American Library, Tulane University. The "Golden Circle" referred to the Knights of the Golden Circle, a pre—Civil War organization dedicated to enlarging the sphere of influence of the South throughout the Caribbean. See Roy Sylvan Dunn, "The KGC in Texas, 1860—61," *Southwestern Historical Quarterly* 70 (1967): 543—573; the origin of the term "Grey-Eyed Man of Destiny" was apparently from an oral tradition that the Indians of Nicaragua would someday be freed from the Spanish by a grey-eyed man. See William O. Scroggs, *Filibusters and Financiers: The Story of William Walker and His Associates*, 218—219.

3. "The Lake of Gold," *Brazilian Bulletin* 1, no. 2 (September 1898): 88—89. Also see Frank P. Goldman, *Os Pioneiros Americanos No Brasil: Educadores, Sacerdotes, Covos e Reis*, 130—138.

4. Ibid.

5. Ibid.

6. "The Lake of Gold."

7. Elizabeth Ann Wright, *James Dyer: Descendents and Allied Families*, [58]; Rachel McMullan White, interview with author, Needham, Massachusetts, April 20, 1975. A search of passenger lists of incoming Irish emigrants shows that a Hugh McMullan sailed from Belfast in 1811 aboard the *Perseverance*. However, positive evidence has not been found that this is John McMullan's son. See J. Dominick Hackett and Charles Montague Earty, *Passenger Lists from Ireland*, 16, 22; James Alfred Sartain, *History of Walker County, Georgia*, 45, 211; U.S. Department of the Interior, Census of 1840, Manuscript Population Schedules, Walker County, Georgia.

8. Wright, *James Dyer*, [57—58]; Hill County, Texas, Affidavit of Simpson C. Dyer, Deed Records, 121 (February 24, 1910): 154—155; Hill County, Texas, Affidavit of Jasper McMullan, Deed Records, 121 (April 29, 1909): 155—156; Virginia McMullan Clark, "Lines to My Old Home," in possession of author. Jasper McMullan continued to live in Hill County until his death in 1929. He was a landowner and farmer and a highly respected member of the community. He maintained his contact with the Hugh McMullan family long after he was freed in 1865. In an affidavit made in 1909, Jasper McMullan noted that he visited Nancy McMullan shortly before her death in 1886 and that he received correspondence from Ney McMullan in Brazil as late as 1908. See Affidavit of Jasper McMullan; Ellis Bailey, *A History of Hill County, Texas: 1838—1965*, 115—117.

9. Affidavit of Jasper McMullan; Wright, *James Dyer*, [57]; U.S. Department of the Interior, Census of 1860, Manuscript Population Schedules, Hill County, Texas, Residence Number 440, 55—56.

10. Wright, *James Dyer*, [7—9]; Nancy Dyer (Owen Dyer's daughter and an aunt of Nancy McMullan), ms. affidavit, c. 1860, in possession of Ella Beatrice Hill, Hillsboro, Texas; copy in possession of author.

11. *A Memorial and Biographical History of Johnson and Hill Counties, Texas,* 235–236; A. Y. Kirkpatrick, *The Early Settlers Life in Texas and the Organization of Hill County,* 34; "Notes from the Field," *Hillsboro Mirror,* April 27, 1921; Texas, General Land Office, File 1831, Hill County, contains the following items relating to the E. S. Wyman 320 acres: Abstract 973, Martha Wyman pre-emption of 320 acres showing patent to Hugh McMullan, August 15, 1861; Martha Wyman to Charles S. Davis, transfer for 320 acres, filed November, 1852; Martha Wyman, pre-emption certificate, Robertson 3rd Class, filed December 11, 1857; Martha Wyman, Special Report, July 24, 1861; Martha Wyman, Field Notes, 320 acres, Robertson 3rd Class, filed January 31, 1854; Charles S. Davis & wife to Hugh McMullan, transfer for 320 acres, filed November, 1854. Texas, General Land Office, file 2432, Hill County, contains the following items relating to the John Carothers 640 acres: John Carothers, Mercer's Colony Certificate filed January 12, 1856; John Carothers to Hugh McMullan, transfer for 640 acres, filed January 12, 1856. Notes in this file show that the property was patented to Hugh McMullan on June 6, 1856.

12. George Scarborough Barnsley, "Notes and Information about the Emigrants from the U. States of 1867–68," George S. Barnsley Papers, Southern Historical Collection, University of North Carolina. Another copy of this manuscript was obtained by the author from Olga Barnsley Schuenstuhl and is in his possession. Also see Ella Beatrice Hill, "The Hill and Allied Stories," in *The Gathering of the Clans* (n.p.: 1957), 56; Edna Rutherford Davey, "The Rutherford Story," in *The Gathering of the Clans,* 22–23; Jules Loh, "A Church Survives Brazos Challenge," *Waco Tribune-Herald,* August 5, 1956, sec. 2, p. 1; Nancy Ethie Eagleton, "The Mercer Colony in Texas, 1844–1883," *Southwestern Historical Quarterly* 39 (October 1935): 275.

13. Charles (Manie) McMullan was the first of the McMullan children to die, but only two of them, Ney and Martha Ann, lived past their thirties. A poignant poem, "Will We Know Each Other There," written by Virginia McMullan Clark, outlines the extraordinary number of early deaths in the family. The original is in the author's possession.

14. Hill County, Texas, Affidavit by A. Y. Kirkpatrick, Deed Records, 121 (February 1910): 159; Hill County, Texas, Deed Records, Vol. G, pp. 40–41; Nancy McMullan became executrix on November 8, 1857, the same day that Frank McMullan signed his last document as executor. Frank was appointed executor in the May term of the Hill County Court. See Hill County, Texas, Deed Records, Vol. H, pp. 662–665.

15. Scroggs, *Filibusters and Financiers,* 218–219. A huge amount of bibliographical material is available on William Walker, and it cannot be reviewed properly here. However, an excellent overview of the expansionist movement in the South is Robert May, *The Southern Dream of a Caribbean Empire, 1854–1861* (Baton Rouge: Louisiana State University Press, 1973).

16. Scroggs, *Filibusters and Financiers,* 320–322; Fayssoux, "Notebook"; James Jeffrey Roche, *The Story of the Filibusters, to Which is Added the Life of Colonel David Crockett,* 165.

17. Ibid.

18. Ibid.

19. Edwin Ney McMullan, "Texans Established Colony in Brazil Just After Civil War," *Semi-Weekly Farm News* (Dallas), January 25, 1916.

20. Fayssoux, "Notebook"; U.S. Congress, House, "Nicaragua—Seizure of General Walker," 35th Cong., 1st sess., *House Exec. Doc. 24*, 77—79.

21. The old McMullan home still stands east of the city of Hillsboro. It is now owned by descendants of the Wood family, as it has been for over 100 years. A poignant poem describing the old home place was written by Frank McMullan's sister Virginia. See Virginia McMullan Clark, "Lines to My Old Home," in possession of author.

22. *Annual Catalogue of the Students and Faculty of McKenzie College, Near Clarksville, Texas, for the Session of 1860—61*, 1—20; *Northern Standard* (Clarksville, Texas), July 2, 1859, 4; *Northern Standard*, October 27, 1860, 4; John Witherspoon Pettigrew McKenzie, Principal of McKenzie Institute, Account Book, 1857—1858, 245, Bridwell Library, Southern Methodist University, Dallas, Texas.

23. John H. McLean, *Reminiscences of Rev. Jno. H. McLean*, 77; *Annual Catalogue of McKenzie College*, 7. On October 16, 1858, McKenzie sold a small Bible to Frank McMullan in which the following was written: "Frank McMullan's Book. Bought of 'Old Master,' October 16, 1858." Underneath the inscription is a note written by Ney McMullan, Frank's brother, which says "Old Master was the name given to the President of the College where he [Frank McMullan] was educated, by the young men students." The Bible is now in possession of Rachel McMullan White, Cumberland, Rhode Island.

24. McLean *Reminiscences*, 77—78. Columbus Wasson was the son of Wylie B. Wasson of Anderson, Grimes County, Texas. Like McMullan, he enrolled at McKenzie Institute in October, 1858, although he had begun his studies there one year earlier. See Rupert Norvel Richardson, *Adventuring with a Purpose: Life Story of Arthur Lee Wasson*, 4.

25. James A. Rawley, *Race and Politics: "Bleeding Kansas" and the Coming of the Civil War*, 177—179, 250—252; Stephen B. Oates, *To Purge This Land with Blood: A Biography of John Brown*, 278—361.

26. "Democratic Meeting in Hill County," *Dallas Herald*, February 15, 1860, 2.

27. Ibid.

28. E. N. McMullan, "Texans Established Colony."

29. Ernest W. Winkler, ed., *Journal of the Secession Convention of Texas: 1861*, 252—261. For an expanded view of the secession movement in Texas, see Walter Buenger, *Secession and the Union in Texas* (Austin: University of Texas Press, 1984).

30. John T. Eubank, James H. Dyer, and Jackson Puckett, Fort Graham, Texas, to Governor Sam Houston, December 8, 1860, Petition [of the citizens of Hill and Bosque counties] to his Excellency Gen[era]l Sam Houston (ms., Governor's Letters [Houston], July—December, 1860), as quoted in James Verdo Reese, "A History of Hill County to 1873" (Master's thesis, University of Texas, 1962), 121.

31. Confederate States of America, State Department Records, Dispatches and Legation Records of the Confederate Minister to Mexico, John T. Pickett,

Ramsdell Collection, Microfilm Rolls 192, 193, and 198, Eugene C. Barker Texas History Center, University of Texas.

32. E. N. McMullan, "Texans Established Colony."

33. *Galveston Daily News*, January 8, 1867, 2; James D. Richardson, *A Compilation of the Messages and Papers of the Presidents: 1789–1897*, 6: 310–312.

34. "The Fate of Davis," *Harper's Weekly* 9 (September 23, 1865): 593.

35. "Champ Ferguson," *Harper's Weekly* 9 (September 23, 1865): 593; "The Execution of Champ Ferguson," *Harper's Weekly* 9 (November 11, 1865): 716.

36. "Letter From Bill Arp to His Old Friend, John Happy," *Dallas Herald*, February 10, 1866, 4.

37. Carl Shurz, as quoted by John Hope Franklin, *Reconstruction after the Civil War*, 2. A relatively recent study that minimizes the idea of an avenging North is Kenneth M. Stampp, *The Era of Reconstruction*.

38. John Cardwell, "Letter to the Editor," *Galveston Tri-Weekly News*, December 16, 1866, 3; Eliza F. Andrews, *Wartime Diary of a Georgia Girl*, 153–155.

2. THE SEARCH FOR LANDS

1. David P. Kidder, *Sketches of Residence and Travels in Brazil, Embracing Historical and Geographical Notices of the Empire and its Several Provinces;* Charles Lee Lewis, *Matthew Fontaine Maury* (Annapolis: n.p., 1927), 118.

2. Aureliano Candido Tavares Bastos, *Os Males do Presente e as Esperanças do Futuro*, 91–97; this reference contains the basic provisions of the September 27, 1860, law. Blanche Henry Clark Weaver, "Confederate Emigration to Brazil," *Journal of Southern History* 27, no. 1 (February 1961): 35.

3. *Richmond Examiner*, December 8, 1864, as quoted in Grier, "Confederate Emigration to Brazil," 62; Gaston, *Hunting a Home in Brazil*, 374.

4. George S. Barnsley, Quatis de Barra Mansa, Brazil, to Julia Von Schwartz, Kingston, Georgia, January 20, 1874, Manuscript Section 204, Tennessee State Library and Archives; José Arthur Rios, "Assimilation of Emigrants from the Old South in Brazil," *Social Forces* 26, no. 2 (December 1947): 146.

5. Weaver, "Confederate Emigration to Brazil," 37. Betty Antunes de Oliveira, *Movimento de Passageiros Norte-Americanos no Porto do Rio de Janeiro: 1865–1890*, 6.

6. Weaver, "Confederate Emigration to Brazil," 37–38; Joaquim Maria Nascentes de Azambuja, Minister of Brazil to the United States, New York, to Antonio Francisco de Paula e Souza, Secretary of State for Trade for Agriculture, Commerce, and Public Works, Rio de Janeiro, January 24, 1866, in *Revista de Imigração e Colonização* 4 (June 1943): 274–277; Dunn, [ed.], *Brazil, The Home for Southerners*, 153–179.

7. Hastings was an attorney from Mt. Vernon, Ohio, who went to Oregon with the first larg expedition of settlers. After a disagreement concerning the train's leader, Elijah White, Hastings became the new captain, a position he retained all the way to Oregon. Soon dissatisfied, Hastings went from Oregon to California, where he developed dreams of a presidency. To do so, he encouraged wagon trains to abandon the Oregon Trail and go instead to Cali-

fornia on the Hastings Cutoff, a desert trail. He hoped that a large Anglo-American population would set the stage for a Texas-like revolution with him at its head. See Lansford Warren Hastings, *The Emigrant's Guide to Oregon and California;* Charles Kelly, *Salt Desert Trails: A History of the Hastings Cutoff and Other Early Trails Which Crossed the Great Salt Desert Seeking a Shorter Road to California;* George R. Stewart, *The California Trail: An Epic with Many Heroes* (New York: McGraw-Hill, 1962), 182–183.

8. J. M. Nascentes de Azambuja to Jose Antonio Savaira, June 18, 1866, in *Revista de Imigração e Colonização,* 290–291; A. Foster Elliot, Vice-Consul of Brazil, New Orleans, to J. M. Nascentes de Azambuja, New York, May 23, 1866, in ibid., 291–292; Martim Francisco Rebeiro de Andrade, Honorary Consul of Brazil, Havana, to J. M. Nascentes de Azambuja, New York, May 31, 1866, in ibid., 292–293; "Shipwreck of a Brazilian Colony," *New Orleans Daily Crescent,* January 29, 1866, 2; Lansford Warren Hastings, On Board Steamship *North America,* near Pará, Brazil, to William Matthews, in *Dallas Herald,* December 1, 1866, 2.

9. Antonio Francisco de Paula e Souza, Rio de Janeiro, to J. M. Nascentes de Azambuja, New York, "Order Number 3," March 9, 1866, in *Dallas Herald,* December 1, 1866, 2; Weaver, "Confederate Emigration to Brazil," 43; A. M. Smith, "Still in Exile, 61 Years After War; Pot of Gold They Sought in Brazilian Jungle Never Found, Say Confederate Colonists," *Detroit News,* January 6, 1929, 12.

10. Manoel Pinto de Souza Dantas, President of the Province of Pará, and Lansford Warren Hastings, "Termo de Contracto celebrado com o Major Lansford Warren Hastings, para estabelecer uma colonia de compatriotas seus nesta provincia," Archives of the Brazilian Institute of History and Geography, November 7, 1866, *Lata 632, Pasta 2,* Rio de Janeiro; Hastings to Matthews, *Dallas Herald,* December 1, 1866, 2.

11. Weaver, "Confederate Emigration to Brazil," 42. The *Red Gauntlet* was sold at auction in November, 1866, shortly before Hastings' last trip. See *Texas Baptist* (Anderson, Texas), March 5, 1856, 3; *New Orleans Times,* November 2, 1866, 3.

12. Lawrence F. Hill, "Confederate Exiles to Brazil," *Hispanic American Historical Review* 7, no. 2 (May 1927): 192–210; Cicero Jones, Vila Americana, São Paulo Province, Brazil, to J. N. Heiskell, Little Rock, Arkansas, September 25, 1915, J. N. Heiskell Library, *Arkansas Gazette* Foundation, Little Rock; Robert Norris, Sitio Cinco Palentes, Province of São Paulo, Brazil, to the Editor of the *Elmore Standard* (Wetumka, Alabama), June 21, 1867, 1, copy in the Blanche Henry Clark Weaver Papers, in possession of author; Mark Jefferson, "An American Colony in Brazil," *Geographical Review* 18, no. 2 (April 1928): 226–231; Martha Norris, Rio de Janeiro, Brazil, to Peter A. Brannon, Editor of the *Alabama Historical Quarterly,* February 5, 1926, copy in the Weaver Papers; Mrs. E. Broadnax, "My Father, Cornal [sic] Norris," ms. copied by Mame A. Minchen, Nova Odessa, Brazil, September 29, 1935, Weaver Papers; Joseph Long Minchen, "A Confederate in South America," ms. copied by Mame A. Minchen, January 3, 1936, Weaver Papers.

13. William F. Pyles, Vila Americana, State of São Paulo, Brazil, to J. N.

Heiskell, Little Rock, Arkansas, September 28, 1915, J. N. Heiskell Library, *Arkansas Gazette* Foundation, Little Rock; Gaston, *Hunting a Home in Brazil;* William F. Pyles, Vila Americana, ms., Weaver Papers. Also see numerous documents concerning the Gaston colony in the National Archives of Brazil, Rio de Janeiro. Photocopies of a number of these papers, as yet unedited and unpublished, are in the author's files.

14. Lawrence F. Hill, *The Confederate Exodus to Latin America,* [53−67]; Peter A. Brannon, "Southern Emigration to Brazil, Embodying the Diary of Jennie R. Keyes, Montgomery, Alabama," *Alabama Historical Quarterly* 1, no. 2 (Summer 1930): 74−75; and no. 3 (Fall 1930): 280−305; Julia L. Keyes, "Our Life in Brazil," *Alabama Historical Quarterly* 28, nos. 3 and 4 (Fall and Winter 1966): 127−399; "Return of the Confederate Colonists from Brazil," *Talldega Watch-Tower* (Talldega, Alabama), August 11, 1869, 2; "With Alabama Émigrés in Brazil—1867−70," *Montgomery Advertiser,* August 4, 1940, 2.

15. Agatha Abney Woodson, Edgefield, South Carolina, to My Dear Miss Owen, March 21, 1930, copy in Weaver Papers; "Shall Southerners Emigrate to Brazil," *De Bow's Review,* After the War Series 2 (July 1866): 30−38; [Cornelius K.] Garrison and Allen, Agents, the New York Mail Steamship Company, New York, to Hugh A. Shaw, Augusta, South Carolina, as published in the *Edgefield Advertiser* (Edgefield, South Carolina), December 19, 1866, 1; James E. Edmonds, "They've Gone, Back Home!" *Saturday Evening Post,* January 4, 1941, 30−47; also see several articles in the *Edgefield Advertiser* from August 16, 1865, to December 14, 1866.

16. "The Southern Emigration to Brazil," *Mobile Weekly Advertiser,* November 4, 1865, 3; "Brazilian News," *Mobile Register and Advertiser,* July 18, 1865, 1; Hill, *The Confederate Exodus to Latin America,* [40−41]. *Herva-mate,* sometimes known as "Brazilian tea," is a stimulating native drink. See *Brazil 1940/41: An Economic, Social, and Geographic Survey,* 132−133. The original director of the colony at Assunguay was G. W. Waley. See *Diário Oficial Do Imperio* (Rio de Janeiro), November 21, 1866.

17. Dunn, [ed.], *Brazil, The Home for Southerners,* i; The Reverend Sidney Vail, New Orleans, to Blanche Henry Clark, Nashville, Tennessee, October, 1942, Weaver Papers; Herman Cape Duncan, *The Diocese of Louisiana: Some of Its History, 1838−1888,* 232; Andrew B. Booth, comp., *Records of Louisiana Soldiers and Louisiana Confederate Commands,* 2: 716; Eliza Kerr Shippey, "When Americans Were Emigrants," *Kansas City Star,* June 16, 1912, sec. B, p. 4. Also, see Ballard S. Dunn, *How the "Banner Church of the South" Obtained a Baptismal Font: A Plain Statement of the Facts, That Refute Many Slanders* (New Orleans: n.p., 1868).

18. Oliveira, *Movimento de Passageiros Norte-Americanos,* 9, shows the name Silas S. Totten. However, a Samuel Sherman Totten is named in the *Diário Oficial Do Imperio* of August 28, 1867; McLennan County, Texas, Inventory of Property of Elizabeth Bowen, Deceased, Probate Records, Vol. E, pp. 184−185; Frank McMullan, "Letter to the Editor," *Galveston Tri-Weekly News,* November 14, 1866, 3; E. N. McMullan, "Texans Established Colony." S. S. Totten was famous for his leadership as a Confederate captain in the Battle of Dove Creek on January 8, 1865. See William C. Pool, "The Battle of Dove

Creek," *Southwestern Historical Quarterly* 53 (April 1950): 367–385. Totten later became a partner in a sawmill on the Garahu River that employed more than 100 persons and did a volume of about $120,000 yearly. See Tavares Bastos, *Os Males do Presente e as Esperanças do Futuro*, 71n.

19. Antonio Francisco de Paula e Souza, Secretary of State for Agriculture, Commerce, and Public Works, Rio de Janeiro, to the President of the Intermediate (Coastal) Steamship Line, Rio de Janeiro, January 8, 1866, Section of Executive Authority, *Simbolo* IA⁶3, *Caixa* F.V, National Archives of Brazil, Rio de Janeiro; E. N. McMullan, "Texans Established Colony."

20. Frank McMullan, "Official Report of Messrs. McMullan and Bowen, of Texas, to the Minister of Agriculture," in Dunn, [ed.], *Brazil, The Home for Southerners*, 152–179; George Scarborough Barnsley, "Original of Reply to a Circular Asking for Information of the Ex-Confederate Emigrants, April, 1915," George Scarborough Barnsley Papers, Southern Historical Collection, University of North Carolina. Another copy of this important Barnsley document is in the estate of Olga Barnsley Scheuenstuhl, Rio de Janeiro, Brazil, who died on June 26, 1985. Scheuenstuhl was one of Barnsley's grandchildren. See Diana Margaret Barnsley Scheuenstuhl, Rio de Janeiro, to William C. Griggs, Houston, Texas, January 27, 1986. Arthur M. Hanson remained in Brazil for many years, and in 1876, he was in partnership with Murray Gilmour. Arthur M. Hanson, Todos os Santos, São Paulo Province, Brazil, to George Scarborough Barnsley, September 24, 1876, George S. Barnsley Papers, Harold Barnsley Holland Collection, Jacareí, São Paulo State.

21. McMullan, "Official Report," 152; "The Lake of Gold," *Brazilian Bulletin* 1, no. 2 (September 1898): 88–89.

22. Ibid.

23. Street probably knew of the legends of treasure, but in all likelihood he did not believe them valid. Virtually all lands offered for colonization in Brazil were offered at the same price—twenty-two and one-half cents per acre.

24. McMullan, "Official Report," 157–161.

25. Ibid.

26. Ibid., 168–169.

27. Ibid., 170. By August 28, 1867, S. S. Totten was reported to be a part of a group that planned to conduct explorations on the Amazon River. See *Diário Oficial Do Império* (Rio de Janeiro), August 28, 1867.

28. McMullan, "Official Report," 170.

29. Ibid. Actually the McMullan grant was divided into two separate parts. The first, which adjoined Ballard S. Dunn's grant on the Juquiá River, was officially called the Territorios do Rio São Lourenço, and the second, east of the first, was called Territorios dos Rios Preto, Conceição, Guanhanhã, Azeite e Peixe, and was located between the cities of Peruibe and Conceição. It was on this second block of land that the colonists settled. The first block was the one on which the Lake of Gold was presumed to be located.

30. Bernardo Augosto Nascentes de Azambuja, Third Director of Public Lands and Colonization, Rio de Janeiro, to Frank McMullan and Guilherme Bowen, "Response to the Nine Questions Presented by Frank McMullau [*sic*]

and Guilherme Bowen," June 2, 1866, *Lata* 632, *Pasta* 4, Brazilian Institute of History and Geography, Rio de Janeiro.

31. Ernesto Dinez Street, Inspector General of Public Lands of Brazil, to Joaquim Floriano de Toledo, Vice-President of the Province of São Paulo, April 5, 1866, ord. 930, c. 135, p. 2, D. 98, Archives of the State of São Paulo, São Paulo.

32. McMullan, "Official Report," 170.

33. Ibid., 172.

34. Ibid., 173.

35. Ibid.

36. Ibid., 178.

37. B. A. Nascentes de Azambuja to McMullan and Bowen, "Response to Nine Questions."

3. STEAMERS FROM THE SOUTH

1. Oliveira, *Movimento de Passageiros Norte-Americanos,* 19; Ernesto Dinez Street, Inspector-General of Public Lands of the Province of São Paulo, São Paulo, Brazil, to Joaquim Floriano de Toledo, Vice-President of the Province of São Paulo, São Paulo, Brazil, April 4, 1866, ord. 930, c. 135, p. 2, D. 98/1 fl.; Ernesto Dinez Street, "Declaration of the Boundaries of the McMullan-Bowen Grant," April 5, 1866, ord. 930, c. 135, p. 2, D. 98 C/2 fl. (anexo); Ernesto Dinez Street, "Validity of Title [of the McMullan-Bowen lands]," April 18, 1866, ord. 930, c. 135, p. 2, D. 98 D/3 fls. (anexo); José Joaquim M. de Oliveira, Department of Public Lands and Colonization of the Province of São Paulo, to Joaquim Floriano de Toledo, Vice-President of the Province of São Paulo, São Paulo, Brazil, April 26, 1866, ord. 930, c. 135, p. 3, D. 8/1 fl.; José Joaquim de Oliveira to Joaquim F. de Toledo, May 4, 1866, ord. 930, c. 135, p. 3, D. 9/2 fls.; José Joaquim M. de Oliveira to José Tavares Bastos, President of the Province of São Paulo, March 12, 1866, ord. 930, c. 135, p. 4, D. 2A/1 fl. (anexo), Archives of the State of São Paulo, São Paulo.

2. *Correio Mercantil* (Rio de Janeiro), June 4, 1866, as quoted in a letter from Betty Antunes de Oliveira, Rio de Janeiro, to William C. Griggs, Canyon, Texas, June 23, 1980, in possession of author; United States, National Archives, *List of Passengers Arriving in New York, 1820–1897,* Microfilm Publication, Microcopy 237, Roll 268; Joaquim Maria Nascentes de Azambuja, Minister of Brazil to the United States, New York, to Antonio Francisco de Paula e Souza, Rio de Janeiro, July 5, 1866, in *Revista de Imigração e Colonização* 4 (June 1943): 296–297. The complete text of the agreement between Brazil and the United States and Brazil Steamship Company is found in "Contracto que celebram, de um lado o governo imperial do Brasil, do outro B. Caymari como representante da compania United States and Brasil Steam Ships, para o transporte de emigrantes," June 20, 1866, *Lata* 632, *Pasta* 1, Brazilian Institute of History and Geography, Rio de Janeiro.

3. A confirmation of the waiver of the citizenship residence requirement for McMullan as well as Ballard S. Dunn is found in Marquez de Olinda to Antonio Francisco de Paula e Souza, Secretary of State for Agriculture, Com-

merce, and Public Works, Rio de Janeiro, June 26, 1866, *Simbolo* IA⁶4, *Caixa* 33V, National Archives of Brazil, Rio de Janeiro; Bernardo Augosto Nascentes de Azambuja to Frank McMullan and William Bowen, Official Letter, June 2, 1866, *Lata* 632, *Pasta* 4, Brazilian Institute of History and Geography, Rio de Janeiro; Joaquim Maria Nascentes de Azambuja to Manoel Pinto de Souza Dantas, Minister of the Secretary of Agriculture, Commerce, and Public Works, Rio de Janeiro, September 30, 1866, in *Revista de Imigração e Colonização* 4 (June 1943): 295–296.

4. Joaquim Maria Nascentes de Azambuja to Frank McMullan, July 5, 1866, *Revista de Imigração e Colonização* 4 (June 1943): 295–296.

5. Joaquim Maria Nascentes de Azambuja to Antonio Francisco de Paula e Souza (letter no. 1), July 5, 1866, ibid., 296; J. M. Nascentes de Azambuja to Paula e Souza (letter no. 2), July 5, 1866, ibid., 296.

6. J. M. Nascentes de Azambuja to Paula e Souza, August 26, 1866, ibid., 297.

7. Bernardo de Azambuja's letter is printed in its entirety in Dunn, [ed.], *Brazil, The Home For Southerners*, 47–49.

8. J. M. Nascentes de Azambuja to Souza Dantas, September 22, 1866, in *Revista de Imigração e Colonização* 4 (June 1943): 308.

9. "Biography of George Lafayette Clark, Written by Himself During the Year A.D. 1913," unpublished typescript, copy in possession of author.

10. A contemporary New Orleans business directory lists a James Dyer as a painter living at Lyon, between Jefferson City and New Orleans. Although this entry may or may not be Judge Dyer, another entry must certainly be the judge's wife. Amanda W. [Webb] Dyer is listed as living at a boarding house at 174 Camp Street, New Orleans. See *Gardner's New Orleans Directory for 1867, Including Jefferson City, Gretna, Carrollton, Algiers, and McDonough; With a Street and Levee Guide, A Complete Map of the City, Business Directory, and an Appendix of Much Useful Information*, 49. Also see Hill, "The Hill and Allied Stories," 26.

11. R. P. Thomas, Santa Barbara, São Paulo Province, Brazil, to H. A. Tupper, April 26, 1886, Archives of the Southwestern Theological Seminary, Fort Worth. Elijah H. Quillin came to Hill County, Texas, in 1850 and by 1858 he was a minister at the Missionary Baptist Church of Christ in Hillsboro. He was also the pastor of Providence Baptist Church at Bush Creek, Navarro County, and at Chatfield Baptist Church, Navarro County. He was clerk of the Richland Baptist Association in 1858. In 1859 he was a pastor of Pin Oak Baptist Church, Richland Crossing, Navarro County. Ben Rogers, Archivist, Southwestern Baptist Theological Seminary, Fort Worth, Texas, to William C. Griggs, Canyon, Texas, July 11, 1979, in possession of author. Other information about Quillin's life before the Civil War may be found in *Texas Baptist* (Anderson, Texas), October 21, November 18, 25, 1858; March 31, December 22, 1859; January 26, August 23, 1860.

12. Alfred Iverson Smith was born on November 4, 1818. As a young man he settled in Walker County, Georgia, where he taught school and became a close friend of the McMullan family. He moved to Navarro County, Texas, in about 1856, where he was given a homestead by Hugh McMullan. He served

as a private in a reserve company commanded by Captain M. T. French, Beat No. 5 (Navarro County), Nineteenth Brigade, Texas Militia, enlisting in August, 1861. For more detailed information on Smith and his family before they emigrated to Brazil, see Sarah Bellona Smith Ferguson, "Emigrating to Brazil in 1866–67: An Account of the McMullan-Bowen Colony," ms., May 29, 1935, in the Blanche Henry Clark Weaver Papers, in possession of author; Ferguson, "The American Colonies Emigrating to Brazil"; "Emigrating to Brazil," *Farm and Ranch* (Dallas, Texas), December 2, 1916; Betty Antunes de Oliveira, Rio de Janeiro, to William C. Griggs, Canyon, Texas, August 3, 1979, in possession of author; Texas, Militia Muster Rolls, Nineteenth Brigade, Texas State Archives, Austin; Goldman, *Os Pioneiros Americanos No Brasil*, 44–45; Vera Smith Lowrie, "Yankee-Hating Southerners after Civil War Vainly Sought to Establish Brazilian Homes," *Dallas Morning News*, August 20, 1939, 8.

13. During the Civil War, Cortez Fielder was a private in the Captain Thomas J. Haynes Reserve Company, Beat No. 1, Navarro County, Texas, Nineteenth Brigade, Texas Militia. He enlisted in August, 1861. See Texas, Militia, Muster Rolls, Nineteenth Brigade, Texas State Archives, Austin. No service record or pre–Civil War information has been located on Zeno Fielder; additional data on emigrant families are included as they are introduced in this work. For estimates of numbers of families, see Frank McMullan to Joaquim Maria Nascentes de Azambuja, October 23, 1866, in *Revista de Imigração e Colonização* 4 (June 1943): 315. J. M. Nascentes de Azambuja wrote that sixty families were planning to emigrate from New Orleans. See J. M. Nascentes de Azambuja to Manoel Pinto de Souza Dantas, October 19, 1866, ibid., 307.

14. Frank McMullan to J. M. Nascentes de Azambuja, October 23, 1866, ibid., 315. The photograph of Frank McMullan was secured by the author from Rachel McMullan White, Providence, Rhode Island. White is the granddaughter of Ney McMullan, Frank McMullan's youngest brother. Rachel McMullan White, Needham, Massachusetts, to William C. Griggs, Lubbock, Texas, August 7, 1976, in possession of author.

15. J. M. Nascentes de Azambuja to Souza Dantas, September 20, 1866, in *Revista de Imigração e Colonização* 4 (June 1943): 305.

16. Ibid.

17. Frank McMullan to J. M. Nascentes de Azambuja, October 18, 1866, in ibid., 313–314; J. M. Nascentes de Azambuja to Souza Dantas, October 19, 1866, ibid.

18. Frank McMullan to J. M. Nascentes de Azambuja, October 18, 1866, ibid.

19. J. M. Nascentes de Azambuja to Souza Dantas, October 19, 1866, in ibid., 307. The person named Waley is identified as G. W. Waley, the former director of the colony of Assunguay. Waley sailed for New York on the *South America* on April 3, 1866. See Oliveira, *Movimento de Passageiros Norte-Americanos*, 15.

20. Frank McMullan to J. M. Nascentes de Azambuja, October 23, 1866, in ibid., 315–316.

21. Ibid.

22. Ibid.; J. M. Nascentes de Azambuja to Souza Dantas, October 21, 1866, in ibid., 311.

23. Cardwell left for Brazil to see the country in 1866 with plans to return to Texas by Christmas. Cardwell's colony, had its leader not decided against emigration to Brazil, would have left in April, 1867. Josephine Henry (Mrs. William Henry), Columbia, Brazoria County, Texas, to Aunt (Laura Perry?), (Madison, Georgia?), Laura L. Perry Papers, 1861–1891, Texas Collection, Baylor University; Galveston Tri-Weekly News, October 19, 1866, 1.

24. Frank McMullan, "Letter to the Editor," Galveston Tri-Weekly News, November 16, 1866, 3.

25. John Cardwell, "Letter to the Editor," ibid., December 16, 1866, 3.

26. Frank McMullan, "To My Friends in Texas, And To All Good Southerners Who Think of Going to Brazil," New Orleans Times, January 24, 1867, 4.

27. Walter Prescott Webb, ed., The Handbook of Texas, 1: 295.

28. J. M. Nascentes de Azambuja to Frank McMullan, November 16, 1866, Revista de Imigração e Colonização 4 (June 1943): 317.

29. Frank McMullan to J. M. Nascentes de Azambuja, November 6, 1866, ibid., 317–319.

30. Frank McMullan, "To My Friends in Texas"; Foreign Clearance, Ships Sailing from the Port of New Orleans, June, 1862, to January, 1875, Record Group 36, National Archives, Washington, D.C.; Works Progress Administration, Survey of Federal Archives in Louisiana: Passenger Lists Taken from the Manifests of the Customs Service, Port of New Orleans, 1864–1867 (carbon copy of typescript), 1941, p. 186-E, Louisiana Collection, Tulane University. A further search for information on both the Derby and Captain Causse has yielded little additional information; Frank McMullan to J. M. Nascentes de Azambuja, November 6, 1866, in Revista de Imigração e Colonização 4 (June 1943): 317–319.

31. Frank McMullan to J. M. Nascentes de Azambuja, November 6, 1866, in Revista de Imigração e Colonização 4 (June 1943): 317–319.

32. Ibid. An advertisement in the New Orleans Daily Picayune by Creeny on November 27, only a few days later, said that the company was "Forming a Regular Semi-Weekly Line of Fine Ocean Steamships" that would provide service to Brazil. For freight or passage, persons interested were to apply to William Creeny, Agent, 33 Carondelet Street, New Orleans. See the Daily Picayune, November 27, 1866, 4. By the date of the advertisement, however, McMullan already had returned to Texas.

33. J. M. Nascentes de Azambuja to Frank McMullan, November 17, 1866, in Revista de Imigração e Colonização 4 (June 1943): 319. Quintino de Souza Bocayuva arrived in New York in November, 1866, with B. Caymari, the Brazilian who negotiated the June 24, 1866, contract with C. K. Garrison and the United States and Brazil Steamship Company. J. M. Nascentes de Azambuja to Souza Dantas, November 27, 1866, ibid., 319–320.

34. "Emigration to Brazil," New York Times, November 25, 1866, 1; "Letter to the Editor," New York Tribune, November 30, 1866, 1.

35. "Emigration to Brazil," *New York Times*, November 25, 1866, 1; "Emigration to Brazil," *New York Tribune*, November 26, 1866, 1.

36. "The Emigration From the South Destined to Prove A Success," *New Orleans Times*, February 10, 1867, 3.

4. GATHERING AT GALVESTON

1. Millican, because of its railroad connection to the Gulf of Mexico, was an important shipping point during the Civil War. In 1867 it had a population of 600. It is located about twelve miles southeast of College Station, Texas. See Webb, ed., *The Handbook of Texas*, 2: 199; Ferguson, "Emigrating to Brazil in 1866−67."

2. Only a few scattered houses remained at the site of Spring Hill when visited by the author in 1978. It was Navarro County's oldest settlement, dating to 1838. See Webb, ed., *The Handbook of Texas*, 2: 564; Betty Antunes de Oliveira, Rio de Janeiro, to William C. Griggs, Canyon, Texas, August 3, 1979, in possession of author; William R. Bowen, Homesite on Ariado River, McMullan-Bowen Grant, to Joaquim Saldanha Marinha, President of the Province of São Paulo, São Paulo, Brazil, November 9, 1867, ord. [930], 29 fls., Archives of the State of São Paulo, São Paulo. This letter contains a census of the colony of that date prepared by Bowen for the president of the province. In subsequent citations it will be referred to as the Bowen Census. Alfred Iverson Smith was a private in a reserve company of the Nineteenth Brigade, Texas Militia, during the Civil War. This brigade was composed of men from Navarro, Ellis, Freestone, and Limestone counties. See Texas, Militia, Muster Roll, Reserved Company, Beat No. 5, Navarro County, August 17, 1861, Texas State Archives, Austin. Also see Ferguson, "Emigrating to Brazil in 1866−67"; Ferguson, "The American Colonies Emigrating to Brazil," December 18, 1866, 18. Other listings of members of the McMullan colony also show the Smith family. See Barnsley, "Original of Reply to a Circular." Also see a list by Martha Norris compiled on February 5, 1926, in Brannon, "Southern Emigration to Brazil," 81−82, hereafter referred to as the Norris List. Also see Thomas H. Steagall and others, "Lista de Americanos Vindos ao Brasil," in Goldman, *Os Pioneiros Americanos No Brasil*, 107, hereafter referred to as the Steagall List. Also see Alfredo Ellis, Jr., *Um Parlamentar Paulista Da Republica: Subsídos para a História da Republica em S. Paulo e Subsídos para a História Economica de São Paulo*, 41.

3. Ferguson, "Emigrating to Brazil in 1866−67." The Green family, like the Smiths, is included in Barnsley, "Original of Reply to a Circular"; Bowen Census; Ellis, *Um Parlamentar Paulista*. A photograph of one of the Greens is found in Judith McKnight Jones, *Soldado Descansa! Uma Epopéia Norte Americana Sob Os Céus Do Brasil*, 155.

4. Ferguson, "Emigrating to Brazil in 1866−67"; Bowen Census; Norris List; Steagall List; Barnsley, "Original of Reply to a Circular." Considerable information about Thomas Wright is available in Wright, *James Dyer*, [50−51]. The Wrights were distant relatives of the McMullans. A J. R. Wright is listed in

Texas, Militia, Muster Roll, Mile Creek Cavalry, Nineteenth Brigade, Texas State Troops, Ellis County, Texas, in Texas State Archives, Austin. In the same muster roll are listed two men, one of whom may have been the husband of widow Rachel Russell. One is named E. Russell; the other is Henry E. Russell.

5. Calvin McKnight's name appears in the land records of Hill County in the General Land Office, State of Texas, Austin. Thirty-six years old at the time of his enlistment in April, 1862, at Dresden, Navarro County, McKnight was described as five feet, ten inches in height, with gray eyes and black hair. A later photograph of McKnight shows him as a pleasant-looking man with large side-whiskers. See Jones, *Soldado Descansa!*, 118; Texas, Militia, Muster Roll, Volunteer Company of Mounted Men, Beat No. 8, Nineteenth Texas Brigade, Texas State Archives, Austin. McKnight is also shown in Norris List; Ellis, *Um Parlamentar Paulista;* Norris List; Steagall List; and Barnsley, "Original of Reply to a Circular." Military records of Thomas Steret McKnight may be found in Texas, Militia, Muster Roll, Nineteenth Brigade, Reserve Company, Beat No. 4, Navarro County, Texas State Archives, Austin.

6. Bowen Census; Steagall List; Ferguson, "Emigrating to Brazil in 1866–67."

7. George Scarborough Barnsley, "Foreign Colonization in Brazil; The American (and English) Attempt at Colonization in Brazil—1866–67," *Brazilian American* (Rio de Janeiro), March 10, 1928, 6; George Scarborough Barnsley, "Confederate Colonists Who Left Their Native Land for a Home in Brazil," *Courant-American* (Cartersville, Bartow County, Georgia), May 16, 1889 (this article is almost identical to the one Barnsley published in the *Brazilian-American*, cited above, in 1928); Ferguson, "Emigrating to Brazil in 1866–67."

8. Ibid.

9. Ferguson, "The American Colonies Emigrating to Brazil," December 18, 1866, 18.

10. *Daily Telegraph* (Houston, Texas), December 16, 1866, 4.

11. Ibid., December 13, 1866, 4.

12. *Galveston Daily News*, January 8, 1867, 2.

13. Frank McMullan, "To My Friends in Texas," 4.

14. Barnsley, "Foreign Colonization in Brazil," 6.

15. "Relação das cartas revebidas pela Legação e Consulado Brasileiros em o anno de 1865 de Habitantes das Estados Unidos que depois da guerra tem manifestado o desejo de emigrar para o Imperio," *Revista de Imigração e Colonização* 4 (June 1943): 280. Woodlands, the old estate of the Barnsley family, still exists as a ruin a few miles west of Adairsville, Georgia. In November, 1979, when visited by the author, it was owned by Earl McCleskey.

16. *Catalogue of the Officers, Alumni & Students of Oglethorpe University (Near Millidgeville), Georgia, 1857–1858* (Macon, Georgia: Lewis H. Andrews Book and Job Printing, 1858), 10; George Scarborough Barnsley, Rezendi, Province of Rio de Janeiro, to Julia Baltzelle (Barnsley's sister), Kingston, Georgia, September 14, 1879, Barnsley Papers, Tennessee State Library and Archives, Knoxville. Nelson Miles Hoffman, Jr., "Godfrey Barnsley, 1805–1873: British Cotton Factor in the South" (Ph.D. diss., University of Kansas, 1964). This

work is an excellent study of Godfrey Barnsley but touches only very marginally on the emigration of George and Lucian to Brazil.

17. George Scarborough Barnsley, Quatis de Barra Mansa, Province of Rio de Janeiro, to Julia Baltzelle, Kingston, Georgia, January 20, 1874, Barnsley Papers, Tennessee State Library and Archives, Knoxville.

18. Godfrey Barnsley, New Orleans, to Lucian Barnsley, Galveston, December 11, 1866, Barnsley Papers, Southern Historical Collection, University of North Carolina; *Gardner's New Orleans Directory for 1867*, 49; Godfrey Barnsley, New Orleans, to Lucian Barnsley, Galveston, December 11, 1866, Barnsley Papers, Southern Historical Collection, University of North Carolina; Godfrey Barnsley, New Orleans, to George Barnsley, Galveston, December 4, 1866, Barnsley Papers, Southern Historical Collection, University of North Carolina.

19. George Scarborough Barnsley, "Notes and Information about the Emigrants from the U. States of 1867–68," Barnsley Papers, Southern Historical Collection, University of North Carolina; Joaquim Maria Nascentes de Azambuja, New York, to J. S. Diggs, Cahaba, Alabama, January 12, 1867, in *Revista de Imigração e Colonização* 4 (June 1943): 325.

20. Clarence E. Moore (William Turner Moore's great-nephew), Fort Worth, Texas, to William C. Griggs, Lubbock, Texas, December 20, 1973, in possession of author; U.S. Department of the Interior, Census of 1860, Manuscript Population Schedules, McLennan County, Texas, Residence no. 276 (June 19, 1860), Microfilm Publication, National Archives, Washington, D.C.; Effie Smith Arnold (granddaughter of William T. Moore and Virginia McMullan Moore), interview with author, San Antonio, Texas, March 20, 1973.

21. Barnsley, "Notes and Information"; Frank McMullan, Galveston, to Joaquim Maria Nascentes de Azambuja, New York, January 6, 1867, in *Revista de Imigração e Colonização* 4 (June 1943): 327; Hill County, Texas, Affidavit of Jasper McMullan, Deed Records, 121 (April 29, 1909): 155–156.

22. Robert Shaw to Hugh McMullan, deed of 320 acres, Land Certificate 854, Robertson 3rd, January 6, 1855, File 3187 (Hill County, Texas), General Land Office, Austin.

23. U.S. Department of Interior, Census of 1860, Manuscript Population Schedules, Milam County, Texas, Residence no. 362, p. 1358; McLennan County, Probate Records, Vol. E, pp. 184–185. The probate records list one of the children as Susan, as does the Bowen Census, although the 1860 census lists her as Sarah.

24. Ferguson, "Emigrating to Brazil in 1866–67"; Bowen Census; Barnsley, "Notes and Information"; Barnsley, "Original of Reply to a Circular"; Ellis Bailey, *A History of Hill County, Texas 1838–1965*, 38. One of the Tarver children was named Ben F. Tarver. It is not known whether any connection existed, but Callender I. Fayssoux and other officers who served under William Walker in 1857 stayed in the home of a Ben F. Tarver in Alabama in 1858 after their capture and release. See Fayssoux, Notebook, ms. no. 136.

25. Bowen Census; Barnsley, "Notes and Information."

26. At one time, Frank McMullan listed some of the professions in the colony ranks, including farmers, stock raisers, mechanics, civil engineers,

ministers, schoolteachers, a physician, and former soldiers. "No politicians," he remarked. See Frank McMullan, "Loss of the Brig Derby," *Flake's Daily Galveston Bulletin*, March 6, 1867, 2; Bowen Census; Ferguson, "Emigrating to Brazil in 1866–67"; various state militia muster rolls in the Texas State Archives, Austin; McKenzie College Papers, Theological Library, Southern Methodist University; Barnsley, "Notes and Information."

27. *Galveston Daily News*, January 18, 1867, 3.

28. Frank McMullan, "To My Friends in Texas."

29. Ibid.

30. E. N. McMullan, "Texans Established Colony"; Ferguson, "The American Colonies Emigrating to Brazil," December 18, 1936, 18; Frank McMullan, "To My Friends in Texas."

31. Foreign Clearance, Ships Sailing from the Port of New Orleans, June, 1862, to January, 1875, Bound Volume, Record Group 36, National Archives, Washington, D.C.; Godfrey Barnsley, New Orleans, Louisiana, to Lucian Barnsley, Galveston, Texas, December 24, 1867, George S. Barnsley Papers, Southern Historical Collection, University of North Carolina.

32. Frank McMullan, "To My Friends in Texas"; "Wrecked Emigrants," *New York Times*, March 28, 1867, 2.

33. Barnsley, "Foreign Colonization in Brazil."

34. Frank McMullan, Galveston, Texas, to Joaquim Maria Nascentes de Azambuja, New York, January 6, 1867, in *Revista de Imigração e Colonização* 4 (June 1943): 327–328.

35. Ibid.

36. *Galveston Daily News*, January 8, 1867, 3.

37. George Scarborough Barnsley, "Notes on Brazil, Especially with reference to its adaptability to English and American Emigrants," George S. Barnsley Papers, Southern Historical Collection, University of North Carolina; *New Orleans Times*, November 15, 1866, 2.

38. *Daily Evening Bulletin* (*Flake's Evening Bulletin*, Galveston), January 22, 1867.

39. Ferguson, "The American Colonies Emigrating to Brazil," December 18, 1936; Ferguson, "Emigrating to Brazil in 1866–67."

40. Barnsley, "Foreign Colonization in Brazil."

41. *The South-Western* (Shreveport, Louisiana), September 13, 1865, 1; Lawrence F. Hill, *The Confederate Exodus to Latin America*, [18], cites a revised version of the poem from the New Orleans *Daily Picayune*, March 18, 1866, which was supposed to have come from the *Galveston Daily News*.

5. THE ISLES OF THE LOTUS EATERS

1. Frank McMullan, "Loss of the Brig Derby," 2; George Scarborough Barnsley, "Letter to the Editor of the New Orleans Times," February 15, 1867, in "Notebook," George S. Barnsley Papers, Southern Historical Collection, University of North Carolina. Other dates of sailing varied considerably. Eugene B. Smith set the date at February 22, 1867, and Sarah Bellona Smith Ferguson erroneously remembered, in different accounts, both March 18 and

January 22, 1867. See Eugene B. Smith, "Sailing Down to Rio in 1866–67," *Brazilian American* (Rio de Janeiro), March 9, 1931, 8–9; Ferguson, "Emigrating to Brazil in 1866–67."

2. Barnsley, "Foreign Colonization in Brazil," 6; Barnsley, "Confederate Colonists Who Left their Native Land."

3. Ibid.

4. Ibid.

5. Ibid. Also see E. N. McMullan, "Texans Established Colony"; Barnsley, "Letter to the Editor of the New Orleans Times."

6. Barnsley, "Letter to the Editor of the New Orleans Times"; Barnsley, "Foreign Colonization in Brazil."

7. Barnsley, "Foreign Colonization in Brazil"; E. N. McMullan, "Texans Established Colony."

8. Ibid.

9. Frank McMullan, "Loss of the Brig Derby," attributes the shortage of drinking water to leakage of casks. Barnsley, "Letter to the Editor of the New Orleans Times," says only two casks of water were on board. Ferguson, "The American Colonies Emigrating to Brazil," December 18, 1936, 18–19; Barnsley, "Foreign Colonization in Brazil," says that adequate water was available for only five days. The same writer, in "Letter to the Editor of the New Orleans Times," says there was enough for fourteen days. The five-day figure is more believable. If water for two weeks had been available, there would have been little or no need for concern.

10. Barnsley, "Foreign Colonization in Brazil"; Barnsley, "Letter to the Editor of the New Orleans Times."

11. Barnsley, "Foreign Colonization in Brazil."

12. Ibid.

13. Ibid.

14. Ferguson, "The American Colonies Emigrating to Brazil"; Frank McMullan, "Loss of the Brig Derby"; Barnsley, "Foreign Colonization in Brazil."

15. E. N. McMullan, "Texans Established Colony"; Barnsley, "Foreign Colonization in Brazil"; Ferguson, "The American Colonies Emigrating to Brazil"; Barnsley, "Letter to the Editor of the New Orleans Times."

16. Smith, "Sailing Down to Rio."

17. Barnsley, "Foreign Colonization in Brazil."

18. E. N. McMullan, "Texans Established Colony."

19. Ferguson, "The American Colonies Emigrating to Brazil."

20. Frank McMullan, "Loss of the Brig Derby."

21. E. N. McMullan, "Texans Established Colony." It is interesting that Frank McMullan mentions neither the lifeboat incident nor the trip to the captain's cabin with drawn pistols. Both accounts come from very reliable narratives. It is likely that McMullan did not want to be accused of mutiny and did not want to make any statement that might be considered an admission of such.

22. E. N. McMullan, "Texans Established Colony."

23. Frank McMullan, "Loss of the Brig Derby"; Ferguson, "The American Colonies Emigrating to Brazil."

24. Barnsley, "Foreign Colonization in Brazil."

25. Ibid.; Smith, "Sailing Down to Rio"; Frank McMullan, "Loss of the Brig Derby."

26. Frank McMullan, "Loss of the Brig Derby."

6. A HANKERING FOR BRAZIL

1. George Scarborough Barnsley, Plaza de Banes, Cuba, to Godfrey Barnsley, Bartow County, Georgia, February 19, 1867, George S. Barnsley Papers, Manuscript Department, William R. Perkins Library, Duke University. Bahia Honda is a small bay on the northwest coast of Cuba. A July 2, 1903, agreement allowed the United States to lease Bahia Honda along with Guantanamo Bay. However, the lease option on the former was allowed to lapse. See U.S. Department of the Interior, *Boundaries, Areas, Geographic Centers and Altitudes of the United States and the Several States*, 2d ed., Geographical Survey Bulletin 817, 56.

2. George Barnsley to Godfrey Barnsley, February 19, 1867, George S. Barnsley Papers, Duke University; E. N. McMullan, "Texans Established Colony"; Frank McMullan, "Loss of the Brig Derby," 2.

3. Ferguson, "The American Colonies Emigrating to Brazil," December 18, 1936, 19; E. N. McMullan, "Texans Established Colony."

4. E. N. McMullan, "Texans Established Colony"; also see Barnsley, "Letter to the Editor of the New Orleans Times"; Frank McMullan, "Loss of the Brig Derby"; Ferguson, "The American Colonies Emigrating to Brazil," December 18, 1936, 19; Barnsley, "Foreign Colonization in Brazil," 8.

5. Ferguson, "The American Colonies Emigrating to Brazil," December 18, 1936, 19.

6. George Barnsley to Godfrey Barnsley, February 19, 1867, Barnsley Papers, Duke University.

7. Ferguson, "The American Colonies Emigrating to Brazil," December 18, 1936, 19; Ferguson, "Emigrating to Brazil in 1866–67"; Frank McMullan, "Loss of Brig Derby"; George Barnsley to Godfrey Barnsley, February 19, 1867, Barnsley Papers, Duke University. A sketch of Vermay's home also appeared in George Barnsley's February 19, 1867, letter.

8. Barnsley, "Letter to the Editor of the New Orleans Times."

9. Ibid.; Barnsley, "Foreign Colonization in Brazil," 8.

10. Frank McMullan, "Loss of the Brig Derby"; Barnsley, "Letter to the Editor of the New Orleans Times"; Barnsley, "Foreign Colonization in Brazil," 8; E. N. McMullan, "Texans Established Colony."

11. Frank McMullan, "Loss of the Brig Derby"; George Barnsley to Godfrey Barnsley, February 19, 1867, Barnsley Papers, Duke University; Barnsley, "Letter to the Editor of the New Orleans Times"; Fernando de Gávez e Fínaz, Consul General of Portugal in the Archipelago of the Spanish Antilles, Havana, to the Minister Plenipotentiary of the Empire of Brazil in the United States, New York, February 13, 1867, in *Revista de Imigração e Colonização* 4 (June 1943): 329–330.

12. Barnsley, "Letter to the Editor of the New Orleans Times"; Frank McMullan, "Loss of the Brig Derby."

13. United States, National Archives, *List of Passengers Arriving in New York, 1820–1897*, Microfilm Publication, Microcopy 237, Roll 268; Quintino de Souza Bocayuva, Agent for Emigration for Brazil, New York, to Henrique Cavalcanti de Albuquerque, Director of Trade of Brazil with the United States, New York, February 19, 1867, in *Revista de Imigração e Colonização* 4 (June 1943): 330–331.

14. Quintino de Souza Bocayuva to Henrique Cavalcanti de Albuquerque, February 19, 1867, in *Revista de Imigração e Colonização* 4 (June 1943): 330–331.

15. Henrique Cavalcanti de Albuquerque, New York, to Quintino de Souza Bocayuva, New York, February 20, 1867, in *Revista de Imigração e Colonização* 4 (June 1943): 332.

16. Henrique Cavalcanti de Albuquerque, New York, to Antonio Coelho de Sá e Albuquerque, Rio de Janeiro, February 22, 1867, in *Revista de Imigração e Colonização* 4 (June 1943): 328–329.

17. Frank McMullan, "Loss of the Brig Derby."

18. Barnsley, "Letter to the Editor of the New Orleans Times"; George Barnsley to Godfrey Barnsley, February 19, 1867, Barnsley Papers, Duke University.

19. Julia Baltzelle, Bartow County, Georgia, to Godfrey Barnsley, New Orleans, February 16, 1867, Godfrey Barnsley Papers, Robert W. Woodruff Library for Advanced Studies, Emory University; C. Berrian, Rome, Georgia, to Godfrey Barnsley, New Orleans, March 1, 1867, Godfrey Barnsley Papers, Manuscript Department, William R. Perkins Library, Duke University.

20. George Barnsley to Godfrey Barnsley, February 19, 1867, Barnsley Papers, Duke University.

21. Ferguson, "The American Colonies Emigrating to Brazil," December 18, 1836, 19; George Barnsley to Godfrey Barnsley, February 19, 1867, Barnsley Papers, Duke University.

22. Ibid.

23. J. P. Baltzelle, Bartow County, Georgia, to Godfrey Barnsley, New Orleans, March 18, 1867, Barnsley Papers, Emory University.

24. "The Brig Derby," *Flake's Daily Galveston Bulletin*, February 23, 1867, 3.

25. Wright, *James Dyer*, [51]. Thomas Wright moved to Comanche County, Texas, in 1870. He died there on August 6, 1880. See ibid., [40]. Causse sailed on the schooner *Mischief*, M. Oliphant, Master, and arrived in New Orleans on March 18. See U.S. Works Progress Administration, Survey of Federal Archives in Louisiana, Passenger Lists Taken From Manifests of the Customs Service, Port of New Orleans, 1864–1867, typescript, 1941, p. 186-E, Louisiana Collection, Library, Tulane University; Barnsley, "Foreign Colonization in Brazil."

26. Barnsley, "Letter to the Editor of the New Orleans Times." A later account by the press lowered this figure to one-half and stated that the amount salvaged was so damaged by seawater that it was almost worthless. See

"Wrecked Emigrants," *New York Times*, March 28, 1867, 2; Ferguson, "Emigrating to Brazil in 1866–67"; Barnsley, "Notes and Information about the Emigrants from the U. States."

27. Wright, *James Dyer*, p. [57]; E. N. McMullan, "Texans Established Colony"; Frank McMullan, "Loss of the Brig Derby."

28. Frank McMullan, "Loss of the Brig Derby."

29. Ibid.

30. Barnsley, "Letter to the Editor of the New Orleans Times."

31. Ibid.; "Wrecked Emigrants"; E. N. McMullan, "Texans Established Colony"; Ferguson, "The American Colonies Emigrating to Brazil," December 18, 1936, 19.

32. "Wrecked Emigrants"; George Barnsley, "A letter [undated], published in Havana Papers, about the time we left that city for New York, to resume the voyage to Brazil (at request, by Dr. Barnsley)," "Notebook," hereafter cited as "Letter Published in Havana Papers"; Frank McMullan, "Loss of the Brig Derby."

33. Ferguson, "The American Colonies Emigrating to Brazil," December 18, 1936, 19.

34. Ibid.; George Barnsley recalled the meal at Guanajay as a "public dinner." See Barnsley, "Foreign Colonization in Brazil."

35. Ibid.

36. "Wrecked Emigrants"; George Barnsley, Havana, to Godfrey Barnsley, Bartow County, Georgia, March 1, 1867, Barnsley Papers, Duke University.

37. Ferguson, "The American Colonies Emigrating to Brazil," December 18, 1936, 19; Barnsley, "Foreign Colonization in Brazil"; Barnsley, "Letter Published in Havana Papers." It is not known why Barnsley referred to the consul of Portugal as Don Fernando de Gavare Toscar. All other evidence names Fernando de Gávez e Fínaz.

38. Departures from the Port of New Orleans, U.S. Vessels Cleared July 1865 to Aug. 1886, Record Group 36, National Archives, Washington, D.C. Also see *Daily Picayune* (New Orleans), November 27, 1866.

39. Barnsley, "Foreign Colonization in Brazil."

40. Ibid.; Ferguson, "The American Colonies Emigrating to Brazil," December 18, 1936, 19; E. N. McMullan, "Texans Established Colony"; Ferguson, "Emigrating to Brazil in 1866–67"; Smith, "Sailing Down to Rio in 1866–67," 8.

41. Ferguson, "The American Colonies Emigrating to Brazil," December 18, 1936, 19.

42. Smith, "Sailing Down to Rio"; "Marine Intelligence," *New York Times*, March 27, 1867, 5; "Wrecked Emigrants."

43. Ferguson, "The American Colonies Emigrating to Brazil," December 18, 1936, 19.

44. "Texas Brazilians," *Galveston Daily News*, April 1, 1867, 2.

45. George Barnsley, New York, to Godfrey Barnsley, Bartow County, Georgia, March 27, 1867, Barnsley Papers, Duke University.

46. Barnsley, "Foreign Colonization in Brazil."

47. Ibid.; Ferguson, "The American Colonies Emigrating to Brazil," December 18, 1936, 19.

48. "Marine Intelligence."

7. THE PROMISED LAND

1. "Wrecked Emigrants," 2; George Barnsley, New York, to Godfrey Barnsley, Bartow County, Georgia, March 27, 1867, Barnsley Papers, Duke University.

2. "Wrecked Emigrants." There is little question but that the "tall youth" mentioned in the article who was reported to be dying of consumption was Frank McMullan.

3. Ferguson, "Emigrating to Brazil in 1866–67."

4. Ibid. The *Mobile Daily News*, April 3, 1867, reported that 350 Texas emigrants bound for Brazil were stranded in New York. Also see Ferguson, "The American Colonies Emigrating to Brazil," December 18, 1936, 19–20.

5. George Barnsley to Godfrey Barnsley, March 27, 1867, Barnsley Papers, Duke University.

6. Ibid.

7. George Barnsley, New York, to Godfrey Barnsley, Bartow County, Georgia, April 17, 1867, Barnsley Papers, Duke University.

8. Ferguson, "The American Colonies Emigrating to Brazil," December 18, 1936, 20.

9. Ibid., 19.

10. The *North America* was originally constructed by Sneeden, New York City, in 1851. Its tonnage was 1,440 pounds, and it had a vertical beam engine with a cylinder diameter of 66 inches and a stroke of 12 feet. See James P. Baughman, *Charles Morgan and the Development of Southern Transportation*, 243. The *North America* arrived in New York from Rio de Janeiro on March 23, 1867, commanded by Louis F. Timmerman. See United States, National Archives, *Passenger Lists of Vessels Arriving at New York, 1820–1897*, Microfilm Publication, Roll 276, Microcopy 237, February 12–March 20, 1867 (List nos. 105–206). Also see George Barnsley to Godfrey Barnsley, April 17, 1867, Barnsley Papers, Duke University; James McFadden Gaston to Dr. H. A. Shaw, April 2, 1867, as printed in the Atlanta *Constitutionalist*, April 6, 1867.

11. George Barnsley to Godfrey Barnsley, April 17, 1867, Barnsley Papers, Duke University; *Dallas Herald*, June 8, 1867, 1.

12. The Irish, according to some observers, were one of the main reasons that it was generally reported that the "Americans" were destitute in Brazil. See Lucian Barnsley, Teite, Province of São Paulo, to Godfrey Barnsley, Bartow County, Georgia, August 5, 1871, Barnsley Papers, Duke University.

13. Barnsley, "Foreign Colonization in Brazil"; George Barnsley, Rio de Janeiro, to Godfrey Barnsley, Bartow County, Georgia, May 23, 1867, Barnsley Papers, Duke University.

14. Ferguson, "The American Colonies Emigrating to Brazil," December 18, 1936, 20.

15. Barnsley, "Foreign Colonization in Brazil," 9. Five *contos* amounted to approximately $2,500 in U.S. currency. See Keyes, "Our Life in Brazil," 274.

16. Ferguson, "Emigrating to Brazil in 1866–67."

17. George Barnsley to Godfrey Barnsley, May 23, 1867, Barnsley Papers, Duke University.

18. The "palace" in which the colonists were lodged, also known as the Casa de Saúde, was located on the Morro de Saúde, on the north side of the old main city. An address for the "hospice for emigrants," 173 Rua de Imperatriz, was noted in the *Diário Oficial Do Império*, June 10, 1867. Even with the address, however, the site of the mansion is difficult to locate because of the major changes, including renaming of streets, that have occurred in Rio de Janeiro in the past 120 years. An inspection and search of the area revealed that the chapel is still intact, but that the house itself is gone. The old iron gate is still intact, however, and the winding road to the top of the hill is still in partial use. Even with a physical inspection of the area, however, the site was not identified with certainty until the completion of exhaustive research by Betty Antunes de Oliveira of Rio de Janeiro. See Betty Antunes de Oliveira to William C. Griggs, April 10, April 12, April 30, May 19, and August 7, 1986, in possession of author. The best contemporary description of the house is in Keyes, "Our Life in Brazil," 142. Also see Brannon, "Southern Emigration to Brazil," 95. Brannon states that Colonel Broome, employed by Brazil to manage the hospice, was probably from La Grange, Georgia, and that he was termed "very gallant." Also see E. N. McMullan, "Texans Established Colony."

19. Keyes, "Our Life in Brazil," 139.

20. Ibid.

21. A diary of the journey of the *Marmion* may be found in Brannon, "Southern Emigration To Brazil." Also see George Barnsley to Godfrey Barnsley, May 23, 1867, Barnsley Papers, Duke University; Sarah Bellona Smith Ferguson, "Emigrating to Brazil," *Farm and Ranch* (Dallas), December 2, 1916; E. N. McMullan, "Texans Established Colony"; Ferguson, "Emigrating to Brazil in 1866–67."

22. Ferguson, "Emigrating to Brazil in 1866–67"; Keyes, "Our Life in Brazil," 140–141; Josephine Foster, Letter to the Editor, *New Orleans Times*, April 26, 1868, as quoted in Lawrence F. Hill, "The Confederate Exodus to South America," *Southwestern Historical Quarterly* 39 (October 1935, January 1936, and April 1936): 113.

23. Keyes, "Our Life in Brazil," 140–142.

24. George Barnsley to Godfrey Barnsley, May 23, 1867, Barnsley Papers, Duke University.

25. Barnsley, "Original of Reply to a Circular"; Ferguson, "The American Colonies Emigrating to Brazil," December 18, 1936, 20.

26. Ferguson, "Emigrating to Brazil in 1866–67."

27. Ibid.

28. Barnsley, "Notes and Information about the Emigrants from the U. States."

29. Ibid.; Dunn, *Brazil, The Home for Southerners*, 70; Barnsley, "Notes and Information about the Emigrants from the U. States." It is of interest that as

early as November, 1866, the Demaret family made arrangements for transportation to Iguape. A note in the *Diário Oficial Do Império*, November 24, 1866, authorized the first ship from Rio de Janeiro to Iguape to carry "Sra. Demaret, three adult sons, and three minor children to Iguape."

30. George Barnsley to Godfrey Barnsley, May 23, 1867, Barnsley Papers, Duke University; Ferguson, "The American Colonies Emigrating to Brazil," December 18, 1936, 20.

31. Ibid.; Ferguson, "Emigrating to Brazil in 1866–67."

32. Ibid.; George Barnsley, Rio de Janeiro, to Godfrey Barnsley, Bartow County, Georgia, June 14, 1867, Barnsley Papers, Duke University; Barnsley, "Original of Reply to a Circular."

33. Ibid.

8. UNDER THE SOUTHERN CROSS

1. It is unlikely that any McMullan colonists other than Barnsley and Dyer (and their families) were briefed by McMullan concerning the Aranzel legend and the possibility of gold on the McMullan grant, although they could have heard of it from residents of the region. J. M. Keith undoubtedly learned of the legend from George Barnsley and worked with Barnsley for years in the search for minerals on the property. Other McMullan colonists such as John "Dad" McMains searched for gold in Brazil, but evidence does not suggest that they knew about the stories of mineral wealth on the McMullan grant itself.

2. José Hygino Xavier, Accountant of the Plantation of São Paulo, Accounting Report, March 5, 1867, Archives of the State of São Paulo, São Paulo, Brazil; José Joaquim de Oliveira, Department of Public Lands and Colonization of the State of São Paulo, São Paulo, to José Tavares Bastos, President of the Province of São Paulo, São Paulo, March 12, 1867, Archives of the State of São Paulo; José Tavares Bastos to Manoel Pinto de Souza Dantas, Minister of the Secretary of Agriculture, Commerce, and Public Works, Rio de Janeiro, March 13, 1867, Register Book of Correspondence of the Governor with the Minister of Agriculture, Commerce, and Public Works, 1861–1869, Archives of the State of São Paulo. The complete survey of the McMullan-Bowen grant is located in the Historical Section of the National Archives of Brazil, Rio de Janeiro. A Brazilian league is about three miles.

3. "1867—Jornal Do Lucian Barnsley," copied by George Barnsley in "Notes and Memoranda from old pocket note-books," George S. Barnsley Papers, Harold Barnsley Holland Collection, Jacareí, São Paulo State.

4. Ibid.

5. Ibid.

6. Ibid.

7. Ibid.; in December, 1866, the Minister of Fazenda of the empire was authorized (probably by the legislature) to pay 3:500$000 (3,500 *contos*) for the construction of a house for William Bowen and his partner Frank McMullan in the Province of São Paulo. See *Diário Oficial Do Império*, December 27, 1866. It is of interest that the same periodical, on June 28, 1867, authorized

another payment of the same amount to William Bowen without mentioning McMullan.

8. "1867—Jornal Do Lucian Barnsley."

9. Ibid.

10. Ibid.

11. Ferguson, "Emigrating to Brazil in 1866–67"; Ferguson, "The American Colonies Emigrating to Brazil," September 18, 1936, 21. Information on J. Thomas Cook, his wife Ann, and their children may be found in Ferguson, "Emigrating to Brazil in 1866–67"; Jones, *Soldado Descansa!*, 133, 139.

12. Jones, *Soldado Descansa!*, 133, 139.

13. Ibid.

14. Ibid. According to Sarah Bellona Smith Ferguson, Wilmot later established a cotton gin, or "factory," near Vila Americana. See Ferguson, "Emigrating to Brazil in 1866–67."

15. Ibid.

16. Ibid. Jacob Wingutter is well established as a member of the McMullan colony. He, his wife Susan, and their daughter Amy are included in a listing by Sarah Bellona Smith Ferguson in "Emigrating to Brazil in 1866–67." Also see Barnsley, "Original of Reply to a Circular"; Barnsley, "Notes and Information about the Emigrants from the U. States." According to Barnsley, Wingutter married again in later years to a Brazilian and became a colporteur, selling Bibles and religious tracts. Richard Ratcliff, a Baptist minister, and his wife Eunice are well-documented members of the McMullan group. Like Wingutter, they are listed in Ferguson, "Emigrating to Brazil in 1866–67." Also see Brannon, "Southern Emigration to Brazil," 81–82; Steagall and others, "Lista de Americanos Vindos ao Brasil," Goldman, *Os Pioneiros Americanos No Brasil*, 107; Jones, *Soldado Descansa!*, 101, 133, 201, 202, 216, 244.

17. Ferguson, "Emigrating to Brazil in 1866–67"; Ferguson, "The American Colonies Emigrating to Brazil," December 18, 1936, 21.

18. Ferguson, "The American Colonies Emigrating to Brazil," December 18, 1936, 41.

19. Ibid.

20. Ibid.

21. Ferguson, "Emigrating to Brazil in 1866–67."

22. Ibid.; Ferguson, "The American Colonies Emigrating to Brazil," December 18, 1936, 41.

23. George Barnsley, Iguape, São Paulo Province, to Godfrey Barnsley, Bartow County, Georgia, July 13, 1867, Barnsley Papers, Duke University.

24. Ibid. *Pinga* is also known as *cachaça*, and a celebration is held in Paratý every year called the Festival da Cachaça, or the Festival da Pinga de Paratý. The author was present at one of these events in 1983.

25. Frank McMullan and William Bowen, Morro Redondo, on the Juquiá River, São Paulo Province, to José Tavares Bastos, President of São Paulo Province, São Paulo, June 13, 1867, in a letter from Antonio Augusto de Costa Aguiar, São Paulo, to Joaquim Saldanha Marinha, November 28, 1867, Archives of the State of São Paulo.

26. Frank McMullan and William Bowen, Morro Redondo, on the Juquiá

River, São Paulo Province, to the President (José Tavares Bastos) and Members of the Provincial Legislative Assembly, São Paulo, June 17, 1867, in a letter from Antonio Augosto de Costa Aguiar to Joaquim Saldanha Marinha, November 28, 1867, Archives of the State of São Paulo, São Paulo.

27. Frank McMullan, Casa de Col. Bowen, to Dr. Octaviano da Rocha (home on the Juquiá River, São Paulo Province), July 8, 1867, Historical Section, National Archives of Brazil, Rio de Janeiro.

28. Antonio Augosto de Costa Aguiar to Joaquim Saldanha Marinha, November 28, 1867; Barnsley, "Foreign Colonization in Brazil," 28.

29. Barnsley, "Foreign Colonization in Brazil"; George Barnsley, "Notes on Brazil: Especially With Reference to its adaptibility to English and American Emigrants," Barnsley Papers, University of North Carolina.

30. Ibid.

31. The Two Republics, November 27, 1867, as quoted by Frank A. Knapp, Jr., "A New Source on the Confederate Exodus to Mexico: The Two Republics," Journal of Southern History 19 (February 1953): 372; Josephine Foster, Gunter Colony, Espiritu Santo Province, to the Editor of the New Orleans Times, April 26, 1868.

32. Ferguson, "The American Colonies Emigrating to Brazil," December 18, 1836, 20.

33. Ferguson, "Emigrating to Brazil in 1866–67"; Ferguson, "The American Colonies Emigrating to Brazil," December 18, 1936, 41; Ferguson, "Emigrating to Brazil," December 2, 1916.

34. Ibid.

35. Ibid.; Ferguson, "The American Colonies Emigrating to Brazil," December 18, 1936, 41.

36. Ferguson, "Emigrating to Brazil," December 2, 1916.

37. The New Orleans Daily Picayune, November 2, 1867, carried a news brief about Bowen's marriage: "Southerners going to Brazil will have a good crop of children," the newspaper editorialized. "Col. Bowen is about to lead to the altar a blooming rosebud of Brazil. He has joined the Roman Catholic Church." Also see Ferguson, "Emigrating to Brazil in 1866–67."

38. "Articles Taken From a Brazilian Newspaper Shortly Before the Centennial of the Arrival of the Americans in Brazil," typescript included in a letter from Nattie Quillin Jacobs (Elijah H. Quillin's granddaughter), Ontario, California, to William C. Griggs, Canyon, Texas, March 3, 1980, in possession of author; Ferguson, "Emigrating to Brazil in 1866–67."

39. Ferguson, "Emigrating to Brazil in 1866–67."

40. Ferguson, "The American Colonies Emigrating to Brazil," December 24, 1936, 14.

41. Ferguson, "Emigrating to Brazil in 1866–67"; Joaquim Saldanha Marinha, President of São Paulo Province, São Paulo, to Manoel Pinto de Souza Dantas, Minister of the Secretary of Agriculture, Commerce, and Public Works, Rio de Janeiro, November 7, 1867, Oficio no. 111, Livro (Letterbook of Joaquim Saldanha Marinha), p. 227, Archives of the State of São Paulo, São Paulo.

42. Ferguson, "The American Colonies Emigrating to Brazil," December

18, 1936, 41. A *caboclo* is a mestizo of mixed white and Indian blood. See *Brazil 1940/41: An Economic, Social, and Geographic Survey*, 26.

43. Ferguson, "Emigrating to Brazil in 1866–67"; Corsicana *Observer*, quoted in *Flake's Semi-Weekly Bulletin* (Galveston, Texas), December 25, 1867.

44. Ferguson, "The American Colonies Emigrating to Brazil," December 18, 1936, 20.

45. Ibid.

46. *A Memorial and Biographical History of Johnson and Hill Counties, Texas*, 215.

47. Guilherme (William) Bowen, American Settlement, São Lourenço River, São Paulo Province (November 9, 1867), to His Excellency, the Minister of Agriculture of the Empire of Brazil (Antonio Francisco de Paula e Souza), Archives of the State of São Paulo, São Paulo.

48. Guilherme (William) Bowen, American Settlement, São Lourenço River, São Paulo Province, to the President of São Paulo (Joaquim Saldanha Marinha), São Paulo, November 10, 1867, Archives of the State of São Paulo, São Paulo.

49. Ibid.

50. Barnsley, "Notes and Information about the Emigrants from the U. States."

51. Antonio Augusto de Costa Aguiar to Joaquim Saldanha Marinha, November 10, 1867, Archives of the State of São Paulo, São Paulo.

52. Barnsley, "Notes and Information about the Emigrants from the U. States"; U.S. Works Progress Administration, Survey of Federal Archives in Louisiana, p. 186-E, Louisiana Collection, Library, Tulane University.

9. LIFE IN EL DORADO

1. Godfrey Barnsley, Bartow County, Georgia, to George Barnsley, Iguape, São Paulo Province, Brazil, December 12, 1867, Barnsley Papers, Duke University; George Barnsley, Iguape, São Paulo Province, to Godfrey Barnsley, Bartow County, Georgia, February 6, 1868, Barnsley Papers, Duke University; George Barnsley, Iguape, São Paulo Province, to Godfrey Barnsley, Bartow County, Georgia, March 9, 1868, Barnsley Papers, Duke University.

2. The directions to the Lake of Gold are outlined in "The Lake of Gold," *Brazilian Bulletin* 1, no. 2 (September 1898): 88–89.

3. Richardson, *Adventuring with a Purpose*, 5–6. For information concerning the purchase of lands by Dyer and Wasson, see W. S. Dyer, C. L. Wasson, and Helen Domm Curry, Power of Attorney to E. N. McMullan, Hill County, Texas, February 8, 1916, in possession of Rachel McMullan White, Cumberland, Rhode Island.

4. Richardson, *Adventuring with a Purpose*, 5–6; George Barnsley, Iguape, São Paulo Province, to Godfrey Barnsley, Bartow County, Georgia, May 24, 1868, Barnsley Papers, Duke University.

5. Ferguson, "The American Colonies Emigrating to Brazil," December 24, 1936, 14; Ferguson, "Emigrating to Brazil in 1866–67."

6. Ferguson, "Emigrating to Brazil in 1866–67."

7. Ibid.
8. Ibid.
9. Ibid. *Cará* is actually *cará taro*, a staple foodstuff introduced from Africa. "Parvilha" is *polvilho*, a product of manioc. *Canja* is a corn dish. See *Brazil 1940/41: An Economic, Social, and Geographic Survey*, 26.
10. Ferguson, "Emigrating to Brazil in 1866–67."
11. Ferguson, "The American Colonies Emigrating to Brazil," December 24, 1936, 15.
12. Ibid.
13. Ferguson, "Emigrating to Brazil in 1866–67."
14. Ferguson, "The American Colonies Emigrating to Brazil," December 24, 1936, 15.
15. Ibid., 20; Ferguson, "Emigrating to Brazil in 1866–67."
16. Ibid.
17. A passenger list of the *Guerriere* is found in *Flake's Semi-Weekly Bulletin* (Galveston), July 3, 1869. Also see U.S. Works Progress Administration, Survey of Federal Archives in Louisiana, 239; Ferguson, "Emigrating to Brazil in 1866–67"; Oliveira, *Movimento de Passageiros Norte-Americanos*, 98–99.
18. Carlos Nathan and Manoel Pinto de Souza Dantas, Minister and Secretary of State of the Business of Agriculture, Commerce, and Public Works, "Contracto celebrado entre o Governo Imperial de uma parte e Carlos Nathan da outra, para o transporte de mil familias procedents dos Estados do Sul da Uniao Americana, por vapores dos portos abaixos declaradas," July 23, 1867, *Lata 632, Pasta 72*, Archives of the Brazilian Institute of History and Geography, Rio de Janeiro.
19. George Barnsley, Iguape, São Paulo Province, to Godfrey Barnsley, Bartow County, Georgia, June 22, 1868, Barnsley Papers, Duke University.
20. These figures are derived from a variety of sources, but principally from Guilherme (William) Bowen, American Settlement, São Lorenso [*sic*] River, to His Excellency, the President of São Paulo (Joaquim Saldanha Marinha), November 9, 1867, Archives of the State of São Paulo, São Paulo; Ferguson, "Emigrating to Brazil in 1866–67"; George Scarborough Barnsley, "List of the Names and Families of the American Emigrants on the River Juquia," in "Original of Reply to a Circular."

10. STRAITENED FORTUNES AND BAPTIZED SOULS

1. Cicero Jones, Vila Americana, State of São Paulo, to J. N. Heiskell, Little Rock, Arkansas, September 25, 1915, J. N. Heiskell Library, *Arkansas Gazette Foundation*, Little Rock.
2. Henry O. McKnight, Santa Barbara, State of São Paulo, interview with Mary Helen Clark, São Paulo, State of São Paulo, notes of interview, c. 1939, Blanche Henry Clark Weaver Papers, in possession of author. This note states that "Tom McKnight had the first iron plow in São Paulo, others used wooden plows. He also had a still and for the first time, perhaps, whiskey was made in Brazil." Also see *Brazil 1940/41: An Economic, Social, and Geographic Survey*, 98.

3. Richard Ratcliff and W. H. (Robert) Meriwether, Santa Barbara, São Paulo Province, to Corresponding Secretary, Foreign Mission Board, Southern Baptist Convention, Richmond, Virginia, January 11, 1873, in Henry Allen Tupper, *The Foreign Missions of the Southern Baptist Convention,* 10.

4. Robert Meriwether, Robert Broadnax, and David Davis, Santa Barbara, São Paulo Province, to (Corresponding Secretary, Foreign Mission Board, Richmond, Virginia), n.d., in Tupper, *Foreign Missions,* 10–11.

5. Richard Ratcliff, Minden, Louisiana, to H. A. Tupper, Richmond, Virginia, October 1, 1878, in Tupper, *Foreign Missions,* 12–13, 479; "Report of the Committee on New Fields," *Proceedings of the Southern Baptist Convention* [1879], 54.

6. Tupper, *Foreign Missions,* 12–13; "Report of the Committee on New Fields," *Proceedings,* 54; Tupper, *Foreign Missions,* 13–14, 479; "The Station Baptist Church," *Proceedings of the Southern Baptist Convention* [1880], 51.

7. R. P. Thomas, Santa Barbara, São Paulo Province, to Henry A. Tupper, Richmond, Virginia, April 26, 1886, Serials Department, Library, Southwestern Baptist Theological Seminary, Fort Worth.

8. Betty Antunes de Oliveira, *North American Immigration to Brazil: Tombstone Records of the "Campo" Cemetery, Santa Barbara D'Oeste—São Paulo State, Brazil,* 11.

9. Lucian Barnsley, Tatuhy, São Paulo Province, to Godfrey Barnsley, Bartow County, Georgia, September 11, 1870, Barnsley Papers, Duke University.

10. George Barnsley, Tiete, São Paulo Province, to Godfrey Barnsley, Bartow County, Georgia, March 10, 1871, Barnsley Papers, Duke University; Lucian Barnsley, Tiete, São Paulo Province, to Godfrey Barnsley, Bartow County, Georgia, March 28, 1871, Barnsley Papers, Duke University.

11. Hill, "Confederate Exiles to Brazil," 192–210; U.S. Congress, "Papers Relating to the Foreign Relations of the United States," 42d Cong., 3d sess., *House Executive Document 1,* 90–91; Weaver, "Confederate Emigration to Brazil," 51–53.

12. "The Self-Exiled Southerners: Terrible Sufferings of the Planters Who Went to Brazil," *New York Times,* May 21, 1871.

13. Ibid.; Barnsley, "Notes and Information about the Emigrants from the U. States"; George Barnsley, Quatis de Barra Mansa, Rio de Janeiro Province, to Godfrey Barnsley, Bartow County, Georgia, September 29, 1871, Barnsley Papers, Duke University.

14. George Barnsley, Quatis de Barra Mansa, Rio de Janeiro Province, to the Editor of the *New Orleans Times,* August 20, 1871, Barnsley Papers, Duke University.

15. Lucian Barnsley, Tiete, São Paulo Province, to Godfrey Barnsley, Bartow County, Georgia, August 5, 1871, Barnsley Papers, Duke University; Lucian Barnsley, Tatuhy, São Paulo Province, to Godfrey Barnsley, Bartow County, Georgia, April 27, 1870, Barnsley Papers, Duke University.

16. *Dallas Herald,* June 8, 1867, 1; George Barnsley, Rio de Janeiro, to Godfrey Barnsley, Bartow County, Georgia, June 22, 1868, Barnsley Papers, Duke University.

17. *San Antonio Express,* March 4, 1870, 1.

18. Hill, "Confederate Exiles to Brazil," 192–210; U.S. Congress, "Papers Relating to the Foreign Relations of the United States"; Weaver, "Confederate Emigration to Brazil," 51–53.

19. George Barnsley, Quatis de Barra Mansa, Rio de Janeiro Province, to the Editor of the *New Orleans Times*, August 20, 1871, Barnsley Papers, Duke University.

20. Barnsley, "Notes and Information about the Emigrants from the U. States"; Richardson, *Adventuring With a Purpose*, 5–6.

21. Barnsley, "Notes and Information about the Emigrants from the U. States."

22. Ferguson, "Emigrating to Brazil in 1866–67"; Ferguson, "The American Colonies Emigrating to Brazil," December 18, 1936, 20; George L. Clark, "G. L. Clark's Ancestors," typescript, April 13, 1913, in possession of author; Hill County, Texas, Affidavit of Jasper McMullan, Deed Records 121 (April 9, 1909): 155–156; Effie Smith Arnold (granddaughter of William T. and Victoria Moore), San Antonio, Texas, interview with author, March 28, 1973, tape recording in possession of author.

23. Jones, *Soldado Descansa!*, 246–247; Laura Bennett Turner (great granddaughter of Hervey Hall), typescript, May, 1942, Weaver Papers, in possession of author.

24. Godfrey Barnsley, Bartow County, Georgia, to George Barnsley, Rio de Janeiro, November 15, 1869, Godfrey Barnsley Papers, in possession of Alice B. Howard, Adairsville, Georgia, as quoted in Nelson Miles Hoffman, Jr., "Godfrey Barnsley, 1805–1873: British Cotton Factor in the South" (Ph.D. diss., University of Kansas, 1964), 268. As of 1986, the author was unable to locate the Howard Papers. Alice Howard was said to be in a nursing home in Atlanta, and friends did not know where the papers were located. Also see George Barnsley, Tatuhy, São Paulo Province, to Godfrey Barnsley, Bartow County, Georgia, June 8, 1870, Barnsley Papers, Duke University.

25. George Barnsley, Rio de Janeiro, to Godfrey Barnsley, Bartow County, Georgia, June 22, 1868, Barnsley Papers, Duke University.

26. Ibid.; H. C. Tucker, "Confederates in Brazil," *United Daughters of the Confederacy Magazine* (July 1951): 22.

27. George Barnsley, Rio de Janeiro, to Godfrey Barnsley, Bartow County, Georgia, June 22, 1868, Barnsley Papers, Duke University; Tucker, "Confederates in Brazil," 22.

28. Ibid.; Goldman, *Os Pioneiros Americanos No Brasil*, 25.

29. George Barnsley, Rio de Janeiro, to Godfrey Barnsley, Bartow County, Georgia, June 22, 1868, Barnsley Papers, Duke University.

30. Ibid.

11. THE END OF EL DORADO

1. Goldman, *Os Pioneiros Americanos No Brasil*, 122–123; Barnsley, "Notes and Information about the Emigrants from the U. States"; David Gueiros Vieira (University of Brasilia), "The Confederate Immigration and the Growth of Protestantism in Brazil," paper given at the annual meeting of the South-

ern Historical Association, Louisville, Kentucky, 1984. Vieira further states that one of Vassão's descendants is Reverend Amantino Vassão, rector of the Presbyterian Cathedral in Rio de Janeiro.

2. Barnsley, "Notes and Information about the Emigrants from the U. States"; George Barnsley, Tatuhy, São Paulo Province, to Godfrey Barnsley, Bartow County, Georgia, June 8, 1870, Barnsley Papers, Duke University; George Barnsley, Sorocaba, São Paulo Province, to Godfrey Barnsley, Bartow County, Georgia, December 13, 1870, Barnsley Papers, Duke University.

3. Charles Henry Von Schwartz, Bartow County, Georgia, to H. Howard [Bartow County, Georgia], December 10, 1874, Barnsley Papers, University of Georgia Library; Barnsley, "Notes and Information about the Emigrants from the U. States"; George Barnsley, Quatis de Barra Mansa, Rio de Janeiro Province, to Julia Von Schwartz, Bartow County, Georgia, January 20, 1874, Barnsley Papers, Manuscript Section 204, Tennessee State Library and Archives, Knoxville.

4. George Barnsley, Quatis de Barra Mansa, Rio de Janeiro Province, to Julia Von Schwartz, Kingston, Georgia, February 2, 1878, Barnsley Papers, Tennessee State Library and Archives, Knoxville; George Barnsley, Rezende, Rio de Janeiro Province, to Julia Von Schwartz, Kingston, Georgia, September 14, 1879, Tennessee State Library and Archives, Knoxville.

5. Goldman, *Os Pioneiros Americanos No Brasil*, 133–138.

6. George Barnsley, "Requerimento de Renovação do Decreto n° 6.625, Palacio do Governo da Provinca de São Paulo," March 16, 1881, Archives of the Camara de Itapetininga, São Paulo Province, as quoted by Goldman, *Os Pioneiros Americanos No Brasil*, 137. Barnsley drew maps of the entire region and indicated several specific areas where he believed minerals to be located. The author has copies of these drawings, the originals of which are in the George S. Barnsley Papers, Harold Barnsley Holland Collection, Jacareí, São Paulo State, Brazil.

7. George Barnsley, Rio de Janeiro, Rio de Janeiro Province, to Julia [Von Schwartz], Kingston, Georgia, July 5, 1882, Special Collections, Robert W. Woodruff Library for Advanced Studies, Emory University; Barnsley, "Notes and Information about the Emigrants from the U. States."

8. Ibid.

9. George Barnsley, Sorocaba, São Paulo Province, to Julia Von Schwartz, Kingston, Georgia, September 12, 1882, Barnsley Papers, Emory University; George Barnsley, Botucatu, São Paulo Province, to Julia Von Schwartz, Kingston, Georgia, September 12, 1883, Tennessee State Library and Archives, Knoxville.

10. George Barnsley, Rio de Janeiro, to Charles Henry Von Schwartz, Kingston, Georgia, February 27, 1883, Barnsley Papers, Tennessee State Library and Archives, Knoxville.

11. George Barnsley, Piraçununga, São Paulo Province, to Julia Von Schwartz, Kingston, Georgia, February 1, 1887, Barnsley Papers, Tennessee State Library and Archives, Knoxville; Barnsley, "Notes and Information about the Emigrants from the U. States."

12. George S. Barnsley, "Notes on the Barnsley Estate, Bartow Co., Geor-

gia, U.S.A.," Barnsley Papers, Harold Barnsley Holland Collection, Jacareí, São Paulo State, Brazil.

13. Ibid.

14. George S. Barnsley, "Private Circular," Woodlands, near Hall's Station W. & A. R. R., Bartow County, Georgia, August, 1891, George S. Barnsley Papers, Harold Barnsley Holland Collection, Jacareí, São Paulo State, Brazil.

15. Barnsley, "Notes on the Barnsley Estate."

16. Ibid.

17. Ibid.

18. José Maria Bello, *A History of Modern Brazil: 1889–1964*, 5–6, 9, 11, 22, 37–45, 50; Mary Wilhelmine Williams, *Dom Pedro the Magnanimous: Second Emperor of Brazil*, 282–287, 321–343.

19. Ibid.

20. Williams, *Dom Pedro the Magnanimous*, 327–343.

21. Barnsley, "Notes and Information about the Emigrants from the U. States."

22. Barnsley, "Notes on the Barnsley Estate"; George Barnsley, São Paulo, State of São Paulo, to B. F. Armington Saylor, Bartow County, Georgia, December 30, 1908, Barnsley Papers, Emory University.

12. THE LAST EXILE

1. George L. Clark, "Biography of George Lafayette Clark, Written by Himself During the Year A.D. 1913," typescript in possession of author.

2. Ibid.; Leddin's Actual Business College, Memphis, Tennessee, Diploma to E. N. McMullan, September 22, 1873, in possession of Rachel McMullan White, Cumberland, Rhode Island.

3. Mary Pearl Clark, interview with author, Burleson, Texas, June 15, 1960, notes in possession of author.

4. *A Memorial and Biographical History of Johnson and Hill Counties, Texas,* 217.

5. Wright, *James Dyer,* [60]; Effie Smith Arnold, interview with author, San Antonio, Texas, March 28, 1973, tape recording in possession of author; Virginia McMullan Clark, "For Trudie," ms. in possession of author; Clark, "Lines to My Old Home"; Thelma C. Griggs, interview with author, Lubbock, Texas, June 3, 1977, notes in possession of author.

6. Richardson, *Adventuring with a Purpose,* 8–9; Wright, *James Dyer,* [66]; *A Memorial and Biographical History of Johnson and Hill Counties, Texas,* 220.

7. Bailey, *A History of Hill County, Texas,* 115–117; *A Memorial and Biographical History of Johnson and Hill Counties, Texas,* 270.

8. "White and Others vs. Jones," *Southwestern Reporter* 4 (April 15, 1887): 161; Roy C. Clark, interview with author, Lubbock, Texas, June 3, 1981, notes in possession of author; Hill County, Texas, Affidavit of William L. Booth, Deed Records 22 (January 25, 1889): 243; Hill County, Texas, Affidavit of William L. Booth, Deed Records 23 (April 9, 1889): 117.

9. E. N. McMullan, "Texans Established Colony."

10. Ibid.; Ney McMullan kept a diary of his trip to Brazil that, in 1975, was

in possession of his granddaughter, Rachel McMullan White, Needham, Massachusetts. In a move of the White family to Bolivia, then to Bermuda, then back to Rhode Island, the little book was evidently lost.

11. Patsy Miles (granddaughter of Martha Ann McMullan Williams), Van, Texas, to Thelma C. Griggs, Lubbock, Texas, March 8, 1973, in possession of author; Patsy Miles, Van, Texas, to William C. Griggs, Lubbock, Texas, April 4, 1973, in possession of author.

12. Patsy Miles to Thelma C. Griggs, March 8, 1973.

13. Ibid. A short biography of Coon Williams may be found in *A Memorial and Biographical History of Johnson and Hill Counties, Texas*, 39–40.

14. Frank McMullan (Ney McMullan's son), interview with author, São Paulo, Brazil, November 26, 1983, notes in possession of author.

15. Ibid.; Effie Smith Arnold, interview with author, San Antonio, Texas, March 28, 1973; Patsy Miles to Thelma C. Griggs, March 8, 1973.

16. Rachel McMullan White, interview with author, Needham, Massachusetts, April 20, 1975, notes in possession of author.

17. Wright, *James Dyer*, [66]; W. S. Dyer, C. L. Wasson, and Helen Domm Curry, Power of Attorney to E. N. McMullan (Rebouças, State of São Paulo), Hill County, Texas, February 8, 1916, in possession of Rachel McMullan White, Cumberland, Rhode Island.

18. Effie Smith Arnold, San Antonio, Texas, interview with author, March 28, 1973; Patsy Miles to Thelma C. Griggs, March 8, 1973.

19. Edwin Ney McMullan, Rebouças, State of São Paulo, to (Hugh Clark), Burleson, Texas, May 31, 1918, in possession of author.

20. Ibid.

21. Cicero Jones, Vila Americana, State of São Paulo, to J. N. Heiskell, Little Rock, Arkansas, September 25, 1915, J. N. Heiskell Library, *Arkansas Gazette* Foundation, Little Rock. On June 23, 1917, Jones wrote a letter to the *Confederate Veteran* in which he reaffirmed his belief that the emigrants to Brazil remained patriotic Americans. See Cicero Jones, "Patriotism of the American Colony in Brazil," *Confederate Veteran* 25 (September 1917): 392.

22. Jones, *Soldado Descansa!*, 305, 348, 401; Nattie Quillin Jacobs, Ontario, California, to William C. Griggs, Canyon, Texas, January 2, 1980, in possession of author. This letter contains a genealogical chart of the Quillin family compiled by Nattie Quillin Jacobs.

23. U.S. State Department, Consular Service, "Report of the Death of an American Citizen [James Monroe Keith]," São Paulo, State of São Paulo, November 25, 1921, by E. M. Lawton, Consul; E. M. Lawton, São Paulo, State of São Paulo, to the Honorable Secretary of State, Washington, D.C., March 26, 1923; Wilber J. Carr (Director of the Consular Service), Washington, D.C., to S. W. Hughes and Company, Brady, Texas, May 21, 1923; S. W. Hughes, Brady, Texas, to Department of State, Division of Consular Service, June 12, 1923; A. T. Haeberle (American Consul), São Paulo, State of São Paulo, to the Honorable Secretary of State, August 20, 1923; Wilber J. Carr, Washington, D.C., to S. W. Hughes and Company, Brady, Texas, September 19, 1923; E. M. Lawton, São Paulo, State of São Paulo, to Aquila A. Amos, San Diego, California, March 20, 1923; A. T. Haeberle, São Paulo, State of São Paulo, to

S. W. Hughes, Brady, Texas, May 17, 1923; A. M. Dobbs, Fort Smith, Arkansas, to E. M. Lawton, São Paulo, State of São Paulo, June 3, 1922; A. T. Haeberle, São Paulo, State of São Paulo, to A. M. Dobbs, Fort Smith, Arkansas, June 27, 1922; Wilber J. Carr, Washington, D.C., to S. W. Hughes and Company, Brady, Texas, June 22, 1923; Wilber J. Carr, Washington, D.C., to Arminius T. Haeberle, Esquire, São Paulo, State of São Paulo, May 31, 1923; E. M. Lawton, São Paulo, State of São Paulo, to the Honorable Secretary of State, Washington, D.C., November 26, 1921; S. W. Hughes, Brady, Texas, to Department of State, Washington, D.C., May 21, 1923. All of the above are located in Papers Relating to the Estate of James M. Keith, Record Group 59, National Archives, Washington, D.C.

24. Ibid.

25. George S. Barnsley, "My Desin [design]—June 5th, 1913," George S. Barnsley Papers, Harold Barnsley Holland Collection, Jacareí, São Paulo State.

26. W. Earl McCleskey, interview with author, Barnsley Gardens, Adairsville, Georgia, November 19, 1979, notes in possession of author; Addie B. Saylor (George Barnsley's niece), "Ghosts of Barnsley Gardens," *Atlanta Journal*, January 11, 1942.

27. Rachel McMullan White, interview with author, Needham, Massachusetts, April 20, 1975.

28. Goldman, *Os Pioneiros Americanos No Brasil*, 152; Jones, *Soldado Descansa!*, 346.

29. William F. Pyles, Vila Americana, State of São Paulo, to J. N. Heiskell, Little Rock, Arkansas, September 28, 1915, J. N. Heiskell Library; E. N. McMullan, Vila Americana, State of São Paulo, to J. N. Heiskell, Little Rock, Arkansas, October 20, 1915, J. N. Heiskell Library.

30. Rachel McMullan White, interview with author, Needham, Massachusetts, April 20, 1975. The author attended the reunion in 1983 at the Campo cemetery.

31. Julia Barnsley Holland Macdonell, interview with author, São Paulo, Brazil, November 13, 1983, notes in possession of author.

32. The author visited the home of Harold Barnsley Holland in Jacareí, São Paulo, on November 27, 1983.

33. Rachel McMullan White, interview with author, Needham, Massachusetts, April 20, 1975.

34. From the *Brazilian Reflector*, Blanche Henry Clark Weaver Papers, in possession of author.

APPENDICES

1. Guilherme [William] Bowen, American Settlement, São Lorenso [*sic*] River, to His Excellency, the President of São Paulo [Joaquim Saldanha Marinha], November 9, 1867, Archives of the State of São Paulo, São Paulo.

2. Ferguson, "Emigrating to Brazil in 1866–67."

3. Barnsley, "Original of Reply to a Circular."

Bibliography

ARCHIVAL MATERIAL

"Article Taken from a Brazilian Newspaper Shortly Before the Centennial of the Arrival of the Americans in Brazil." Typescript included in a letter from Nattie Quillin Jacobs, Ontario, California, to William C. Griggs, Canyon, Texas, March 3, 1980. In possession of author, Houston, Texas.

Barnsley, George S., Papers. Harold Barnsley Holland Collection (privately owned). Jacareí, São Paulo State, Brazil.

Barnsley, George S., Papers. Julia Barnsley Macdonell Collection (privately owned). São Paulo, Brazil.

Barnsley, George S., Papers. Olga Barnsley Scheuenstuhl Collection (privately owned). Rio de Janeiro, Brazil.

Barnsley, George S., Papers. Southern Historical Collection. University of North Carolina. Chapel Hill, North Carolina.

Barnsley, Godfrey, Papers. Manuscript Department, William R. Perkins Library. Duke University. Durham, North Carolina.

Barnsley, Godfrey, Papers. Robert W. Woodruff Library for Advanced Studies. Emory University. Atlanta, Georgia.

Barnsley, Godfrey, Papers. Tennessee State Library and Archives. Knoxville, Tennessee.

Barnsley, Godfrey, Papers. University of Georgia Library. Athens, Georgia.

Bastos, José Tavares, President of São Paulo Province, São Paulo, to Manoel Pinto de Souza Dantas, Minister of the Secretary of Agriculture, Commerce, and Public Works, Rio de Janeiro, March 13, 1867. Register Book of Correspondence of the Governor with the Minister of Agriculture, Commerce, and Public Works, 1861–1869. Archives of the State of São Paulo, São Paulo, Brazil.

Bowen, Guilherme (William), American Settlement, São Lourenço River, São Paulo Province, to His Excellency, the Minister of Agriculture of the Empire of Brazil (Antonio Francisco de Paulo e Souza), October 28, 1867. Archives of the State of São Paulo, São Paulo.

———, American Settlement, São Lourenço River, São Paulo Province, to Joaquim Saldanha Marinha, President of São Paulo Province, São Paulo.

Letter including a census of the McMullan colony, November 9, 1867. Archives of the State of São Paulo, São Paulo.

———, Homesite on Ariado River, McMullan Grant, São Paulo Province, to Joaquim Saldanha Marinha, President of São Paulo Province, São Paulo, November 9, 1867. Ord [930], 29 fls. Archives of the State of São Paulo, São Paulo.

Clark, George Lafayette. "Biography of George Lafayette Clark, Written by Himself During the Year A.D. 1913." Copy in possession of author, Houston, Texas.

———. "G. L. Clark's Ancestors." Typescript, April 13, 1913. Copy in possession of author, Houston, Texas.

Clark, Virginia McMullan. "For Trudie." In possession of author, Houston, Texas.

———. "Lines to My Old Home." In possession of author, Houston, Texas.

Confederate States of America. State Department Records. Dispatches and Legation Records of the Confederate Minister to Mexico, John T. Pickett. Ramsdell Collection. Eugene C. Barker Texas History Center. University of Texas, Austin, Texas.

"Contracto que celebram, de um lado o Governo Imperial do Brasil, do outro B. Caymari como representante da Compania [companhia] United States and Brasil Steam Ships, para o transporte de emigrantes," June 20, 1866. *Lata 632, Pasta 1.* Brazilian Institute of History and Geography, Rio de Janeiro.

Costa Aguilar, Antonio Augosto de. To Joaquim Saldanha Marinha, President of São Paulo Province, São Paulo, November 28, 1867. Archives of the State of São Paulo, São Paulo.

Dyer, Nancy. Ms. Affidavit, c. 1860. In possession of Ella Beatrice Hill, Hillsboro, Texas.

Dyer, W. S., C[olumbus] L. Wasson, and Helen Domm Curry. Power of Attorney to E. N. McMullan, Hill County, Texas, February 8, 1916. In possession of Rachel McMullan White, Cumberland, Rhode Island.

Eubank, John T., James H. Dyer, and Jackson Puckett, Fort Graham, Texas, to Governor Sam Houston, (Austin, Texas), December 8, 1860. "Petition [of citizens of Hill, McLennan and Bosque Counties] to His Excellency Gen-[eral] Sam Houston." Ms., Governor's Letters (Houston), July–December, 1860. Archives of the State of Texas, Austin, Texas.

Fayssoux, Callender Irvine. Collection of William Walker Papers. Latin American Library. Tulane University. New Orleans, Louisiana.

Ferguson, Sarah Bellona Smith. "Emigrating to Brazil in 1866–67: An Account of the McMullan-Bowen Colony." Ms., May 29, 1935. Blanche Henry Clark Weaver Papers. In possession of author, Houston, Texas.

Foreign Clearance, Ships Sailing from the Port of New Orleans, June, 1862, to January, 1875. Ms. bound volume. Record Group 36. National Archives of the United States, Washington, D.C.

Hill County, Texas. Affidavit of Jasper McMullan. Deed Records 121 (April 29, 1909): 155–156.

———. Civil Minutes, 1905–1907 M (September Term, 1905): 14.

Jacobs, Nettie Quillin, Ontario, California, to William C. Griggs, Canyon, Texas, January 2, 1980. In possession of author, Houston, Texas.

———, Ontario, California, to William C. Griggs, Canyon, Texas, March 3, 1980. In possession of author, Houston, Texas.

Jones, Cicero, Vila Americana, São Paulo Province, Brazil, to J. N. Heiskell, Little Rock, Arkansas, September 25, 1915. J. N. Heiskell Library, *Arkansas Gazette* Foundation. Little Rock, Arkansas.

Leddin's Actual Business College. Diploma to E. N. McMullan, September 22, 1873. In possession of Rachel McMullan White, Cumberland, Rhode Island.

McKenzie College Papers. Perkins Theological Seminary Library. Southern Methodist University, Dallas, Texas.

McLennan County, Texas. "Inventory of Community Property of Elizabeth Bowen, Deceased." Probate Records, Vol. E, pp. 184–185.

McMullan, Edwin Ney [Rebouças, State of São Paulo], to [Hugh Clark], Burleson, Texas, May 31, 1918. In possession of author, Houston, Texas.

———, Vila Americana, State of São Paulo, to J. N. Heiskell, Little Rock, Arkansas, September 25, 1915. J. N. Heiskell Library, *Arkansas Gazette* Foundation. Little Rock, Arkansas.

McMullan, Frank, and William Bowen [Morro Redondo, on the Juquiá River], São Paulo Province, to José Tavares Bastos, President of São Paulo Province, São Paulo, June 13, 1867. Ms. copy in a letter from Antonio Augusto de Aguilar, São Paulo, São Paulo Province, to Joaquim Saldanha Marinha, President of São Paulo Province, November 28, 1867. Archives of the State of São Paulo, São Paulo.

———, and William Bowen [Morro Redondo, on the Juquiá River], São Paulo Province, to the President [José Tavares Bastos] and members of the Provincial Legislative Assembly, São Paulo, June 17, 1867. Ms. copy in a letter to Joaquim Saldanha Marinha, President of São Paulo Province, São Paulo, November 28, 1867. Archives of the State of São Paulo, São Paulo.

———, "Casa de Col. Bowen [Morro Redondo]," on the Juquiá River, São Paulo Province, to Dr. Octaviano da Rocha (camp on the Juquiá River), São Paulo Province, July 8, 1867. National Archives of Brazil, Rio de Janeiro.

McMullan, Wiley Dyer, São Paulo, State of São Paulo, to William C. Griggs, Lubbock, Texas, June 27, 1973. In possession of author, Houston, Texas.

———, São Paulo, State of São Paulo, to William C. Griggs, Lubbock, Texas, December 28, 1974. In possession of author, Houston, Texas.

Marinha, Joaquim Saldanha, President of São Paulo Province, São Paulo, to Manoel Pinto de Souza Dantas, Minister of the Secretary of Agriculture, Commerce, and Public Works, Rio de Janeiro, November 7, 1867. *Oficio* (letterbook of Joaquim Saldanha de Marinha), p. 227. Archives of the State of São Paulo, São Paulo.

Miles, Patsy, Van, Texas, to William C. Griggs, Lubbock, Texas, March 8, 1973. In possession of author, Houston, Texas.

———, Van, Texas, to William C. Griggs, Lubbock, Texas, April 4, 1973. In possession of author, Houston, Texas.

Miller, R. R., Search Department, Public Records Office, Kew, Surry, England, to William C. Griggs, Canyon, Texas, October 18, 1978. In possession of author, Houston, Texas.

Moore, Clarence E., Fort Worth, Texas, to William C. Griggs, Lubbock, Texas, December 20, 1973. In possession of author, Houston, Texas.

Nascentes de Azambuja, Bernardo Augosto, Third Secretary of Public Lands and Colonization, Rio de Janeiro, to Frank McMullan and William Bowen, "Response to Nine Questions Presented by Franck McMullau [sic] and Guilherme [William] Bowen," June 2, 1866. *Lata* 632, *Pasta* 4. Brazilian Institute of Geography and History, Rio de Janeiro.

———, Third Secretary of Public Lands and Colonization, Rio de Janeiro, to Frank McMullan and William Bowen, Official Letter, June 2, 1866. *Lata* 632, *Pasta* 4. Brazilian Institute of Geography and History, Rio de Janeiro.

Nathan, Carlos, and Manoel Pinto de Souza Dantas, Minister and Secretary of State of the Business of Agriculture, Commerce, and Public Works, "Contracto celebrado entre o Governo Imperial de uma parte e Carlos Nathan da outra, para o transporte de mil familias procedentes dos Estados do Sul da Uniao Americana, por vapores d'aqulles [aqueles] Estados para Rio de Janeiro, sob as condiçoes abaixo declaradas," July 23, 1867. *Lata* 632, *Pasta* 72. Archives of the Brazilian Institute of History and Geography. Rio de Janeiro.

Olinda, Marquez de. To Antonio Francisco de Paula e Souza, Secretary of State for Agriculture, Commerce, and Public Works, Rio de Janeiro, June 26, 1866. *Simbolo* 1A⁶4, *Caixa* 33V. National Archives of Brazil, Rio de Janeiro.

Oliveira, Betty Antunes de, Rio de Janeiro, to William C. Griggs, Canyon, Texas, June 23, 1980. In possession of author, Houston, Texas.

———, Rio de Janeiro, to William C. Griggs, Canyon, Texas, August 3, 1979. In possession of author, Houston, Texas.

Oliveira, José Joaquim M. de, Department of Public Lands and Colonization of São Paulo Province, São Paulo, to Joaquim Floriano de Toledo, Vice-President of São Paulo Province, São Paulo, April 26, 1866. Ord. 930, C. 135, p. 3, D. 8/1 fl. Archives of the State of São Paulo, São Paulo.

———, Department of Public Lands and Colonization of São Paulo Province, São Paulo, to José Tavares Bastos, President of São Paulo Province, São Paulo, May 4, 1866. Ord. 930, C. 135, p. 3, D. 9/2 fls. Archives of the State of São Paulo, São Paulo.

———, Department of Public Lands and Colonization of São Paulo Province, São Paulo, to José Tavares Bastos, President of São Paulo Province, São Paulo, March 12, 1867. Ord. 930, C. 135, p. 4, D. 2A/1 fl. (anexo). Archives of the State of São Paulo, São Paulo.

Paula e Souza, Antonio Francisco de, Secretary of State for Agriculture, Commerce, and Public Works, Rio de Janeiro, to the President of the Intermediate (Coastal) Steamship Line, Rio de Janeiro, January 8, 1866. Section of Executive Authority. *Simbolo* 1A⁶3, *Caixa* F.V. National Archives of Brazil, Rio de Janeiro.

Perry, Laura L. Papers. The Texas Collection. Baylor University, Waco, Texas.

Pyles, William F., Vila Americana, State of São Paulo, to J. N. Heiskell, Little

Rock, Arkansas, September 28, 1915. J. N. Heiskell Library, *Arkansas Gazette* Foundation, Little Rock, Arkansas.

Rogers, Ben, Fort Worth, Texas, to William C. Griggs, Canyon, Texas, July 11, 1979. In possession of author, Houston, Texas.

Shaw, Robert. To Hugh McMullan. Deed of 320 acres. Land Certificate 854, Robertson 3rd, January 6, 1855. File 3187 (Hill County, Texas). General Land Office of Texas, Austin, Texas.

Souza Dantas, Manoel Pinto de, President of Para Province, and Lansford Warren Hastings. "Termo de Contracto celebrado com o Major Lansford Warren Hastings, para establecer uma colonia de compatriotas seus nesta provincia." *Lata 632, Pasta 2.* Archives of the Brazilian Institute of History and Geography, Rio de Janeiro.

Street, Ernesto Dinez, Inspector General of Public Lands of São Paulo Province, São Paulo, to Joaquim Floriano de Toledo, Vice-President of São Paulo Province, São Paulo, April 4, 1866. Ord. 903, c. 135, p. 2, D. 98/1 fl. Archives of the State of São Paulo, São Paulo.

———, Inspector General of Public Lands of São Paulo Province, São Paulo, to Joaquim Floriano de Toledo, Vice-President of São Paulo Province, April 5, 1866. Ord. 930, c. 135, p. 2, D. 98. Archives of the State of São Paulo, São Paulo.

———. "Declaration of the Boundaries of the McMullan-Bowen Grant," April 5, 1866. Ord. 930, c. 135, p. 2, D. 98, C/2 fl. (anexo). Archives of the State of São Paulo, São Paulo.

———. "Declaration of the Inspector General About the Public Lands in the Province of São Paulo." Ord. 930, D. 98 C/2, fl. 1 (anexo). Archives of the State of São Paulo, São Paulo.

———. "Validity of Title [of the McMullan-Bowen Grant]," April 18, 1866. Ord. 930, c. 135, p. 2, D. 98D/3 fls. (anexo). Archives of the State of São Paulo, São Paulo.

Texas, Militia, Muster Rolls. 2nd Regiment, Texas Volunteer Infantry. Texas State Archives. Austin, Texas.

———. Nineteenth Brigade, Reserve Company, Beat No. 4, Navarro County, Texas. Texas State Archives. Austin, Texas.

———. Nineteenth Brigade, Mile Creek Cavalry Company, Texas State Troops, Ellis County, Texas. Texas State Archives. Austin, Texas.

———. Nineteenth Brigade, Reserved Company, Beat No. 5, Navarro County, Texas, August 17, 1861. Texas State Archives. Austin, Texas.

———. Nineteenth Brigade, Volunteer Company of Mounted Men, Beat No. 8, Hill County, Texas. Texas State Archives, Austin, Texas.

Texas, General Land Office. File No. 1831, Hill County. Archives of the General Land Office. Austin, Texas.

———. File No. 2432, Hill County. Archives of the General Land Office. Austin, Texas.

Thomas, R. P., Santa Barbara, São Paulo Province, to H. A. Tupper, April 26, 1866. Archives of Southwestern Theological Seminary, Fort Worth, Texas.

United States, National Archives. Record Group 36, Papers Relating to Clearance of Ships at New Orleans. Washington, D.C.

————. Record Group 59, Papers Relating to the Estate of James M. Keith. Washington, D.C.

Weaver, Blanche Henry Clark, Papers. In possession of author, Houston, Texas.

White, Rachel McMullan, Needham, Massachusetts, to William C. Griggs, Lubbock, Texas, August 7, 1975. In possession of author, Houston, Texas.

————, Needham, Massachusetts, to William C. Griggs, Lubbock, Texas, August 7, 1976. In possession of author, Houston, Texas.

Works Progress Administration. Survey of Federal Archives in Louisiana: Passenger Lists Taken from the Manifests of the Customs Service, Port of New Orleans, 1864–1867. Bound Volume (carbon copy of typescript), 1941, p. 186-E. Louisiana Collection. Library, Tulane University, New Orleans, Louisiana.

Xavier, José Hygino, Accountant of the Plantation of São Paulo. Accounting Report on Surveys of Public Lands Designated for American Emigrants, March 5, 1867. Archives of the State of São Paulo, São Paulo.

BOOKS AND DISSERTATIONS

Abstract of Land Titles of Texas; Comprising the Titled, Patented, and Located Lands in the State. 2 vols. Galveston: Shaw & Blaylock, 1878.

Andrews, Eliza F. *Wartime Diary of a Georgia Girl.* New York, n.p., 1908.

Annual Catalog of the Students and Faculty of McKenzie College, Near Clarksville, Texas, for the Session of 1860–61. Nashville: Southern Methodist Publishing House, 1861.

Bailey, Ellis. *A History of Hill County, Texas: 1838–1965.* Waco: Texian Press, 1966.

• Barney, William L. *The Secessionist Impulse: Alabama and Mississippi in 1860.* Princeton: Princeton University Press, 1974.

• Basso, Hamilton. *A Quota of Seaweed: Persons and Places in Brazil, Spain, Honduras, Jamaica, Tahiti, and Samoa.* London: Collins, 1961.

Baughman, James P. *Charles Morgan and the Development of Southern Transportation.* Nashville: Vanderbilt University, 1968.

• Bello, José Maria. *A History of Modern Brazil: 1889–1964.* Stanford: Stanford University Press, 1966.

Booth, Andrew B., comp. *Records of Louisiana Soldiers and Louisiana Confederate Commands.* 3 vols. New Orleans: n.p., 1920.

Brazil 1940/41: An Economic, Social, and Geographic Survey. Rio de Janeiro: Ministry of Foreign Affairs, 1941.

• Brown, Charles H. *Agents of Manifest Destiny: The Life and Times of the Filibusters.* Chapel Hill: University of North Carolina Press, 1980.

Bruchy, Stuart, ed. *Cotton and the Growth of the American Economy.* New York: Harcourt, Brace, and World, 1967.

Burton, Richard F. *Explorations of the Highlands of Brazil: With a Full Account of the Gold and Diamond Mines . . .* London: Tinsley Brothers, 1869.

• Crabtree, A. R. *Baptists in Brazil.* Rio de Janeiro: Baptist Publishing House, 1953.

Crenshaw, Ollinger. *The Slave States in the Presidential Election of 1860.* Baltimore: Johns Hopkins Press, 1945.

Dozer, Donald Marquand. *Latin America: An Interpretive History.* New York: McGraw-Hill, 1962.

Duncan, Herbert Cape. *The Diocese of Louisiana: Some of Its History, 1838–1888.* New Orleans: A. W. Wyatt, 1888.

˻ Dunn, Ballard Smith, [ed.]. *Brazil, The Home for Southerners, or, A Practical Account of What the Author, and Others, Who Visited That Country For the Same Objects, Saw and Did While in That Empire.* New Orleans: Bloomfield & Steel, 1866.

————. *How the "Banner Church of the South" Obtained a Baptismal Font: A Plain Statement of the Facts, That Refute Many Slanders.* New Orleans: n.p., 1868.

Edwards, John N. *Shelby's Expedition to Mexico. An Unwritten Leaf of the War.* Kansas City: Kansas City Times Book and Job Printing House, 1872.

Ellis, Alfredo, Jr. *Um Parlamentar Paulista Da Republica: Subsídos para a História da Republica em S. Paulo e Subsídos para a História Economica de São Paulo.* São Paulo: n.p., 1949.

Fehrenbacher, Don E. *The Dred Scott Case: Its Significance in American Law and Politics.* New York: Oxford University Press, 1978.

Ferrez, Gilberto. *Um Panorama Do Rio de Janeiro de 1775.* Rio de Janeiro: Instituto Historico e Geografico Brasileiro, 1957.

Foner, Eric. *Free Soil, Free Labor, Free Men: The Ideology of the Republican Party before the Civil War.* New York: Oxford University Press, 1970.

Franklin, John Hope. *Reconstruction after the Civil War.* Chicago: University of Chicago Press, 1961.

Gardner's New Orleans Directory for 1867, Including Jefferson City, Gretna, Carrollton, Algiers, and McDonough; With a Street and Levee Guide, A Complete Map of the City, Business Directory, and An Appendix of Much Useful Information. New Orleans: Charles Gardner, 1867.

Garrison, George Pierce. *Westward Expansion: 1841–1850. The American Nation: A History.* New York: Harper & Brothers, 1906.

Gaston, James McFadden. *Hunting a Home in Brazil: The Agricultural Resources and Other Characteristics of the Country.* Philadelphia: King and Baird, 1867.

• Gill, Everett, Jr. *Pilgrimage to Brazil.* Nashville: Broadman Press, 1954.

Goldman, Frank P. *Os Pioneiros Americanos No Brasil: Educadores, Sacerdotes, Covos e Reis.* São Paulo: Livraria Pioneiro Editora, 1972.

Grier, Douglas. "Confederate Emigration to Brazil: 1865–1870." Ph.D. dissertation, University of Michigan, 1965.

• Griggs, William C. "Frank McMullan's Brazilian Colony." Ph.D. dissertation, Texas Tech University, 1982.

Guilhon, Norma de Azevedo. *Confederados em Santarem.* Belem and Para: Conselho Estadual de Cultura, 1979.

Hackett, J. Dominick, and Charles Montague Earty. *Passenger Lists from Ireland.* Baltimore: Genealogical Publishing Company, 1965.

Hamilton, Holman. *Prologue to Conflict: The Crisis and Compromise of 1850.* N.p.: University of Kentucky Press, 1964.

Hastings, Lansford Warren. *The Emigrant's Guide to Oregon and California.* 1845. Reprint. Princeton: Princeton University Press, 1932.

Hesler, Samuel B. *A History of Independence Baptist Church, 1839–1969, and Related Organizations.* N.p.: Executive Board of the Baptist General Convention of Texas, 1970.

Hill, Lawrence F. *The Confederate Exodus to Latin America.* Austin: Texas State Historical Association, 1936.

• ———. *Diplomatic Relations between the United States and Brazil.* Durham, North Carolina: Duke University Press, 1932.

Hoffman, Nelson Miles, Jr. "Godfrey Barnsley, 1805–1873: British Cotton Factor in the South." Ph.D. dissertation, University of Kansas, 1964.

Howard, Benjamin C. *Report of the Decision of the Supreme Court of the United States, and The Opinions of the Judges Thereof, In the Case of the Dred Scott vs. John F. A. Stanford, December Term, 1856.* Washington: Cornelius Wendell, 1857.

Jamison, James Carson. *With Walker in Nicaragua, or Reminiscences of An Officer of the American Phalanx.* Columbia, Missouri: E. W. Stephens, 1909.

Jones, Judith McKnight. *Soldado Descansa! Uma Epopéia Norte Americana Sob Os Céus Do Brasil.* São Paulo: Jarde, 1967.

Kelly, Charles. *Salt Desert Trails: A History of the Hastings Cutoff and Other Early Trails Which Crossed The Great Salt Desert Seeking a Shorter Road to California.* Salt Lake City: Western Printing Company, 1930.

Kidder, David P. *Sketches of Residence and Travels in Brazil, Embracing Historical and Geographical Notices of the Empire and its Several Provinces.* 2 vols. Philadelphia: Sorin & Ball, 1845.

Kilpatrick, A. Y. *The Early Settlers Life in Texas and the Organization of Hill County.* Hillsboro: [A. Y. Kirkpatrick], 1909.

Manning, William R., ed. *Diplomatic Correspondence of the United States: Inter-American Affairs, 1831–1860.* 8 vols. Washington: Carnegie Endowment for International Peace, 1934.

A Memorial and Biographical History of Johnson and Hill Counties, Texas. Chicago: Lewis Publishing Company, 1892.

Moore, Glover. *The Missouri Controversy: 1819–1821.* N.p.: University of Kentucky Press, 1953.

McLean, John H. *Reminiscences of Rev. Jno. H. McLean.* Nashville: Smith & Lamar, 1919.

Nash, Roy. *The Conquest of Brazil.* New York: Harcourt, Brace, & Co., 1926.

Oates, Stephen B. *To Purge This Land with Blood: A Biography of John Brown.* New York: Harper & Row, 1970.

Oliveira, Betty Antunes de. *Antonio Teixeira de Albuquerque.* Rio de Janeiro: n.p., 1982.

———. *Centelha em Restolho Seco: Uma Contribuição para a Historia dos Primordios do Trabalho Batista no Brasil.* Rio de Janeiro: n.p., 1985.

———. *Movimento de Passageiros Norte-Americanos no Porto do Rio de Janeiro, 1865–1890.* Rio de Janeiro: B. A. de Oliveira, 1981.

———. *North American Immigration to Brazil: Tombstone Records of the "Campo"*

Cemetery, Santa Barbara D'Oeste—São Paulo State, Brazil. Rio de Janeiro: n.p., 1978.

Overdyke, William Darrell. *The Know-Nothing Party in the South.* N.p.: Louisiana State University Press, 1950.

Rawley, James A. *Race and Politics: "Bleeding Kansas" and the Coming of the Civil War.* Philadelphia: J. B. Lippincott, 1969.

Reese, James Verdo. "A History of Hill County to 1873." Master's thesis, University of Texas, Austin, Texas, 1962.

Richardson, James D. *A Compilation of the Messages and Papers of the Presidents: 1789–1897.* 10 vols. Washington: Government Printing Office, 1897.

Richardson, Rupert Norval. *Adventuring with a Purpose: Life Story of Arthur Lee Wasson.* San Antonio: Naylor Company, 1953.

Riker, David Afton. *O Ultimo Confederado na Amazonia.* Manaus: Imprensa Oficial do Estado do Amazonas, 1983.

⌀ Roark, James L. *Masters without Slaves: Southern Planters in the Civil War and Reconstruction.* New York: W. W. Norton & Co., 1977.

Roche, James Jeffrey. *The Story of the Filibusters, to Which is Added the Life of Colonel David Crockett.* London: F. Fisher Unwin, 1891.

Rolle, Andrew F. *The Lost Cause: The Confederate Exodus to Mexico.* Norman: University of Oklahoma Press, 1965.

Rome (Georgia) Heritage Foundation. *A Plan for Barnsley Gardens.* N.p., 1979.

Russell, Robert R. *A History of the American Economic System.* New York: Appleton-Century-Crofts, 1964.

Sartain, James Alfred. *History of Walker County, Georgia.* 1932. Reprint. Carrollton, Georgia: A. M. Matthews and J. S. Sartain, 1972.

Scroggs, William O. *Filibusters and Financiers: The Story of William Walker and His Associates.* New York: Russell & Russell, 1916.

Smith, Theodore Clark. *Parties and Slavery.* Vol. 18 of *The American Nation: A History.* New York: Harper & Brothers, 1906.

Stampp, Kenneth M. *The Era of Reconstruction.* New York: Alfred A. Knopf, 1965.

Tavares Bastos, Aureliano Candido. *Os Males do Presente E As Esperanças Do Futuro.* São Paulo: Companhia Editora Nacional, 1939.

Texas. 4th Legislature. Special Session. *Journals of the House of Representatives of the State of Texas.* Austin: J. W. Hampton, 1953.

Tupper, Henry Allen. *The Foreign Missions of the Southern Baptist Convention.* Richmond: Foreign Mission Board of the Southern Baptist Convention, 1880.

Walker, William. *The War in Nicaragua.* New York: S. H. Goetzel & Co., 1860.

Webb, Walter Prescott, ed. *The Handbook of Texas.* 2 vols. Austin: Texas State Historical Association, 1952.

Wells, William V. *Walker's Expedition to Nicaragua: A History of the Central American War, and the Sonora and Kinney Expeditions, Including All the Recent Diplomatic Correspondence, Together With a New and Accurate Map of Central America.* New York: Stringer and Townsend, 1856.

Williams, Mary Wilhelmine. *Dom Pedro the Magnanimous: Second Emperor of Brazil.* New York: Octagon Books, 1978.

Winkler, Ernest W., ed. *Journal of the Secession Convention of Texas: 1861.* Austin: Texas Library and Historical Commission, 1912.
Wright, Elizabeth Ann. *James Dyer: Descendents and Allied Families.* Dallas: n.p., 1954.

JOURNAL AND NEWSPAPER ARTICLES

"Americana, Brazil, Residents Trace Confederate Heritage." *Lubbock Avalanche-Journal,* April 21, 1975.
"Americana in São Paulo State Still Has Vestiges of Confederate Americans." *Brazilian Business,* May 1962, 38–39.
Barnsley, George Scarborough. "Foreign Colonization in Brazil: The American (and English) Attempt at Colonization in Brazil—1866–67." *Brazilian American* (Rio de Janeiro), March 10, 1928.
Brannon, Peter A. "Southern Emigration to Brazil, Embodying the Diary of Jennie R. Keyes, Montgomery, Alabama." *Alabama Historical Quarterly* 1 (Summer 1930): 74–95.
Brazilian Emigration Agency. "Letter to the Editor." *New York Tribune,* November 30, 1866.
"Brazilian News." *Mobile Register and Advertiser,* July 18, 1865.
"The Brig Derby." *Flake's Daily Galveston Bulletin,* February 23, 1867.
Cardwell, John. "Letter to the Editor." *Galveston Tri-Weekly News,* December 16, 1866.
"Champ Ferguson." *Harper's Weekly* 9 (December 23, 1865): 593.
"Chevalier D. Azambuja, The New Minister From Brazil." *Harper's Weekly* 9 (December 2, 1865): 765.
"Correspondencia Diplomatica." *Revista de Imigração e Colonização* 4 (June 1943): 268–333.
Davis, William C. "Confederate Exiles." *American History Illustrated* 5 (June 1970): 31–43.
"Democratic Meeting in Hill County." *Dallas Herald,* February 15, 1860.
"Dixie City in Brazil." *Ebony* 22 (November 1966): 89–94.
"Editorial Correspondence." *Dallas Herald,* April 4, 1860.
Edmonds, James E. "They've Gone, Back Home." *Saturday Evening Post,* January 4, 1941, 43–47.
"The Emigration From the South Destined to Prove a Success." *New Orleans Times,* February 10, 1867.
"Emigration to Brazil." *New York Times,* November 25, 1866.
"Emigration to Brazil." *New York Tribune,* November 30, 1866.
"The Exiled Ex-Southerners: Terrible Sufferings of the Planters Who Went to Brazil." *New York Times,* May 21, 1871.
"The Fate of Davis." *Harper's Weekly* 9 (June 17, 1865): 374.
Ferguson, Sarah Bellona Smith. "The American Colonies Emigrating to Brazil." *Times of Brazil* (São Paulo), December 18, 1936; December 24, 1936; December 31, 1936.
———. "Emigrating to Brazil." *Farm and Ranch* (Dallas, Texas), December 2,

1916, December 9, 1916, December 16, 1916, January 13, 1917, January 20, 1917.

Foster, Josephine (Gunter Colony, Lake Juparanão, Espiritu Santo Province), "Letter to the Editor." *New Orleans Times*, April 26, 1868.

"From Brazil." *Advertiser and Register* (Mobile, Alabama), December 13, 1867.

Hill, Lawrence F. "Confederate Exiles to Brazil." *Hispanic American Historical Review* 7, no. 2 (May 1927): 192–210.

Jefferson, Mark. "An American Colony in Brazil." *Geographic Review* 18, no. 2 (April 1928): 226–231.

Jones, Cicero. "Patriotism of the American Colony in Brazil." *Confederate Veteran* 25 (September 1917): 392.

Kelly, Brian J., and Mark London. "Gold! Brazil's Big Find." *Parade (Houston Post)*, March 29, 1981, 8–10.

Keyes, Julia L. "Our Life in Brazil." *Alabama Historical Quarterly* 28, nos. 3 and 4 (Fall and Winter 1966): 127–399.

Knapp, Frank A., Jr. "A New Source on the Confederate Exodus to Mexico: The Two Republics." *Journal of Southern History* 19 (August 1953): 364–373.

"The Lake of Gold." *Brazilian Bulletin* 1, no. 2 (September 1898): 88–89.

"Letter from Bill Arp to His Old Friend, John Happy." *Dallas Herald*, February 10, 1866.

Loh, Jules. "A Church Survives Brazos Challenge." *Waco Tribune-Herald*, August 5, 1956.

"Marine Intelligence." *New York Times*, March 27, 1867.

McMullan, Edwin Ney. "Texans Established Colony in Brazil Just After Civil War." *Semi-Weekly Farm News* (Dallas), January 25, 1916.

McMullan, Frank. "Letter to the Editor." *Galveston Tri-Weekly News*, November 4, 1866.

———. "Letter to the Editor." *Galveston Tri-Weekly News*, November 16, 1866.

———. "Loss of the Brig Derby." *Flake's Daily Galveston Bulletin*, March 6, 1866.

———. "To My Friends in Texas, And To All Good Southerners Who Think of Going to Brazil." *New Orleans Times*, January 24, 1867.

Norris, Robert (Sitio Cinco Palentes, São Paulo Province), "Letter to the Editor." *Elmore Standard* (Wetumka, Alabama), June 21, 1867.

"The Old South That Went South." *United Daughters of the Confederacy Magazine* 11 (May 1948): 2.

Pool, William C. "The Battle of Dove Creek." *Southwestern Historical Quarterly* 53 (April 1950): 367–385.

Reese, James V. "The Murder of Major Ripley A. Arnold." *West Texas Historical Association Yearbook* 41 (October 1965): 144–155.

"Relação Das Cartas Revebidas [recebidas] Pela Legação e Consulado Brasileiros em o Anno de 1865 de Habitantes Das Estados Unidos Que Depois Da Guerra Tem Manifesto o Desejo de Emigrar Para o Império." *Revista de Imigração e Colonização* 4 (June 1943): 280.

"Return of the Confederate Colonists from Brazil." *The Talldega Watch-Tower* (Talldega, Alabama), August 11, 1869.

Rios, José Arthur. "Assimilation of Emigrants from the Old South to Brazil." *Social Forces* 26 (December 1947): 145–152.

Saylor, Addie B. "Ghosts of Barnsley Gardens." *Atlanta Journal*, January 11, 1942.

Shalhope, Robert E. "Race, Class Slavery, and the Antebellum Southern Mind." *Journal of Southern History* 37 (November, 1971): 557–574.

"Shall Southerners Emigrate to Brazil?" *De Bow's Review*. After the War Series 2 (July 1866): 30–38.

Shippey, Eliza Kerr. "When Americans Were Emigrants." *Kansas City Star*, June 16, 1912.

"Shipwreck of a Brazilian Colony." *New Orleans Daily Crescent*, January 29, 1866.

Smith, A. M. "Still in Exile, 61 Years After War; Pot of Gold They Sought in Brazilian Jungle Never Found, Say Confederate Colonists." *Detroit News*, January 6, 1929.

Smith, Eugene C. "Sailing Down to Rio in 1866–67." *Brazilian American* (Rio de Janeiro), March 9, 1931.

Steinberg, Alfred. "Fire-Eating Farmer of the Confederacy." *American Heritage: The Magazine of History* 9 (December 1957): 22–25.

"The Southern Emigration to Brazil." *Mobile Weekly Advertiser*, November 4, 1865.

"Texas Brazilians." *Galveston Daily News*, April 1, 1867.

Tucker, H. C. "Confederates in Brazil." *United Daughters of the Confederacy Magazine*, July 1951, 22.

Weaver, Blanche Henry Clark. "Confederate Emigration to Brazil." *Journal of Southern History* 27 (February 1961): 51–53.

———. "Confederate Immigrants and Evangelical Churches in Brazil." *Journal of Southern History* 18 (November 1952): 446–468.

Wiley, Bell I. "Confederate Exiles in Brazil." *Civil War Times Illustrated* 15 (January 1977): 23.

Williams, Frederick G., and Roberta S. Rohwedder. "Brazil's Confederate Exiles: Where Are They Now?" *California Intermountain News*, March 22, 1973.

"With Alabama Emigres in Brazil—1867–1870." *Montgomery Advertiser*, August 4, 1940.

"Wrecked Emigrants." *New York Times*, March 28, 1867.

NEWSPAPERS

Advertiser and Register (Mobile, Alabama), 1867.

Atlanta Journal (Atlanta, Georgia), 1942.

Brazilian American (Rio de Janeiro), 1928, 1931.

California Intermountain News (Los Angeles), 1973.

The Constitutionalist (Atlanta, Georgia), 1867.

Correio Mercantil (Rio de Janeiro), 1866.

Daily Evening Bulletin [Flag] (Galveston, Texas), 1867.

Daily Picayune (New Orleans, Louisiana), 1866–67.

Daily Telegraph (Houston, Texas), 1866.
Dallas Herald (Dallas, Texas), 1860, 1866–67.
Detroit News (Detroit, Michigan), 1929.
Diário de São Paulo (São Paulo, Brazil), 1865.
Diário Oficial Do Imperio (Rio de Janeiro, Brazil), 1867.
Edgefield Advertiser (Edgefield, South Carolina), 1865–66.
Elmore Standard (Wetumka, Alabama), 1867.
Flake's Daily Galveston Bulletin (Galveston, Texas), 1867.
Flake's Semi-Weekly Bulletin (Galveston, Texas), 1867.
Galveston Daily News (Galveston, Texas), 1867.
Galveston Tri-Weekly News (Galveston, Texas), 1866.
Kansas City Star (Kansas City, Missouri), 1912.
Lubbock Avalanche-Journal (Lubbock, Texas), 1975.
Mobile Daily News (Mobile, Alabama), 1867.
Mobile Register and Advertiser (Mobile, Alabama), 1865.
Mobile Weekly Register (Mobile, Alabama), 1865.
Montgomery Advertiser (Montgomery, Alabama), 1940.
New Orleans Daily Crescent (New Orleans, Louisiana), 1866.
New Orleans Times (New Orleans, Louisiana), 1866–68.
New York Times (New York, New York), 1867, 1871.
New York Tribune (New York, New York), 1866.
Northern Standard (Clarksville, Texas), 1859.
Richmond Examiner (Richmond, Virginia), 1864.
San Antonio Express (San Antonio, Texas), 1870.
Semi-Weekly Farm News (Dallas, Texas), 1916.
The South-Western (Shreveport, Louisiana), 1865.
Talldega Watch-Tower (Talldega, Alabama), 1869.
Texas Baptist (Anderson, Texas), 1856–60.
Times of Brazil (São Paulo, Brazil), 1936.
Two Republics (Mexico, D.F.), 1867.
Waco Tribune-Herald (Waco, Texas), 1956.

PUBLISHED U.S. GOVERNMENT DOCUMENTS

United States. Department of the Interior. Census of 1840. Manuscript Population Schedules, Walker County, Georgia. Microfilm Publication. National Archives of the United States.
———. Census of 1850. Manuscript Population Schedules, Cherokee County, Texas. Microfilm Publication. National Archives of the United States.
———. Census of 1860. Manuscript Population Schedules, Hill County, Texas. Microfilm Publication. National Archives of the United States.
———. Census of 1860. Manuscript Population Schedules, McLennan County, Texas. Microfilm Publication. National Archives of the United States.
———. Census of 1860. Manuscript Population Schedules, Milam County, Texas. Microfilm Publication. National Archives of the United States.
———. Census of 1870. Manuscript Population Schedules, Hill County, Texas. Microfilm Publication. National Archives of the United States.

United States, Congress, House. "Papers Relating to the Foreign Relations of the United States." 42nd Cong., 3rd sess., *House Executive Document 1*. September 30, 1870. Washington, D.C.: Government Printing Office, 1873.
———. "Nicaragua—Seizure of General Walker." 35th Cong., 1st sess., *House Executive Document 24*. Washington, D.C.: Government Printing Office, 1858.
United States, Department of the Interior. *Boundaries, Areas, Geographic Centers and Altitudes of the United States and the Several States*. 2d ed. Geological Survey Bulletin 817. Washington, D.C.: Government Printing Office, 1932.
United States. National Archives. *List of Passengers Arriving in New York, 1820–1897*. Microfilm Publication. Microcopy 237. Roll 268.

INTERVIEWS

Arnold, Effie Smith. Interview with author. San Antonio, Texas, March 20, 1973. Tape recording in possession of author, Houston, Texas.
Clark, Mary Pearl. Interview with author. Burleson, Texas, June 15, 1960. Notes in possession of author, Houston, Texas.
Clark, Roy C. Interview with author. Lubbock, Texas, June 3, 1981. Notes in possession of author, Houston, Texas.
Griggs, Thelma C. Interview with author. Lubbock, Texas, June 3, 1977. Notes in possession of author, Houston, Texas.
McCleskey, W. Earl. Interview with author. Adairsville, Georgia, November 19, 1979.
Macdonell, Julia Barnsley Holland. Interview with author. São Paulo, Brazil, November 13, 1983. Notes in possession of author, Houston, Texas.
McMullan, Frank. Interview with author. São Paulo, Brazil, November 26, 1983. Notes in possession of author, Houston, Texas.
White, Rachel McMullan. Interview with author. Needham, Massachusetts, April 20, 1975.

Index

Ables, Second Mate, 65
Abney, Joseph, viii, 19
Agents of colonization, 16–21
Alabama, 18–19, 83
Alba, Adelaide, x
Albuquerque, Antonio Aoelho de
    Sá e, 68
Albuquerque, Henrique Cavalcanti
    de, 67
Allen, Crawford, 123
*Almanaque Literario da Provinca de
    São Paulo,* 129
Amazon River, 15, 18, 47, 125
Ancheita, Father, 2, 22
Andersonville (Ga.) Prison, 12
Anglo-Brazilian Times, 100
Ann & Lizzie (ship), 20
Antunes de Oliveira, Betty, x
Aranzel, João, 2–3, 21, 24, 129, 146
Ariado River, 101–102, 110–111
Arkansas, 31
Arp, Bill, 12–13
Assunguay River, 20
Attala County, Miss., 136
Austin (Tex.) *Statesman,* 39
Azambuja, Bernardo Nascentes de,
    24, 27, 29, 30
Azambuja, Joaquim de, 28, 33, 34,
    35, 39–40, 52–53
Azeite River, 26, 94, 101, 110

Bahia Honda, Cuba, 64
Baltzelle, Adelaide ("Addie"),
    131–132, 134

Baltzelle, Capt. J. P., 70
Baltzelle, Julia. *See* Barnsley, Julia
Bananal River, 22
Baptist Church, 117, 119, 126
Barbosa, Ruy (Rui), 134
Barnsley, George Scarborough, 50,
    58–59, 63, 71, 77, 78, 81–83, 86,
    88, 90, 105–106, 107–108, 114,
    146, 154; cites reasons for colo-
    nists' return to U.S., 122–123;
    comments on American colony
    entrepreneurs, 97, 124–126;
    comments on Brazil and Bra-
    zilians, 97; conducts burial service
    for Frank McMullan, 99; death of,
    144; decries article in *New York
    Times,* 120–121; descendants of,
    x; describes arrival in Rio de Ja-
    neiro, 84; describes conditions on
    Derby, 59; describes McMullan
    colonists, 70, 109; early life of,
    47–48; financial problems of,
    47, 128–131; helps colonists at
    Iguape, 108; joins McMullan
    Colony, 47; manuscript collections
    of, ix; marriage of, 128; medical
    practice of, 83, 97, 124, 128, 132;
    obtains food for colonists, 106;
    praises Americans in Brazil, 126;
    protests health conditions on
    ships, 78, 83–84; purchases prop-
    erty from James Keith, 134; and
    request for McMullan Colony
    leadership, 104, 108; returns to

Brazil, 132; returns to U.S., 131; searches for gold, 127–129; searches for Lake of Gold, 91; shares house with Moores in Iguape, 89; spirit of, said to have returned, 144; writes to *New Orleans Times*, 69, 120; writes to Cuban newspapers, 75–76; years to return to Georgia, 128–132

Barnsley, Godfrey, 47–48, 69, 108, 124, 128

Barnsley, Julia (Julia Baltzelle; later Julia Von Schwartz), 69, 128–132

Barnsley, Julia (daughter of George and Mary), 128

Barnsley, Lucian, 48, 50, 60–61, 69, 70, 81, 93, 98, 128, 131, 154; decries article in *New York Times*, 121; descendants of, x; diary of, 92–94; joins McMullan colony, 47; manuscript collections of, ix

Barnsley, Mary Laniera Emerson, 128, 132

Barr, Alwyn, xi

Bartow County, Ga., 69

Bastos, José Tavares, 98

Baxter, Catherine, 151

Baxter, John, 151; family of, 114

Baxter, Oscar, 151

Beasley, Cary, 149

Beasley, Julia, 112, 149

Beasley, W. H. T., 149, 155; family of, 101, 155

Biquá River, 25

Blue, John H., 20

Bocayuva, Quintino de Souza, 39, 41, 82–83, 132, 134; appeals for assistance for shipwrecked Texans, 67; authorizes passage to Brazil for Texan colonists, 68; meets with Frank McMullan in New York, 67

Bom Jesus de Iguape (church), 21

Bom Reteiro, São Paulo, Brazil, 116

Booth, William L., 138–139

Bosque County, Tex., 139

Bosqueville, Tex., 31, 48

Botucatu, São Paulo, Brazil, 19

Botujuru, São Paulo, Brazil, 22

Bowen, Adam L. (Berry?), 49, 151, 153

Bowen, Anna Martins, 101, 151

Bowen, Elizabeth B. ("Betty"), 49, 151

Bowen, Leonidas Sanders ("Lon"), 49, 102, 106, 151, 153, 155

Bowen, Mary H., 49, 151, 153

Bowen, Susan S. ("Sue"), 49, 110, 151

Bowen, William, 25–28, 37, 39, 49, 93, 96, 105–106, 110, 150, 155; arrives at Rio de Janeiro, 20; assumes leadership of McMullan Colony, 104; family of, 151, 155; marries Anna Martins, 101; military record of, 20; prepares census of McMullan Colony, 105; protests attempt of Barnsley and Dyer to take over colony, 104, 108; requests money for road to coast, 98; settles on Ariado River, 101; travels with Frank McMullan to Brazil, 20–21

Bowen, William R. ("Bill," son of William), 49, 151

Boyd (colonist), 155

Braxton, Alexander, 88, 155; family of, 155

Brazil, 33, 49, 63, 70–71, 77–78, 85, 88, 97–98, 103, 105, 114–117, 126–127, 136–142, 146–147; House of Deputies of, 133; reasons Americans wanted to leave, 119–123; reasons southerners wanted to emigrate to, 13–14, 16; refuses to comply with Union demands, viii; southern interest in, before Civil War, 15

Brazilian-Americans: patriotism of, 143

Brazilian Emigration Agency (New York), 41, 79, 80, 82, 132

Brazilian Legation (New York), 41

Brazoria, Tex., 11
Brazoria County, Tex., 38
Brazos County, Tex., 32, 43, 46
British Lion (ship), 114
Broome, Col. James A., 85
Brown, Ellen, x
Brown, John, 9
Broyles, William, 150
Brunswick (ship), 7
Bryan (or Bryant), L. M., 105, 149, 155
Buenos Aires, Argentina, 88
Byrd, Robert L., x

Cain, Virginia J. H., xi
California, viii, 1, 88
Camargo, "Old Man," 103
Campinas, São Paulo, Brazil, 93, 100, 113
Campo Cemetery and Church, 119, 145
Canada, viii
Canal Street (New York), 73, 79–80
Cananea, São Paulo, Brazil, 21
Cape Hattaras, N.C., 77
Cardwell, John, 36–39
Carmaleo, Cuba, 73–75
Carothers, John A., 5, 137–138
Carter, "Parson," 154
Cass County, Tex., 5
Causse, Alexander, 53, 56, 62; as captain of *Derby*, 39–40; conspires to swindle colonists, 51, 56; deserts post during storm, 60–61, 63; evacuates colonists from *Derby*, 64–65; ordered to kangaroo court of colonists, 57–58; returns to New Orleans, 71
Central America, 1, 73
Central American League, 6
Charles W. Lord, 77
Chatard, Frederick, 7
Chester County, S.C., viii
Chestnut Flat, Ga., 32
Civil War, U.S., 16, 47, 49, 50, 73, 99, 117, 136, 139

Clark, George L., 31, 49, 136–137
Clark, Hugh, 142
Clark, Virginia I. *See* McMullan, Virginia I.
Clay, Henry, 37
Cleburne, Tex., 140
Clothing of colonists, 79
Coachman, Dr. R., 129–130
Cobb, Bell C., 149, 153
Cobb, J. C., 105, 149, 153, 155
Cobb, Malinda, 149, 153
Cobb, Mary P., 149, 153
Coffee, cultivation of, 93
Collins, Jacquelin, xi
Collins Hotel (New York), 73, 79–83
Colomie, Juan A., 73, 75
Colorado (state), 1
Columbia, Tex., 36
Comanche County, Tex., 71
Conceição, São Paulo, Brazil, 2, 21–22, 113, 129
Confederate States of America: army of, 50, 88, 129; surrender of, vii, 15; joining of Texas to, 11
Connor, Seymour V., xi
Cook, Ann, 45, 94, 149
Cook, Edward, 45, 96, 149
Cook, J. Thomas, 94, 96, 149, 153, 155
Cook, Lilly, 45, 149
Cook, Mary, 45, 149
Cook, Nancy, 45, 149
Cook, Pet, 45, 112, 150
Cook, Samuel, 45, 149
Cook, Susan, 45, 149
Cook, Thomas, 45
Cook family, 44–45, 95–96, 102, 112–114, 153, 155
Cotton, cultivation of, 119, 145
Crawley, C. A., 63, 71, 105, 110, 112, 150, 154
Crawley, Rachel Russell. *See* Russell, Rachel
Creeny, William, 40
Crony (colonist), 101, 154
Cuba, viii, 59, 73, 78, 79, 80

Curea River, 18
Currie, Edward, 143
Curry, Helen Domm, 142

Dado de Deus (mountain), 129
Daily Missouri Republican, 20
Daingerfield, Tex., 5
Dallas Herald, 83
Danton, M. W., 53–54
Davis, James, 150
Davis, William, 105
Davis (Galveston merchant), 48
De Bow's Review, 15
Demaret, Martin Felix, 71, 88
Demaret, Pamela, 88
Demaret family, 71
Democratic Executive Committee
    (Texas), 39
Democratic Party (Texas), 9–10, 138
Derby (brig), 47, 49, 50, 78, 115, 146;
    becalmed, 58–59; inspected at
    Galveston, 53–54; leased by Frank
    McMullan, 39, 40, 42–43, 48; sold
    for salvage, 70; in storm, 60–63;
    sails to Galveston from New Or-
    leans, 52–53; sails from Gal-
    veston, 56; seized for debt, 51;
    wreck of, 61–65
Diario de São Paulo, viii
Dillard (passenger on *North America*),
    83
Dixie Free and Easy Concert Saloon,
    120
Doce River, viii, 87–88, 100
Dom Affonso (ship), 21
Domm, John, 116, 143
Dom Pedro II, 55; description of,
    86; encourages emigration of
    southerners to Brazil, 16; over-
    throw of, 133–134; visits colonists
    at Emigrant Hotel, 85–86
Dove Creek (Tex.): battle of, 20
Dred Scott decision, 9
Dunn, Rev. Ballard Smith, ix, 145;
    and Brazilian authorities, 30, 35,
    39, 40, 41; complaints about, 122;
    mortgages and abandons colony,

125; plans to establish colony, 20;
    sails to Brazil with colonists, 83,
    85–86
Dunn, Elizabeth, ix, 20
Dyer, Amanda, 5, 31, 123
Dyer, Harriet, 9, 31, 109
Dyer, James (son of James Harrison
    and Amanda), 31
Dyer, James Harrison (Judge), 69,
    100, 144; attempts to take over
    McMullan Colony, 104–105, 108;
    buys land on Una River, 109,
    141–142; death of, 138; in first
    group up Ribeira de Iguape,
    92–94; in Galveston, 48, 56; in
    Hill County, 5–6; in New Orleans,
    31, 39; sawmill built by, 109, 123,
    127; searches for gold, 91, 107,
    109; steamboat owned by, 109,
    123; in storm and shipwreck, 61,
    62; writes to Gov. Houston, 11
Dyer, Nancy. *See* McMullan, Nancy
    Dyer
Dyer, Simpson Cash, 5
Dyer, Wylie (father of Nancy Dyer
    McMullan), 4, 5
Dyer, Wylie (son of James Harrison
    and Amanda), 31

Eagle (ship), 67
Economic conditions in Brazil,
    119–121
Edgefield, S.C., 19, 83
8th Georgia Regiment, 47, 129
El Dorado (McMullan Colony), 4,
    94, 97, 107, 112
Ella S. Thayer (ship), 106
Emerson, Mary Laniera, 128, 132
Emerson, Rev. William C., 128
Emigrant Hotel, 84–85, 87
Emigration association formed in
    Brazil, viii
England, viii, 13, 81
Episcopal Church, 99
Espirito Santo Province, Brazil, viii,
    20, 120
Estrada Real, 93

Eubank, John T., 11
European Hotel (New York), 81
Exel, Antonio, 143

Fairfax, Jennie, 47
Fairfield, Tex., 63
Fashion (ship), 2, 7
Fazenda de Bocudo, 113
Ferguson, Champ, 12
Ferguson, Sarah Bellona Smith. *See* Smith, Sarah Bellona
Fielder, Cortez, 32, 60, 101, 103, 112, 149, 154–155
Fielder, Sarah, 112, 149
Fielder, Zeno, 32, 101, 103, 149, 154–155
"Finger of God," 21
First North American Baptist Missionary Church, 117–118
Fish, Hamilton (U.S. Secretary of State), 122
Flake's Bulletin (Galveston, Tex.), 70
Flores, Dan, xi
Florida (state), 18, 83
Florida (ship), viii
Fonesca, Manoel Deodoro da, 134
Foreign Mission Board, 117, 118
Fortress Monroe, Va., 77–78
Fort Smith, Ark., 5
Foster, Josephine, 100
14th Alabama Infantry, 85
France, 13, 65, 143
Fraternity of Descendants of Americans, 145
Freestone County, Tex., 32
Fulton (ship), 7

Gail, Tex., 138
Galveston, Tex., 10, 33, 36–37, 40, 43, 45, 48–52, 58–59, 88, 115
Galveston Daily News, vii, 46, 50, 55, 77
Galveston Tri-Weekly News, 36–37, 38
Garlington, Allen, 49, 150
Garlington, Sarah, 49, 150, 153
Garlington family, 114, 153
Garner, Thomas, 44, 105, 112, 150

Garner family, 95–96, 102
Garrison, Cornelius K., 31, 40, 76, 78
Gaston, James McFadden, viii, 19, 82–83, 86
Gaston Colony, 83
Gavare Toscar, Fernando de, 75
Gávez e Fínaz, Fernando, 75
Georgia (state), 4, 5, 47, 70, 81, 83, 124, 128–129, 131
German emigrants to Brazil, 120–121
Germany, 41
Gill (unnamed infant), 150
Gill, Frances R., 150, 153
Gill, William A. (Billy), 49, 93–94, 105, 150, 153, 155
Gill family, 114, 153, 155
Gilmour, Murray, 128
Glasgow (mining engineer), 132
Glen (colonist), 87, 154
Goias (state), 145
Goicouria, Gen. Domingo de, 73, 79
Goicouria, Felipe de, 73–74
Government House (on Juquiá River), 93
Government House (Rio de Janeiro). *See* Emigrant Hotel
Graham, Ann, x
Graham, Jimmy, 120
Great Eastern, (ship), 82
Green (teacher), 82
Green, A. J. ("Old Man"), 44, 74, 103, 149, 153, 155
Green, Angeletta, 44, 149
Green, Bonaparte H. ("Bony"), 44, 97
Green, J. J.: *See* Green, A. J.
Green, Joseph, 44, 149
Green, Jurilla, 44, 149
Green, Lewis, 44, 74, 149
Green, Sarah, 103
Green family, 101, 153, 155
Greenwich, Conn., 82
Griggs, Joan, xi
Griggs, John, xi
Griggs, Nancy, xi

Grimes County, Tex., 8, 32, 88
Guanajay, Cuba, 73–75
Guanhanhã River, 101–103, 110
Guerriere (ship), 114, 122
Guiding Star (ship), 18
Gunter, George Grandioson: colony of, 19, 85–87, 100; commented on by George Barnsley, 121, 125; failure of, 125

Hall, Hervey, 123–124
Hall family, 124
Hampton Roads, Va., 78
Hanson, Arthur M., 21
Hargrove, J. D. *See* Hargrove, William
Hargrove, William, 101, 112, 150, 154–155
Harper's Ferry, Va., 9
Harper's Weekly, 12
Hartwell, Reverend, 117
Hastings, Lansford Warren, viii, 17–18
Hastings colony, viii, 17–18; Barnsley's evaluation of, 124; in 1888, 124–125; in 1940, 125
Havana, Cuba, 18, 39, 58–59, 69, 73, 74, 76, 78, 84
Haviland, James E., 53–54
Hayes, Harry, 51
Hayes, Robert, xi
Haynes, L. F. *See* Haynie, S. F.
Haynie, C. B., 150, 153
Haynie, Hugh H., 44, 150
Haynie, J. H., 150
Haynie, Mary A., 50, 150
Haynie, Mary L., 44, 150
Haynie, S. F., 44, 105, 150, 155
Haynie, S. Travis, 150
Haynie, W. Boothe, 150
Haynie family, 113–114, 153, 155
Henderson (colonist), 88, 154
Herva-mate, 20
Hickman, John, 105, 151, 154–155
Hill County, Tex., ix, 9, 11, 32, 49, 137
Hillsboro, Tex., 11, 119, 136,

137–139; land of McMullan family in, 138–139; location of townsite of, 5
Hillsboro Express, 11
Hockaday, P. B., 37–38
Holland, Harold Barnsley, x, 146
Honduras, viii
Houston, Samuel, 11
Houston, Tex., 45
Houston and Texas Central Railway, 43
Houston Daily Telegraph, 46
Hudzeitz, Coon, 140
Hudzeitz, Ileita, 140
Hudzeitz, Lucia, 140
Hudzeitz, Rie, 140
Hudzeitz, Swan, 140
Hudzeitz, Swan, Jr., 140
Hudzeitz family, 140–141
Huguenots, 46

Iguape, São Paulo, Brazil, 21, 26–27, 29, 40, 86, 87–89, 93, 97–98, 100, 104–106, 112, 129
Indiana, 138
Indians on Peixe River, 103
International Society of Immigration, 15
Iowa, 138
Iredell, Tex., 139
Ireland, 4, 41
Irish emigrants to Brazil, 83, 120–121
Isabel, Princess, 133–134
Itapetininga, São Paulo, Brazil, 129
Itariri River, 26, 94, 100–101, 110
Itatins Mountains, 129

Jacareí, São Paulo, Brazil, 146
Jacupiranga River, 22
Jahu River, 17
Jefferson Medical College, 120–121
Johnson (colonist), 87, 154
Johnson, Andrew (U.S. president), 12
Johnson, John, 114, 151, 154–155

Johnson, Molly, 114
Jones, Cicero, 116, 143
Jundiahy, São Paulo, Brazil, 113
Juquiá River, ix, 20–22, 25–27, 93, 96–97, 100

Kansas (state), 9
Kansas (ship), 122
Kansas-Nebraska Act, 9
Keech, Kent, x
Keith, James Monroe, 88, 127; association of, with George Barnsley, 129; death of, 143; heirs of, 143–144; loss of properties in Brazilian revolution, 134; receipt of land grant by, 134
Kent, Gen. Loreh, 53, 56
Kentucky, 5, 12
Kidder, Rev. Daniel P., 15
King, Joseph, xi
Knapp, Dr., 11
Knapp, Sharon E., x
Knights of the Golden Circle, 2
Kosciusko, Miss., 136

Ladies Benevolent Society (Havana), 75
Lake Juparanão, 19
Lake of Gold, 2–4, 24, 129, 146
Lane, Horace Manly, 20, 129–130
Lawrence County, Ky., 5
Lawton, E. M., 143–144
Leddin's Business College (Memphis, Tenn.), 136–137
Lee (colonist), 87, 154
Leite, Captain Lui, 26
Leopard (ship), 7
Lima, Raul, x
Limestone County, Tex., 31, 118
Linn, George A., 153; sister of, 153–54; wife of, 153
Linn family, 106, 153
Lisboa, José Maria, 129
Liverpool, England, 82
Lizzieland, ix, 20, 125
London, England, 81

Louisiana, 17, 20, 30, 88, 120
Lydick (mining engineer), 132, 134–135

McAlpine, Napoleon Bonaparte ("Bony"), 44, 105, 112, 143, 150, 154–155
McCann, William T., 87, 154
Macdonnell, Julia Barnsley Holland, x, 146
McKenzie, John Witherspoon Pettigrew, 8, 10
McKenzie Institute (Red River County, Tex.), 8, 9, 10
McKnight, America, 44, 116
McKnight, Calvin, 44, 50, 82, 87, 98, 153; family of, 153
McKnight, Emma, 87
McKnight, Isabel, 44, 87
McKnight, Thomas Steret, 44, 50, 82, 87, 116, 153; death of, 143; distills *pinga* and whiskey, 117; family of, 153; introduces moldboard plow in Brazil, 116–117
McKnight, Wilber, 124
McLennan County, Tex., ix, 31, 48
McMahon, Albert G., 71–72
McMains, John ("Dad"), 88, 144, 154
McMullan, Caskey, 145
McMullan, Charley, 6
McMullan, Dana, 145
McMullan, Edwin Ney. *See* McMullan, Ney
McMullan, Eugene ("Nuck"), 4
McMullan, Frank, 153; argues for ships for colonists from southern ports, 33–35; appointed to Democratic Party Resolutions Committee, 9; arrives at Rio de Janeiro, 20, 85; asks José Tavares Bastos for support for road, 98; attends state Democratic convention, 10; birth of, 4; blames C. K. Garrison for lack of ships from South, 76; briefs Dyer and Wasson on Lake of Gold, 91; burial of, 99; Civil

War activities of, in Mexico, 11–12; death of, 99, 103, 107; describes wreck of *Derby*, 61; desperation of, in New Orleans, 34–35; as executor of father's estate, 6, 137; early life of, 4; enrolls in McKenzie Institute, 8; eulogy of, by George Barnsley, 99–100; fails to indict Captain Causse and crew, 72; forces captain out of cabin at gunpoint, 61; friendship of, with Judge Dyer, 6; furnishes money to lease *Derby*, 52; illness of, 10–11, 53, 80, 91–92, 97, 103, 107; leases *Derby*, 39; leaves Cuba for New York on *Eagle*, 67; leaves New Orleans for Texas, 52; leaves New York for Texas, 31, 73; leaves Plaza de Banes for Havana, 66; leaves Texas for Brazil, 20; leaves Texas for Mexico, 11; leaves Texas for New Orleans, 6, 50; locates colony lands on upper São Lourenço River, 25–26; meets with Quintino de Bocayuva, 67; moves to White Rock Creek, Tex., 10; naturalized as a Brazilian citizen, 98; newspaper letter debate of, with John Cardwell, 36–39; praises conduct of passengers during and after shipwreck, 63, 68, 69; praises Don Juan Vermay, 73; proficient in Spanish, 12; purchases Morro Redondo on Juquiá River, 26–27; reads directions to Lake of Gold, 3; receives conditional title to colony lands, 27; receives letter of guarantee for ship, 35; requests help from Portuguese embassy in Havana, 66–67; rescues Jesse Wright from Cuban authorities, 66; returns to Havana, 73; returns to Texas to get colonists, 27, 31; sails to Nicaragua under William Walker, 6–8; sets criteria for colonists, 46; trunk of, 146; writes book on Spanish grammar, 12;

writes report to Secretary of Agriculture, 27
McMullan, Frank (son of Ney), x, 144
McMullan, Hugh, 32; comes to the U.S., 4; death of, 6; estate of, 137–138; helps found Hillsboro, Tex., 137; home of, in Hill County, Tex., 5; moves to Mississippi, 5
McMullan, Jasper ("Jap"), 4
McMullan, John, 4
McMullan, Lorin, 145
McMullan, Louise ("Lou"), 100, 153; birth of, 5; death of, 123, 136; marries John Odell, 31, 49
McMullan, Mabe Oldham, 139–141, 144–145
McMullan, Manie. *See* McMullan, Charley
McMullan, Martha Ann ("Matt"), 4, 31, 49, 139
McMullan, Milton ("Bud"), 4
McMullan, Nancy Dyer, 153; accused of stealing gold, 71–72; attends wedding of Virginia McMullan, 31; becomes administrator of Hugh McMullan's estate, 6; death of, 138; fails to prosecute squatters, 137; lives in Santa Barbara, 123; marries Hugh McMullan, 4; moves to Mississippi, 5, 49, 136; moves to Texas, 5, 49; returns to Hillsboro, 137; returns to U.S., 123, 136
McMullan, Ney, 51, 127, 140, 145, 153; adept at writing, 139, 142; attends business college, 136–137; attends wedding of sister, Virginia, 31; birth of, 6; children of, 144–145; describes storm in Caribbean, 61; endeavors to get financial support from U.S. relatives, 141; goes to Brazil with mother, 49; marries, 139; offered McMullan grant by Brazilian government, 141; praises actions of

Judge Dyer during storm, 62; receives power of attorney, 142; returns to Brazil, 139–140; returns to Texas, 137; returns to U.S., 123, 136

McMullan, Rachel "Kelly" (Rachel McMullan White), x, 145

McMullan, Victoria ("Vic"), 61, 142, 153; birth of, 5; daughter of, born, 138; death of, 138; with husband, shares home with George Barnsley, 89; infant child of, dies, 77; joins McMullan colony, 48; marries William T. Moore, 31, 48; moves to Campinas with husband, 100; returns to U.S., 123

McMullan, Virginia I. ("Jennie"): birth of, 5; death of, 138; meets family on their return from Brazil, 136; moves to Mississippi, 136; returns to Texas, 136; wedding of, 31; as wife of George L. Clark, 49

McMullan, Wylie Dyer, x, 144

McMullan colonists: activities of, on *Derby*, 59; ages of, 50; appearance of, 50, 79; arrive at Fortress Monroe, Va., 77; arrive at Galveston, 46; arrive at New York, 78–79; arrive at Norfolk, Va., 77; arrive at Rio de Janeiro, 84; baggage and equipment of, 54, 65–66, 71; camp on Galveston beach, 46; convene court to try Captain Causse, 57–58; deaths of, 143; delayed in Iguape, 89–90; description of, 70; desperation of, 120; discontent of, at Galveston, 52; education of, 8; evacuate wrecked *Derby*, 64–65; gather at Millican, Tex., 43; illness of, in New York, 82; leave Galveston for Brazil, 56; leave Havana for New York, 76; leave Iguape for colony lands, 92; leave McMullan colony lands, 112; leave New York for Brazil, 83; leave Rio de Janeiro for Iguape, 89; money spent by, for supplies, 52; number of, 50, 114–115; occupations of, 50; origins of, 50; pay bribes, 51, 54; pre-war economic status of, 34; protest efforts of Dyer and Barnsley to take over colony, 104–105; purchase supplies in Galveston, 53; rent baggage car to travel to Galveston, 43; return to U.S. by some of, 112, 115, 119–123, 126, 127; settle on McMullan grant, 101; southern philosophy of, 46; status of, in 1870, 114–115; in storm aboard *Derby*, 60–63; in storm aboard *Mariposa*, 76–77; travel by canoe up Ribeira de Iguape, 94–97; travel to Guanajay, Cuba, 73–74; wait in New York for steamship, 82

McMullan colony, 88, 140, 145; census of, 149–152; religious services at, 102; scholarly studies of, ix; size of, 25, 92; survey of, x, 92

McMullan estate (Hill County, Tex.), 138–139

McMullan family, on Ferguson list, 153

McMullan Grant, 141; agreements made by Brazil concerning, 24–25, 27; conditional title to, given, 92; description of, 92, 94; part of, purchased by Dyer and Wasson, 109

McNabb (colonist), 87

Magalhes, Lt. Col. Benjamin Constant Coelho de, 134

Margaret (ship), 18

Marinha, Joaquim Saldanha, 105, 106

Mariposa (ship), 69, 75, 77–79; conditions on, 76–77

Marmion (ship), 85, 87, 89, 91

Martiń, João, 99

Martins, Anna (Anna Bowen), 101, 151

Maryland, 120

Mason (colonist), 154
Masonic Lodge, 118, 133
Maston (colonist), 87, 154
Matto Grosso Province, Brazil, 88
Maury, Matthew P., 15
Memphis, Tenn., 136
Meridien, Miss., 143
Meriwether, Maj. Robert, 86; as representative of Southern Emigration Society, 19, 83
Merrimac (ship), 69, 77
Methodist Church, 8, 80, 97, 119
Mexia, Tex., 118
Mexico, viii, 10, 13, 18
Michigan, 138
Milam County, Tex., 46
Miller, Anna, 87
Miller, Irving, 87
Miller, Sophie, 87
Millican, Tex., 43–45
Mississippi (state), 5, 17, 49, 136–137
Missouri (state), 20
Mobile, Ala., 2, 7, 18, 114
Mobile and Nicaragua Steamship Company, 7
Monserate, Parish of (Havana), 75
Montana (ship), 17
Moore, Juanita, 123
Moore, Montie, 138, 142
Moore, Victoria McMullan. See McMullan, Victoria
Moore, William T., 31, 61, 63, 142, 153; accidentally wounds himself, 49; infant child of, dies, 77, 123; joins McMullan colony, 48; marries Victoria McMullan, 48; moves to Campinas with wife, 100; returns to Texas, 123; shares house with George Barnsley in Iguape, 89; wins money for food by gambling, 89–90
Morgan's Raiders, 12
Morro Redondo, 27, 93, 96, 98, 101

Nathan, Charles, 114
Navarro County, Tex., 32, 46, 103

Negroes, 13, 37, 77, 97
Neptune (ship), 18
Nettles, William B., 77, 153; family of, 153
New Mexico, 17
New Orleans, La., 6–7, 18, 19, 32–35, 37, 39, 42–43, 47–48, 50–52, 58, 69, 76, 78, 106, 114, 125, 131, 136
New Orleans Times, 38, 41–42, 52, 100
New York, N.Y., 17, 28–31, 33, 36, 41–42, 59, 69, 73–75, 77, 79–80, 82–83, 85, 97, 114, 121, 133, 138
New York and Brazil Steamship Company, 40, 41, 76, 84, 114
New York Herald, 16
New York Times, 41, 78, 79–80, 120
New York Tribune, 41
Nicaragua, 2, 4, 6–7, 76
19th Texas Cavalry, 11
Norfolk, Va., 77–78
Norfolk Navy Yard, 8
Norris, Peter, 53, 54
Norris, Robert C., 19
Norris, William Hutchinson, 19, 125
Norris colony, 112, 116; reasons for success of, 125
North America, 114, 120, 123, 127, 146
North America (ship), 28, 82–84, 85, 121
North Carolina, 77

Odell, John, 31, 49, 100, 153
Odell, Louise McMullan. See McMullan, Louise
Oglethorpe University, 47
Oldham, Mabe. See McMullan, Mabe Oldham
Oliver, A. T., 119
Oliver, Beatrice, 119
Oregon, viii
O'Reilly (passenger on North America), 83
O'Reilly, Countess, 75
Oriol, J. M., 39, 43, 50–52
Our Lady of Conceição (church), 22

Paraná Province, Brazil, 20
Paratý, Brazil, 98
Parks, W. E., 49, 151, 153
Partridge, James R., 122
Paula e Souza, Antonio Francisco de,
    20–21, 30, 104–105, 108
Peacock, Ileita Williams, 139, 141
Pecan Creek (Hill County, Tex.), 5, 8
Pedroso, Joaquim, 25
Peixe River, 26, 101–103
Penn, Major, 71, 154
Pennsylvania, 82
Perkins, "Old Man," 113
Peruibe, São Paulo, Brazil, 21, 110,
    112
Philadelphia, Pa., 120
Pickett, John T., 11
Piedade, São Paulo, Brazil, 129
Pilgrim's Progress, 102
Pinga, 98, 117
Piraçununga, São Paulo, Brazil, 131
Pittsburgh, Pa., 134–135
Pizarro, Francisco, 1
Plaza de Banes, Cuba, 65–66, 70
Plows, 116–117, 126
Portsmouth (ship), 122
Presbyterian Church, 119
Puckett, Jackson, 11
Pyles, William F., 145

Quick, Captain, 76–78
Quillin, Aulina, 151
Quillin, Parson Elijah Hupton, 151;
    appointed missionary by Southern
    Baptist Convention, 118, 126; ar-
    rives in Galveston, 49; becomes
    pastor of First North American
    Missionary Baptist Church, 118;
    begins Sunday School in
    McMullan colony, 102; burial of,
    119; death of, 118; family of, 96,
    153, 155; joins McMullan colony,
    32; library of, 97; lives on Ariado
    River, 101; marries Eugene Smith
    and Sue Bowen, 110; moves to
    "the station," 112, 118
Quillin, Leona, 151

Quillin, Leonidas, 151
Quillin, Leroy, 151
Quillin, Parks, 151
Quillin, Sarah, 32, 119, 143, 151
Quinnebaug (ship), 122

Raleigh, Sir Walter, 1
Ratcliff, Eunice, 94, 96, 117–118,
    153
Ratcliff, Maude, 96
Ratcliff, Richard, 94, 117–118, 153
Ratcliff family, 95–96, 117
Rath, Dr. Charles, 3
Rebouças, São Paulo, Brazil, 113
Reconstruction, 136, 138; amnesty
    provisions of, 12; comments on by
    Capt. J. P. Baltzelle, 70; economic
    conditions in the South during, 1;
    attitude of southerners toward
    Negroes during, 13; and northern
    demands for punishment of
    southerners, 12
Red Gauntlet (ship), 18
Red River, 120
Red River County, Tex., 8
Reese, James V., xi
Republican Party (Texas), 138
Review of Reviews, 142
Rhode Island, 81, 123
Ribeira de Iguape, 19, 21, 89–90,
    92–93
Richmond, Va., 47
Richmond Inquirer, 16
Rio Branco Law of 1871, 133
Rio de Janeiro, Brazil, 15, 17, 19, 20,
    22, 25, 27–31, 34, 38–40, 51, 75,
    77, 79, 82–84, 86–90, 100, 106,
    109, 114, 119–120, 128–129, 131
Rio Doce colony. See Gunter, George
    Grandioson
Rio Grande (river), 12
Rio Grande do Sul (Brazilian state),
    123–124
Rio Una de Prelado. See Una River
Rio Verde, Goias, Brazil, 145
Robinson, John, 51
Rocha, Octaviano da, 99

Rogers, Col. William K., 6
Roman Catholic Church, 119, 133
Rome Light Guard, 47
Ross, Lawrence Sullivan, 138
Ross, Margaret, x
Ruffin, Edmund, vii
Russell, Rachel, 44, 45, 112, 150, 153, 155

San Antonio Express, 121
Sanitary Commission of New York, 78
San Juan del Sur, Nicaragua, 7
Santa Barbara, São Paulo, Brazil, 112–117, 119, 125, 127, 140, 145
Santa Maria (ship), 17
Santarem, Pará, Brazil, 125
Santos, Rio de Janeiro state, Brazil, 17, 21, 28, 89, 96, 98, 112–113
São Lourenço Peak, 21, 129
São Lourenço River, ix, 21, 25–26, 28, 92, 94, 96, 98, 100–101, 102, 105, 107, 110, 112, 114–116, 141
São Paulo (city), viii, 3, 19, 89, 93, 100, 112–113, 116, 142–144, 146
São Paulo (province or state), ix; Archives of, ix, x, 17, 19, 21, 28, 86–87, 98, 105–106, 119–120, 122, 129, 134, 143
São Paulo, legislature of, 145
Saratoga (ship), 7
Savannah, Ga., 47, 83
Saylor, Adelaide Baltzelle, 131–132, 134
Saylor, B. F. Armington, 132, 134–135
Schofield, Walter, 60, 154
Schuenstuhl, Olga Barnsley, x
Scott, Dred, 9
Secession Convention of Texas, 11
Serra do Mar, 28
Shaw, Dr. Hugh A., 19, 82–83, 86
Silva, Carlos Ilidro da, 129
Sisters of Charity (Havana), 75
Slavery: abolition of, in Brazil, 133; in Texas, 5; in U.S., vii; relocation of slaves on the Amazon suggested, 15
Smith, Alfred Iverson, 71, 82, 89, 94, 97, 105, 151; builds "American-style" house on Ariado River, 111–112; cooks meal for colonists at Guanajay, 74; death of, 143; decides to leave McMullan grant, 112; family of, 95–96, 101–102, 153, 155; given Texas land by Hugh McMullan, 32; joins McMullan colony, 32; moves to Santa Barbara area, 112–114; purchases house on McMullan grant, 103; settles with family on Ariado River, 101, 110–114; as teacher of Frank McMullan in Georgia, 43
Smith, Bellona. *See* Smith, Sarah Bellona
Smith, Bob, 101
Smith, Eugene, 44, 60, 89, 110, 151
Smith, Fulton ("Fully"), 152
Smith, Marsene, 44, 111
Smith, Masserly, 151
Smith, Pennington ("Penny"), 44, 111, 113, 151
Smith, Preston, 44, 151
Smith, R., 149, 155
Smith, Sailor, 154
Smith, Sarah (A. I. Smith's wife), 89, 112, 151
Smith, Sarah Bellona, ix, 44, 51, 82, 95–96, 100–101, 102, 110–111, 113, 151
Smith, Virgil C., 152
Smith, W. T., 105, 155
Smith County, Tex., 5
Sorocaba, São Paulo, Brazil, 93, 129–130, 134, 144
South America, 36, 42, 44, 47, 71, 83, 124, 132, 136, 139, 141
South America (ship), 17
South Carolina, viii, 11, 19, 82, 83
Southern Baptist Convention, 117–118

Southern Emigration Society, 19
Souza Dantas, Manoel Pinto de, 33, 35, 133
Spring Hill, Tex., 43
Stampley, J., 102, 154
Stars and Bars (Confederate battle flag), 143, 146
Stars and Stripes (U.S. flag), 143
"Station, the," 112
Station Church, 118
Steiner Valley Prison Farm, 138
Steve (former slave), 50; business success of, 127; family of, 127; friendship of, with Judge Dyer, 48; takes surname of Wasson, 127–128; vows to go to Brazil, 48
Stevens, Thaddeus, vii
Street, Maj. Ernesto Dinez, 21, 24–25, 92
Swain, Col. M. S., 20

Talisman (ship), 19
Tapejos River, 18, 125
Tartar (ship), 114
Tarver, Abner, 152
Tarver, Ben F., 152
Tarver, "Dock," 123
Tarver, James, 152
Tarver, Luisa, 152
Tarver, Nelson ("Judge"), 49, 101, 105, 123, 152–153, 155 (incorrectly listed as B. F. Tarver on p. 155)
Tarver, Sarah, 49, 103, 152
Tarver family, 153, 155
Teite River, 17
Tennessee, 12, 132
Texas, 28, 34, 42–43, 49–50, 77, 82–83, 88, 114, 116, 120, 137–138, 141; buffalo plains of, 1; leaves Union, 11; return of Frank McMullan to, 27; secession convention of, 11; Senate of, 138; Supreme Court of, 139
Texas Rangers, 50, 88, 134
Thomas, Rev. R. P., 118

Thweatt, John, x
Totten, S. S., 20
Towash, Tex., 49
Tucker, H. C., 125
Tully (colonist), 93, 94
Tupper, H. A., 118, 119
12th Texas Cavalry, 11
Two Republics, 100

Una River, 21, 109, 141
Una (village), São Paulo, Brazil, 129
United Railway, 74
United States and Brazil Steamship Company, 28, 30, 33, 39
United States of America, 28, 39, 51, 57, 81, 84–85, 106, 113–115, 117, 119, 120, 122–123, 132, 136, 143; Supreme Court of, 9

Vassão: surname of descendants of Steve (former slave), 128
Vermay, Juan, 69–70, 75; leaves for Havana to raise money for Texans, 69; provides assistance for shipwrecked colonists, 65, 69; provides carts to carry colonists to Guanajay, 73–74; warns colonists of possible thieves, 66; wife of, 65
Vila Americana, 145
Virginia, 9, 17
Von Schwartz, Julia. See Barnsley, Julia

Wachusett (ship), viii
Waco Times-Herald, 138
Waley, G. W., 35
Walker, William, 2, 6–7, 73
Walker County, Ga., 4
Wallace, Carolyn, x
Wallace, Ernest, xi
Wasson, Columbus, 93–94, 100, 154; attends McKenzie College, 8–9; borrows money to purchase steamboat, 109; cheers Dom Pedro II at Emigrant Hotel, 86; in first group to leave for colony

lands, 92; makes plans to emigrate to Brazil, 31; marries Harriet Dyer, 109; purchases lands on Una River, 109; remains in Brazil to complete teaching contract, 123; runs for Texas Senate, 138; searches for Lake of Gold, 109; visits McMullan home in Hill County, 9

Wasson, Steve. *See* Steve

Watermelons, 145

Waters-Pierce Oil Company, 140

Weaver, Blanche Henry Clark, ix, xi

Weaver, Daniel, 105, 150

Weaver, Othniel ("Parson"), 49, 50, 105, 150, 153, 155

Weaver, Rebecca, 150

Weaver, Riley, 105, 150

Weaver, W. O. *See* Weaver, Othniel

Weaver family, 32, 49, 102, 114, 153, 155

West Texas, 138

Whitaker, "Uncle" Joe, 145

White, Colonel, 94

White, Rachel McMullan, x, 145

White and Others v. Jones, 138–139

White Rock Creek, 10

Wier, Joseph, 11

Williams, Coon, 140

Williams, Ileita, 139, 141

Williams, John B., 11, 31, 49

Williams, Martha Ann ("Mattie"). *See* McMullan, Martha Ann

Williams, Monk, 139–140

Williams, Nanneita, 140

Williams family, 141

Wilmot, Clement H., 95

Wingutter, Amy, 49, 94, 151

Wingutter, Jacob, 49, 94, 151, 155

Wingutter, Susan, 49, 94, 151

Wingutter family, 95, 96, 155

Wirz, Capt. Henry, 12

Wood, Gen. William Wallace, 17, 19, 35

Woodlands Plantation, 47, 124, 130–132

World's Work, 142

World War I, 143

Wornell, James, 138

Wright, Ambrose, 44, 124, 150

Wright, Boregard, 44, 150

Wright, Jesse R., 105, 150, 153, 155; arrives at Millican, 44; family of, 102, 155; flees to Rio Grande do Sul, 124; hounds of stolen in New York, 80–81; kills Cuban looter at Bahia Honda, 66; murders Hervey Hall, 124; returns to Texas, 124

Wright, Sarah J., 44, 150

Wright, Thomas, 44, 71

Wright, William, 44, 150

Wright family, 32, 153

Wyman, Martha, 5

Xiririca, São Paulo, Brazil, 19

Yankees, 32, 41, 51, 77, 83, 121